Contents

Y0-AGT-078

Introduction

Lessons for Theme 1: Journeys

Lessons for Theme 2: American Stories

Lessons for Theme 3: That's Amazing!

Lessons for Theme 4: Problem Solvers

Lessons for Theme 5: Heroes

Lessons for Theme 6: Nature: Friend and Foe

Blackline Masters

Teaching Masters and Practice Masters

Letter Cards

Teachers' greatest challenges tend to be fitting in special instruction during an already busy day, having appropriate materials and organizing them quickly, and maintaining structure and concentration when interruptions and distractions are frequent.

Houghton Mifflin Reading's universal access materials are a time-saving system of instruction to help teachers meet these challenges. With this group of handbooks you can turn your attention to specific needs in your classroom—to advanced students, students who are struggling below level, or students who are learning English—while other students work independently. The Challenge, Extra Support, and English Language Learners handbooks are each tied to the core instruction in *Houghton Mifflin Reading: A Legacy of Literacy.* For independent work, the *Classroom Management Handbook* provides meaningful activities related to literature selections and to core skills.

As a group, the universal access handbooks:

- help you manage your classroom and organize your time effectively

- provide excellent, additional instruction

- give you the resources you need to help *all* students achieve grade-level expectations

Extra Support Handbook Overview

The *Extra Support Handbook* provides support to enable lower-performing students participate effectively in the instruction and reading opportunities in *Houghton Mifflin Reading.* Lessons in this handbook coincide with the daily skill instruction in your *Houghton Mifflin Reading* Teacher's Edition, providing critical support for students prior to or following core instruction. Handbook lessons are specifically designed for students needing extra support:

- Lessons are presented in a five-day plan for preteaching and reteaching key skills and previewing core literature.

- Lessons focus on essential decoding and comprehension skills.

- Instruction is explicit and systematic, with concepts presented in easy, step-by-step order.

- Student learning is scaffolded through teacher modeling, visual examples, and interactive guided practice.

- Lessons include regular comprehension checks to monitor student understanding.

- The Practice/Apply step provides meaningful independent practice.

Your goal is to advance these students to greater proficiency and ultimately to on-level reading independence.

The *Extra Support Handbook* is one of several options in *Houghton Mifflin Reading* for providing extra support for students who need it. Your Teacher's Edition provides suggestions for each anthology selection and includes a Theme Resources section for support at the theme level. However, the *Extra Support Handbook* targets key skills in greater depth, building fluency and confidence.

Identifying Students Who Need Extra Support

Students who will benefit from Extra Support instruction include those who struggle to read on-level fiction and nonfiction, who read at one or more grades below level, or who are in a Title 1 or similar program. These students may have difficulty with decoding or comprehension or both. They may be able to decode simple words but need help learning to decode longer words. Some may be able to decode or "call" most words but cannot comprehend the meaning of what they read. Others may lack fluency, being unable to read rapidly and accurately enough to grasp the meaning of the text.

Evaluating Student's Needs At the start of the year, and periodically throughout the year, you can evaluate student's instructional needs using the diagnostic assessments included in *Houghton Mifflin Reading*. These instruments include the Baseline Group Test, Leveled Reading Passages, Phonics Decoding Screening Test, and others. More information on diagnostic assessment can be found in the *Teacher's Assessment Handbook*. In general, students who need extra support will likely fall into one of the following groups:

- **Benchmark Group** These students' difficulties tend to be temporary or intermittent. In general, they are meeting their learning goals and are not performing far below grade-level expectations. You can determine specific difficulties using the Diagnostic Checks in the Teacher's Edition. Often, the Reteaching Lessons in the Theme Resources section of the Teacher's Edition provide sufficient support. In some cases, these students may need the more ongoing support provided by the lessons in this handbook.

Frequent, positive feedback supports students' belief that they can do well. Make sure students who are struggling have opportunities for success.

- **Strategic Group** Diagnostic assessment will show that these students' proficiencies are consistently below level, and this will be confirmed by your ongoing observations. These students need the regular, structured preteaching and reteaching support provided in this handbook. They should be evaluated regularly to make sure that they are progressing toward meeting grade level expectations.

- **Intensive Group** These students are likely to be reading two grade levels or more below expectations. Diagnostic testing may reveal significant lack of decoding or comprehension skills. These students should receive intensive intervention or an individualized education plan. In the meantime, they can benefit from the lessons included in this handbook.

Once you have diagnostics underway, the *Classroom Management Handbook* provides guidance for managing groups for differentiated instruction.

Lesson Structure

The number of Extra Support lessons are related to the frequency of word identification and comprehension lessons in the core program. Preteaching prepares students for whole-class instruction; reteaching after core instruction provides more practice. Further, each daily lesson includes a literature focus in the form of guided previews or through revisiting selections or ancillary literature. Lessons are not intended to substitute for core instruction, but are in addition to it.

The handbook provides multiple ways of explaining a concept, flexibility in pacing, levels of complexity, and frequent checks of student understanding.

Five-day Instructional Plan

DAY 1	DAY 2	DAY 3	DAY 4	DAY 5
PRETEACH Structural analysis skill	**PRETEACH** Comprehension skill	**RETEACH** Structural analysis skill	**RETEACH** Grammar skill	**RETEACH** Comprehension skill
PREVIEW Anthology selection, first segment	**PREVIEW** Anthology selection, second segment	**PREVISIT** Anthology selection, apply comprehension skill	**PREVIEW** Reader's Library selection	**REVISIT** Anthology and Reader's Library selection: apply structural analysis skill

A consistent pattern of preteaching, reteaching, and revisiting skills is built into instruction day to day, and week to week. Consistency, repetition, and predictably help students progress more quickly. Skill focus instruction is modeled step-by step for students. Appropriate examples are used to help students comprehend the skill. Student understanding is monitored carefully with reminders to check that every student comprehends.

An application of the skill is presented and modeled, using the Teaching Master. This master introduces the skill in an interactive, visual way. The teacher guides students through the process, and then students practice and apply the skill on their own.

Teacher support for each selection includes:

Skill focus

- Easily scanned objectives and materials
- A warm-up where the skill is defined
- Guided instruction
- Visual examples
- Guided practice using the Teaching Master
- Teaching Master facsimile reference
- Support for Practice Master

Literature focus

- Literature citation
- Support for preview and review

See the Walkthrough on the following pages for more information.

To the Teacher

This walkthrough will familiarize you with the five-day instructional plans for Extra Support. Each plan is based on a selection in this level of *Houghton Mifflin Reading*. Days 1 and 3 are presented here for *Akiak* and show the basic features of a typical lesson.

Instruction Labels

Preteach or Reteach labels note when to use the lesson in relation to core instruction. The type of Skill Focus lesson is shown and a suggested amount of time to spend on it.

Warm-Up Lesson Opener

For Day 1, the easy-to-scan introductory paragraph allows a quick identification of the focus of the skill. Definitions are provided to familiarize students with the academic language related to the skill.

Objectives/Materials

Skill Focus objectives are listed each day. Materials are provided at the back of the handbook; literature needed for the Literature Focus is listed.

Additional Resources

The Get Set for Reading CD-ROM builds background and summarizes the selection. Students can log on to the Education Place site for activities. The theme audiotape helps with listening and comprehension skills. The Lexia Phonics CD-ROM provides phonics intervention.

THEME 1/ SELECTION 1
Akiak

Day 1

PRETEACH

SKILL FOCUS: STRUCTURAL ANALYSIS   25-30 MINUTES

Base Words and Endings -er and -est

Objective
• read base words with inflectional endings -er and -est

Materials
• Teaching Master ES1-1
• Practice Master ES1-1
• Letter Cards a,d,d,e, e,f,g,l,n,n,r,r,s,t,u,y
• Anthology: *Akiak*

Technology

Get Set for Reading CD-ROM
Akiak

Education Place
www.eduplace.com
Akiak

Audiotape
Akiak
Audiotape for **Journeys**

Lexia Phonics CD-ROM
Intermediate Intervention

Warm-Up/Academic Language

Remind students that a **base word** is a word that can have its meaning changed by adding different beginnings and endings. Tell students that they will learn about adding the **endings -er and -est** to base words. Explain that **-er** can be added to many adjectives to **compare two things** and that **-est** can be added to many adjectives to **compare three or more things**.

Teach

Draw a tall building on the board. Have all students draw pictures of a tall building on a piece of paper. Now draw a picture of a building that is *taller* than the first one. Have students follow your example on their papers. Repeat the exercise for the *tallest* building.

Write the word *tall* under the first building and these equations under the second and third buildings: *tall + er = taller*, *tall + est = tallest*. Have students label their buildings and then circle the base words.

Repeat the drawing exercise, this time asking students to make drawings with labels for *small, smaller, smallest* and *fast, faster, fastest*.

Explain that there are some base words that require spelling changes when the -er and -est endings are added to them.

• If a word ends with *e*, drop *e* before adding -er and -est.

• If a word ends with *y*, change *y* to *i* before adding -er and -est.

• If a one-syllable base word ends in a short vowel and a consonant, the consonant must be doubled before adding -er and -est.

Drop Silent *e*	Change final y to *i*	Double final consonant
wid	heav + i	hot+t
wid+er = wider	heavi+er = heavier	hot+t+er = hotter
wid+est = widest	heavi+est = heaviest	hot+t+est = hottest

14 THEME 1: **Journeys**

Blackline Masters

The Teaching Master and Practice Master are shown for reference. See the following pages for descriptions of the masters.

Give students individual letter cards that spell the base word *large*. Next, hand out letter cards that spell each of the endings *-er* and *-est*.

Instruct the students with the cards *l, a, r, g, e* to stand up and arrange themselves to spell out their word. Then have students with *e* and *r* cards join the group and arrange to spell the word *larger*. Note that the student holding silent *e* will need to sit down. Follow the same procedure with the word *largest*.

Repeat this exercise for the words *funny* and *red*. Note that for *funny* the student holding *y* will need to sit down and be replaced by the student holding *i*. For *red*, you will need to hand out a second *d*.

Guided Practice

Display or **distribute** Teaching Master ES1-1. Read the title and discuss the illustration with students.

Tell children to use what they know about the endings *-er* and *-est* to read the story independently.

Help students to underline *-er* and *-est* words as they read the story aloud. Have students read the underlined word aloud, say the meaning, and identify the base word within.

Practice/Apply

Distribute Practice Master ES1-1 to students.

Have students complete the Practice Master independently.

Ask selected students to share their sentences with the class.

Check students' papers to be sure they know which form of comparative to use.

LITERATURE FOCUS: 10-15 MINUTES

Preview *Akiak* Segment 1

Refer to the bottom of page 29 in the Teacher's Edition and preview with students Segment 1 of *Akiak* (pages 29–41).

Note the suggestions in the Extra Support boxes on Teacher's Edition pages 30, 37, and 38.

Teaching Master ES 1-1

**Base Words and Endings
-er and -est**

The Greatest Dog in Town

Our dog Rex is the greatest dog in town. He's braver than any other dog. He's also noisier than any dog! He gets hungrier and thirstier than any of our friends' dogs. He's got the wettest nose and the sharpest ears in the neighborhood. High fives for Rex! No, wait a minute — highest fives for Rex!

Practice Master ES 1-1

Name

**Base Words and Endings
-er and -est**

Write a sentence using each of the numbered words.

Answers will vary.

1. loud
2. louder
3. loudest

Answers will vary.

1. strong
2. stronger
3. strongest

Answers will vary.

1. silly
2. sillier
3. silliest

SELECTION 1: *Akiak* 15

Guided Practice

After teaching the skill, this section allows you to gradually turn the responsibility for practice to the students and to give immediate feedback. See the Teaching Master description on the following page.

Practice/Apply

Student use the Practice Master to work on the skill independently. This provides an additional opportunity to assess student comprehension.

Literature Preview

The selection walkthrough is targeted at the day's reading in the core program, and follows the previewing suggestions in the Teacher's Edition.

Blackline Masters

Shown here are the Teaching Master and Practice Master for Day 1 of *Akiak*.

Skill Title

To familiarize students with the academic language for the skills they are learning, the skill title is shown on both the Teaching and Practice masters.

Guided Practice

Guided practice with the master is the key step prior to independent skill practice. By this point, examples and applications have progressed from the most basic to a readiness for core instruction.

Teaching Master

The Teaching Master is used as a verbal guide to model the process and practice expected of students for applying the skill. Teaching Masters can be held up or displayed for guiding students through the activity, or they can be copied and distributed so that students can follow along individually.

Teaching Master **ES 1–1**   *Akiak*

Base Words and Endings
-er and *-est*

The Greatest Dog in Town

Our dog Rex is the greatest dog in town. He's braver than any other dog. He's also noisier than any dog! He gets hungrier and thirstier than any of our friends' dogs. He's got the wettest nose and the sharpest ears in the neighborhood. High fives for Rex! No, wait a minute — highest fives for Rex!

Grade 4   Theme 1: Journeys   **TMES 1–1**

Copyright © Houghton Mifflin Company. All rights reserved.

Practice Master

Students practice the skill with a brief activity to check mastery. As students explain their answers, you have the opportunity to make corrections immediately and give positive feedback.

Copyright © Houghton Mifflin Company. all rights reserved.

Practice Master **ES 1–1**   *Akiak*

Name_____

Base Words and Endings
-er and -est

Write a sentence using each of the numbered words.

Answers will vary.

1. loud
2. louder
3. loudest

Answers will vary.

1. strong
2. stronger
3. strongest

Answers will vary.

1. silly
2. sillier
3. silliest

Grade 4   Theme 1: Journeys   **PMES 1–1**

Visual Support

Usually an illustration or illustrations are added that can help reinforce the skill concept.

Skill Focus: Reteach

Day 3 lessons typically reteach a skill or skills presented in Day 1. Notice the Reteach label and the skill title, along with the suggested amount of time for instruction.

3-Step Approach

Reteach lessons rely on a **Teach/Practice/Apply** lesson approach, using multiple examples for reinforcement.

Think Aloud

This feature can be present in instruction on any day. Frequent modeling of conceptual processes is key to building proficiency. For visual learners, it's helpful to use gestures or write and draw as you think aloud.

Directive Verbs

For ease of use, the beginning verb of each paragraph is boldfaced.

THEME 1/ SELECTION 1: *Akiak*

Day 3

RETEACH

SKILL FOCUS: STRUCTURAL ANALYSIS   25-30 MINUTES

Base Words and Endings
-er and -est

Objectives

- decode words with endings *-er* and *-est*
- identify meaning of words with the comparative endings *-er* and *-est*

Materials

- Anthology: *Akiak*
- paper clip, pen, and ruler
- index cards

Teach

Write the words *long, longer,* and *longest* on the board. Display a paper clip, pen, and ruler, and ask, *Which is longer, the paper clip or pen?* Then ask, *Which is the longest, the paper clip, the pen, or the ruler?*

Use *long, longer, longest* to review the concepts of *base word* and *ending*. Underline the base word (long) and circle the endings in each of the words. (-er, -est)

Display the following sentence: *Even when trails were confusing, Akiak found the fastest way.* Model decoding the word *fastest*.

> **Think Aloud**
>
> *When I look at the letters in this word, I see it has the -est ending. So, next I'll look for the base word. I see a word I know: fast. Now I'll put the parts together and blend the sounds. I get the word/fast est/. I'll check to see if it makes sense in the sentence. It does.*

Explain that the *-er* and *-est* endings are used to compare things. The letters *-er* show that two things are being compared; the letters *-est* show that three or more things are being compared.

 THEME 1: **Journeys**

Visual Support

Chalkboards and notebook art help organize instruction for visual learning and promote active student involvement.

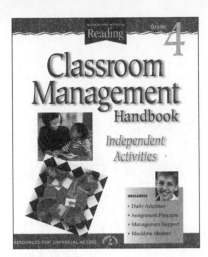

Suggestions for grouping and planners for coordinating small group instruction can be found in the *Classroom Management Handbook*, along with selection-based independent activities.

Practice

Help students practice reading words ending in *-er* and *-est*. Display the following sets of words:

cool	cooler	coolest
deep	deeper	deepest
warm	warmer	warmest
short	shorter	shortest

Read each set aloud with students. Have students use each word in a sentence.

Apply

Write cards with familiar base words and the ending *-er* or *-est*. For example write, *louder, loudest; softer, softest; bigger, biggest*. Have students work in pairs and take turns choosing a card, decoding the word, and using it in a sentence.

LITERATURE FOCUS: 10-15 MINUTES

Review *Akiak*

Guide students through the Comprehension Skill Lesson for **Story Structure** on page 39 of the Teacher's Edition.

Literature Review

By Day 3, students have previewed and read both segments of the anthology selection. Use the Teacher's Edition as noted to review both segments. For Days 4 and 5, students will preview other program literature and revisit the selection.

SELECTION 1: *Akiak* 19

Theme 1

Journeys

Selections

1 Akiak

2 Grandfather's Journey

3 Finding the Titanic

4 By the Shores of Silver Lake

Day 1

Objective

- read base words with inflectional endings *-er* and *-est*

Materials

- Teaching Master ES1-1
- Practice Master ES1-1
- Letter Cards *a,d,d,e, e,f,g,l,n,n,r,r,s,t,u,y*
- Anthology: *Akiak*

Get Set for Reading CD-ROM

Akiak

Education Place

www.eduplace.com
Akiak

Audiotape

Akiak
Audiotape for **Journeys**

Lexia Phonics CD-ROM

Intermediate Intervention

Base Words and Endings -er and -est

Warm-Up/Academic Language

Remind students that a **base word** is a word that can have its meaning changed by adding different beginnings and endings. Tell students that they will learn about adding the **endings -er and -est** to base words. Explain that *-er* can be added to many adjectives to **compare two things** and that *-est* can be added to many adjectives to **compare three or more things**.

Teach

Draw a tall building on the board. Have all students draw pictures of a tall building on a piece of paper. Now draw a picture of a building that is *taller* than the first one. Have students follow your example on their papers. Repeat the exercise for the *tallest* building.

Write the word *tall* under the first building and these equations under the second and third buildings: *tall + er = taller, tall + est = tallest*. Have students label their buildings and then circle the base words.

Repeat the drawing exercise, this time asking students to make drawings with labels for *small, smaller, smallest* and *fast, faster, fastest*.

Explain that there are some base words that require spelling changes when the *-er* and *-est* endings are added to them.

- If a word ends with *e*, drop *e* before adding *-er* and *-est*.
- If a word ends with *y*, change *y* to *i* before adding *-er* and *-est*.
- If a one-syllable base word ends in a short vowel and a consonant, the consonant must be doubled before adding *-er* and *-est*.

Drop Silent *e*	Change final y to i	Double final consonant
wid	heav + i	hot+t
wid+*er* = wider	heavi+*er* = heavier	hot+t+er = hotter
wid+*est* = widest	heavi+*est* = heaviest	hot+t+est = hottest

Give students individual letter cards that spell the base word *large*. Next, hand out letter cards that spell each of the endings *-er* and *-est*.

Instruct the students with the cards *l, a, r, g, e* to stand up and arrange themselves to spell out their word. Then have students with *e* and *r* cards join the group and arrange to spell the word *larger*. Note that the student holding silent *e* will need to sit down. Follow the same procedure with the word *largest*.

Repeat this exercise for the words *funny* and *red*. Note that for *funny* the student holding *y* will need to sit down and be replaced by the student holding *i*. For *red*, you will need to hand out a second *d*.

Guided Practice

Display or **distribute** Teaching Master ES1-1. Read the title and discuss the illustration with students.

Tell children to use what they know about the endings *-er* and *-est* to read the story independently.

Help students to underline *-er* and *-est* words as they read the story aloud. Have students read the underlined word aloud, say the meaning, and identify the base word within.

Practice/Apply

Distribute Practice Master ES1-1 to students.

Have students complete the Practice Master independently.

Ask selected students to share their sentences with the class.

Check students' papers to be sure they know which form of comparative to use.

Preview *Akiak* Segment I

Refer to the bottom of page 29 in the Teacher's Edition and preview with students Segment 1 of *Akiak* (pages 29–41).

Note the suggestions in the Extra Support boxes on Teacher's Edition pages 30, 37, and 38.

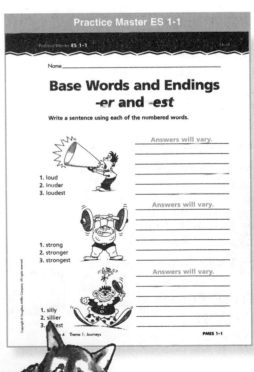

Day 2

Objectives
- identify story characters, setting, and plot
- recognize a story's structure

Materials
- Teaching Master ES1-2
- Practice Master ES1-2
- Anthology: *Akiak*

SKILL FOCUS: COMPREHENSION   25-30 MINUTES

Story Structure

Warm-Up/Academic Language

Explain that stories are alike in some ways. Almost all stories have **characters** (who is in a story), a **setting** (where and when a story takes place), and a **plot** (what happens in a story – the **problem**, the attempts to solve the problem, and finally, the **solution**).

Teach

Read this story with students. Then reread it, asking two volunteers to act out the parts of Brad and Brenna.

Read Aloud

> The singing of birds awakened Brad. He looked at his alarm clock and scratched his head. "My alarm never went off. It's eight o'clock, and I'm going to be late for school!"
>
> Brad leaped out of bed, pulled on his clothes wildly, and raced to the kitchen. He was gulping orange juice when his twin sister, Brenna, walked in. She looked sleepy and was still wearing her pajamas.
>
> "Hurry up! We're going to be late for school," Brad said.
>
> Brenna laughed and pointed to the calendar on the wall. "Today is Saturday, Brad. There's no school today." Then she rolled her eyes and walked away.

Draw the following chart on the board:

Characters	Setting	Plot
Brad, Brenna	Brad's house, Saturday morning	**Problem:** Brad thinks he's late for school **Solution:** It's Saturday

Have students fill in the chart. Assist students as needed.

Guided Practice

Display or **distribute** Teaching Master ES1-2. Students may read the story independently, or if needed, follow along as you read it aloud.

Point out the names of the characters in the story and where the story is set. (a Florida yard on a Saturday)

Summarize the plot by thinking aloud about the problem, events, and solution:

Think Aloud

> *The problem is that Harry wants to help a dog that seems to be hurt, but he can't take it home or to a vet. When he gives the dog water, it drinks and then walks away. The problem is solved.*

Lead students through the story arc, helping them to identify the characters, the events, the problem, and the solution.

Practice/Apply

Distribute Practice Master ES1-2 to students.

Have them read the story independently, and label the characters' names and the setting.

Ask them to fill in the story arc by writing story events in the circles.

Check students' work to ensure that they understand the elements of story structure.

LITERATURE FOCUS: 10-15 MINUTES

Preview *Akiak* Segment 2

Refer to the bottom of page 42 in the Teacher's Edition and preview with students Segment 2 of *Akiak* (pages 42–51).

Note the suggestion in the Extra Support box on Teacher's Edition page 45.

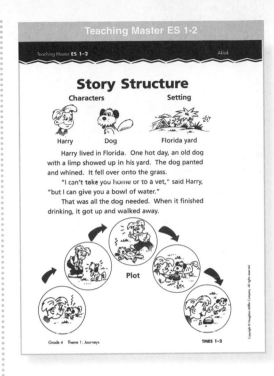

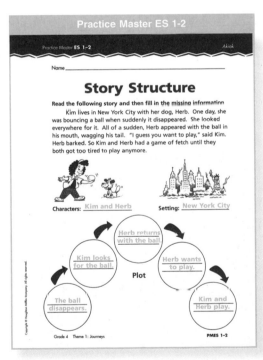

Day 3

Base Words and Endings -*er* and -*est*

Teach

Write the words *long*, *longer*, and *longest* on the board. Display a paper clip, pen, and ruler, and ask, *Which is longer, the paper clip or pen?* Then ask, *Which is the longest, the paper clip, the pen, or the ruler?*

Use *long*, *longer*, *longest* to review the concepts of *base word* and *ending*. Underline the base word (long) and circle the endings in each of the words. (-er, -est)

Display the following sentence: *Even when trails were confusing, Akiak found the fastest way.* Model decoding the word *fastest*.

Think Aloud

When I look at the letters in this word, I see it has the -est ending. So, next I'll look for the base word. I see a word I know: fast. Now I'll put the parts together and blend the sounds. I get the word /fast est/. I'll check to see if it makes sense in the sentence. It does.

Explain that the -*er* and -*est* endings are used to compare things. The letters -*er* show that two things are being compared; the letters -*est* show that three or more things are being compared.

Objectives

- decode words with endings -*er* and -*est*
- identify meaning of words with the comparative endings -*er* and -*est*

Materials

- Anthology: *Akiak*
- paper clip, pen, and ruler
- index cards

Practice

Help students practice reading words ending in *-er* and *-est*. Display the following sets of words:

cool	cooler	coolest
deep	deeper	deepest
warm	warmer	warmest
short	shorter	shortest

Read each set aloud with students. Have students use each word in a sentence.

Apply

Write cards with familiar base words and the ending *-er* or *-est*. For example write, *louder*, *loudest*; *softer*, *softest*; *bigger*, *biggest*. Have students work in pairs and take turns choosing a card, decoding the word, and using it in a sentence.

LITERATURE FOCUS: 10–15 MINUTES

Review *Akiak*

Guide students through the Comprehension Skill Lesson for **Story Structure** on page 39 of the Teacher's Edition.

Objectives

- identify four types of sentences: *statements*, *commands*, *questions*, and *exclamations*
- punctuate the four types of sentences correctly
- write four types of sentences

Materials

- Anthology: *Akiak*
- Reader's Library: *Sky*
- index cards

RETEACH

SKILL FOCUS: GRAMMAR   25–30 MINUTES

Kinds of Sentences

Teach

Write the following sentences about the story *Akiak* on the chalkboard:

> 1. The men tried to catch Akiak.
>
> 2. Why is Akiak running away?
>
> 3. Stay here, Akiak.
>
> 4. There she is!

Point to each sentence type as you describe it.

Point out the appropriate end marks.

> 1. A <u>statement</u> tells something.
>
> 2. A <u>question</u> asks something.
>
> 3. A <u>command</u> gives an order.
>
> 4. An <u>exclamation</u> shows strong feeling.

Have students read the four sample sentences aloud. Discuss how their voices change when they read different kinds of sentences. For example, a high tone of voice usually ends a question, while a lower tone and higher volume usually indicate an exclamation.

Practice

Have students write the words *statement*, *question*, *command*, and *exclamation* on separate index cards. Read page 49 aloud to students. Pause after each sentence, and ask students to raise the index card that names the type of sentence you have just read.

Apply

Have students revisit page 49. Encourage students to work in pairs to locate an example of each sentence type.

Ask students to write an example of each sentence type and label it.

LITERATURE FOCUS: 10-15 MINUTES

Preview *Sky*

Walk students through *Sky*, and discuss illustrations, using words such as *roundup*, *mare*, and *reins*.

Have students predict what the story's setting and plot will be, based on a quick scan of the illustrations. Students may also predict who the characters will be.

Day 5

Objectives
- identify story characters, setting, and plot
- recognize a story's structure

Materials
- Anthology: *Akiak*
- Reader's Library: *Sky*

SKILL FOCUS: COMPREHENSION   25-30 MINUTES

Story Structure

Teach

Write the following story map on the chalkboard. Use the prompts to review and discuss the parts of a familiar story, such as *Cinderella*.

Who is in the story?	characters
Where does it take place? When?	setting
What is the problem the character(s) is trying to solve?	problem
What happens?	action
How does the story end? How is the problem solved?	outcome

Explain that most stories have the basic elements of characters, setting, a problem, action, and a solution, or outcome.

Practice

Have students use the story map to determine the story structure of *Akiak*. Ask students to revisit page 30 of the story. Help them identify the setting. Have a student write it on the story map. Continue in this way until all the elements are identified.

Apply

Have students keep track of story structure with an eye to identifying characters, setting, problem, and outcome in *Sky* by Julia Hanna in the Reader's Library. Ask students to complete the questions and activity on the Responding page.

LITERATURE FOCUS: 10-15 MINUTES

Revisit *Akiak* and *Sky*

Guide students through *Akiak* and *Sky*, helping them to identify base words with endings *-er* and *-est* such as *safest, fastest*, (*Akiak*, page 33) *faster*, and *hotter* (*Sky*, pages 7, 18). Also, briefly review the story structures for *Akiak* and *Sky*, comparing and contrasting when possible.

Day 1

Objective

- form new words by adding the suffixes -*ly* and -*y*

Materials

- Teaching Master ES1-3
- Practice Master ES1-3
- Letter Cards *a, c, d, e, e, f, g, i, k, l, l, o, r, s, u, y, y*
- Anthology: *Grandfather's Journey*

Get Set for Reading CD-ROM
Grandfather's Journey

Education Place
www.eduplace.com
Grandfather's Journey

Audiotape
Grandfather's Journey
Audiotape for **Journeys**

Lexia Phonics CD-ROM
Intermediate Intervention

PRETEACH

SKILL FOCUS: STRUCTURAL ANALYSIS   25-30 MINUTES

Suffixes -*ly* and -*y*

Warm-Up/Academic Language

Remind students that a **base word** can have its meaning changed by adding different beginnings and endings. Tell students that today they will learn about **adding the endings -*y* and -*ly***. Tell students that -*y* and -*ly* words are used for describing things.

Teach

Ask students to demonstrate the word *quiet* by whispering in a quiet way. Write the base word *quiet* on the board and read the word aloud. Write + *ly* = beside *quiet* on the board. Call on a volunteer to complete the equation. Next, have the student use the new word in a sentence that describes the way in which students whispered. (We whispered quietly.)

Explain that *quietly* is the base word *quiet* with the suffix -*ly*. Tell students that this suffix changes the meaning of *quiet* to "in a way that is" quiet.

Repeat the above steps for the words *loud*, *quick*, *rain*, and *wind*. Explain to students that -*ly* doesn't always fit with every base word. Explain that the suffix -*y* has the same meaning as -*ly*.

Write out these equations for the words rain and wind: *rain + y = rainy*, *wind + y = windy*.

Tell students that some base words need spelling changes when adding the -*ly* and -*y* suffixes.

- When adding the suffix -*ly* to a word ending in *y*, the *y* becomes an *i*. (angrily, happily)

- When adding the suffix -*y* to many words ending in a short vowel and a consonant, the consonant is doubled before adding the ending. (baggy, funny)

Write *luck*, *lucky*, and *luckily* on the board. Guide students to observe that an -*ly* suffix was added to the base word *lucky* to form *luckily*. Point out that the *y* changed to *i* when the suffix was added.

Distribute the letter cards *l, u, c, k,* and *y* to five students. Have them come to the front and spell out *lucky*. Give three students the letter cards *i, l,* and *y*. Have them work with the first group to spell out *luckily*. Note that the first *y* student will need to sit down.

Repeat the procedure with the words *sleep*, *rude*, *fog*, and *easy*.

Guided Practice

Display or **distribute** Teaching Master ES1-3, and read the story with students.

Reread the story, pausing at the end of each sentence to review each boldfaced word.

Help students to cross out each bolded word and write the *-ly* or *-y* form above it to make a new word that means "in the manner of."

Practice/Apply

Distribute Practice Master ES1-3 to students and go over the directions.

Instruct students to complete the worksheet independently.

Check students' understanding of *-ly* and *-y* by calling on them to read their answers.

LITERATURE FOCUS: 10-15 MINUTES

Preview *Grandfather's Journey*

Segment 1

Refer to the bottom of page 62 in the Teacher's Edition and preview with students Segment 1 of *Grandfather's Journey* (pages 62–69).

Note the suggestions in the Extra Support boxes on Teacher's Edition pages 65 and 68.

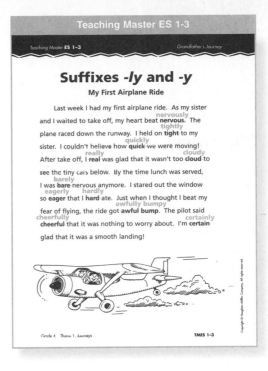

Teaching Master ES 1-3

Teaching Master **ES 1-3**   *Grandfather's Journey*

Suffixes *-ly* and *-y*
My First Airplane Ride

Last week I had my first airplane ride. As my sister and I waited to take off, my heart beat **nervous**. (nervously) The plane raced down the runway. I held on **tight** (tightly) to my sister. I couldn't believe how **quick** (quickly) we were moving! After take off, I **real** (really) was glad that it wasn't too **cloud** (cloudy) to see the tiny cars below. By the time lunch was served, I was **bare** (barely) nervous anymore. I stared out the window so **eager** (eagerly) that I **hard** (hardly) ate. Just when I thought I beat my fear of flying, the ride got **awful bump**. (awfully bumpy) The pilot said **cheerful** (cheerfully) that it was nothing to worry about. I'm **certain** (certainly) glad that it was a smooth landing!

Grade 4   Theme 1: Journeys   **TMES 1–3**

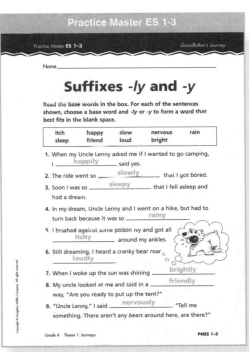

Practice Master ES 1-3

Practice Master **ES 1-3**   *Grandfather's Journey*

Name_____

Suffixes *-ly* and *-y*

Read the base words in the box. For each of the sentences shown, choose a base word and *-ly* or *-y* to form a word that best fits in the blank space.

| itch | happy | slow | nervous | rain |
| sleep | friend | loud | bright | |

1. When my Uncle Lenny asked me if I wanted to go camping, I _____ happily _____ said yes.

2. The ride went so _____ slowly _____ that I got bored.

3. Soon I was so _____ sleepy _____ that I fell asleep and had a dream.

4. In my dream, Uncle Lenny and I went on a hike, but had to turn back because it was so _____ rainy _____

5. I brushed against some poison ivy and got all _____ itchy _____ around my ankles.

6. Still dreaming, I heard a cranky bear roar _____ loudly _____

7. When I woke up the sun was shining _____ brightly _____

8. My uncle looked at me and said in a _____ friendly _____ way, "Are you ready to put up the tent?"

9. "Uncle Lenny," I said _____ nervously _____. "Tell me something. There aren't any *bears* around here, are there?"

Grade 4   Theme 1: Journeys   **PMES 1–3**

Day 2

Objective

- make inferences from story clues to identify an author's feelings, attitude, and purpose

Materials

- Teaching Master ES1-4
- Practice Master ES1-4
- Anthology: *Grandfather's Journey*

SKILL FOCUS: COMPREHENSION   25-30 MINUTES

Author's Viewpoint

Warm-Up/Academic Language

Explain that a **writer** may show his or her **attitude** or **feelings** on a topic by giving readers important **clues**. Among these clues are an author's **word choices**, **opinions**, **focus** and **purpose** for writing. Any combination of these clues can help to show an **author's viewpoint**.

Teach

Read the story aloud. Then reread it and have three volunteers act out the parts of Mom, Tim, and Chen.

Read Aloud

Mom gave me a pep talk on the first day of school. "Relax, Tim," she said. "Just be yourself."

Mom said that fourth grade would be a new beginning. I hoped so. In third grade, I didn't have many friends.

Fourth grade got off to a bad start. No one sat beside me on the bus. But things got better during lunch. A boy from my neighborhood sat down beside me. He showed me a cardinal feather that he found at summer camp. Chen said he always carried the feather with him for good luck.

"I could use a lucky feather, too!" I exclaimed.

Chen suggested that we go out looking for my lucky feather that very day, right after school.

Guide students to identify the author's viewpoint in this story by using the following Think Aloud:

Think Aloud

Tim is nervous about making friends. The author doesn't give many details about the school, but focuses on the idea of friendship. She uses words such as "new beginning." Maybe the author wrote the story to help kids who don't easily make friends.

Copy the word web below on the board. Have students record their inferences on it.

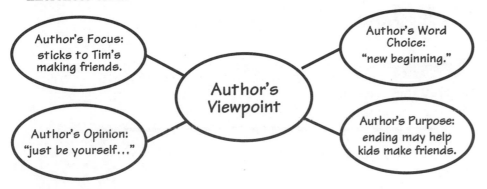

Guided Practice

Display or **distribute** Teaching Master ES1-4, and read the story with students.

Discuss the story and ask questions such as *How does the author feel about Heidi?* and *What clues in the story tell you that?*

Guide students to interpret the author's viewpoint. Complete the graphic organizer together.

Practice/Apply

Distribute Practice Master ES1-4 to students.

Instruct students to read the story and complete the Practice Master. Prompt students to compare and contrast the author's feelings in the two stories.

Sum up the Author's Viewpoint based on student responses.

Check that students understand the various elements used to determine Author's Viewpoint.

LITERATURE FOCUS: 10-15 MINUTES

Preview *Grandfather's Journey*

Segment 2

Refer to the bottom of page 70 in the Teacher's Edition and preview with students Segment 2 of *Grandfather's Journey* (pages 70–75).

Note the suggestions in the Extra Support boxes on Teacher's Edition pages 72, 73, and 74.

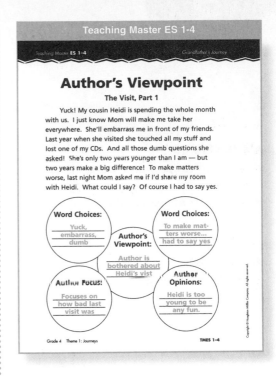

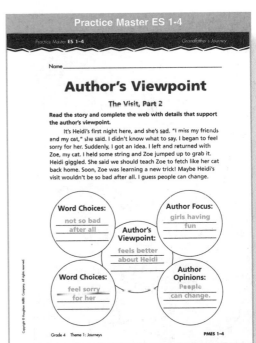

Day 3

Objectives

- recognize when words have the suffix *-ly* or *-y*
- decode words with suffixes *-ly* and *-y*

Materials

- Anthology: *Grandfather's Journey*

SKILL FOCUS: STRUCTURAL ANALYSIS   25-30 MINUTES

Suffixes *-ly* and *-y*

Teach

Display these sentences:

> We have had a week of cold and <u>wind</u>y nights.
>
> It was three weeks before land <u>final</u>ly appeared.

Review the concepts *base word* and *suffix*, and underline *final* and *wind*; circle *-ly* and *-y*. Explain that in these words, *-ly* and *-y* are suffixes, or word parts added to the end of a base word. Remind students that the following tips can help them decode words with the suffixes *-y* and *-ly*:

- A suffix always appears *after* the base word.

- A suffix is usually a syllable.

- A suffix has the same pronunciation in different words.

Practice

Help students identify the base words and suffixes in the following words:

quickly	rainy
weekly	bumpy

Apply

Write these words on the board: *speedy*, *bravely*, *muddy*. Have students identify the base word and suffix in each word. Ask students to use each word in a sentence.

Review *Grandfather's Journey*

Guide students through the Comprehension Skill Lesson for **Author's Viewpoint** on page 65 of the Teacher's Edition.

SKILL FOCUS: GRAMMAR   25-30 MINUTES

Subjects and Predicates

Teach

Write the following on the board:

> ### The family traveled far.
>
> | What or whom is the sentence about? | Which words tell what the subject does or is? |
> |---|---|
> | [subject] | [predicate] |

Ask students the first question. Help students understand that *The family* is the complete subject; it tells whom this sentence is about. Underline *The family*.

Ask the next question. Help students understand that *traveled far* is the complete predicate of this sentence. It tells what the subject did. Draw a double line under *traveled far*.

Remind students that a sentence needs both a subject and a predicate to express a complete thought.

Explain that the main word in a complete subject is the *simple subject*. It tells exactly what or whom the sentence is about. Ask students for a one-word answer to the question, *What or whom is this sentence about?* (family) Ask students for a one-word answer to the question, *Which word tells what the subject does or is?* (traveled) Explain that the main word in a complete predicate is the simple predicate. It tells exactly what the subject does or is.

Practice

Display this sentence: *My grandfather bought a house in a large city.*

Ask students to identify the complete subject (My grandfather), the complete predicate (bought a house in a large city), the simple subject (grandfather), and the simple predicate. (bought)

Objectives

- identify complete subjects and complete predicates in sentences
- write complete sentences
- identify simple subjects and simple predicates in sentences

Materials

- Reader's Library: *Elena in America*

Apply

Have students fold a piece of paper lengthwise, and mark the left column *complete subject*, the right column *complete predicate*.

Direct students to write a subject or a predicate and pass the paper left. The receiver completes the sentence and passes the paper left. Repeat the process.

Have students take turns reading a favorite sentence when enough of them are written. Choose one sentence, display it on the board, and ask volunteers to identify the simple subject and the simple predicate.

LITERATURE FOCUS: 10-15 MINUTES

Preview *Elena in America*

Walk students through *Elena in America* and discuss the illustrations, using words from the story such as *Russian*, *village*, and *stranger*.

Ask students to predict the author's viewpoint relating to Elena's experiences in America. Is it positive or negative? Have students give reasons to support their responses.

Day 5

Objectives

- use story words to infer author's viewpoint
- explain author's viewpoint

Materials

- Anthology: *Grandfather's Journey*
- Reader's Library: *Elena in America*

SKILL FOCUS: COMPREHENSION   25-30 MINUTES

Author's Viewpoint

Teach

Encourage students to recall the first time they went to a new place. Ask them to write two sentences to describe their feelings.

Read one student's sentences to the class. Ask students whether or not the writer has a positive attitude toward the place, and what makes them think so. Repeat this process several times.

Explain that by taking a closer look at the words an author uses, students will often be able to tell how the author feels about the topic she or he is writing about.

Have students reread pages 64–66 of *Grandfather's Journey* silently. Then model how to identify an author's viewpoint.

Think Aloud

As I read these pages, I see that Allen Say used lively words and phrases such as amazed, excited, marveled, longed to see new places, never thought of returning home. *I know that the author is talking about his grandfather's experiences. But if I add up all those lively words, I begin to see that Allen Say's own feelings and attitudes about America are probably also positive. Otherwise, he might not have used such lively, positive words to describe America.*

Practice

Have students read page 68 and identify words and phrases that describe either the character's feelings or the character's actions. Have students record their findings on a graphic organizer such as the one shown. It will help students decide how the author feels about America and Japan by the end of the story.

Feelings		Actions		Author's viewpoint
He could not forget his homeland.	+	He returned to his home-land.	=	He loves Japan.

Apply

Have students keep track of the author's viewpoint with an eye to the author's choice of words as they read *Elena in America*, by Robin Bloksberg, in the Reader's Library. Ask students to complete the questions and activity on the Responding page.

LITERATURE FOCUS: 10-15 MINUTES

Revisit *Grandfather's Journey* and *Elena in America*

Guide students through *Grandfather's Journey* and *Elena in America*, helping them look for words using suffixes *-ly* and *-y* such as *finally*, *funny*, (*Grandfather's Journey*, pages 63 and 74) and *lonely* (*Elena in America*, page 30). Also review the author's viewpoint in each of these selections.

Day 1

Objectives

- identify syllables within words
- use syllabication to decode long words
- use the Phonics/Decoding strategy to decode longer words

Materials

- Teaching Master ES1-5
- Practice Master ES1-5
- Anthology: *Finding the Titanic*

Technology

Get Set for Reading CD-ROM
Finding the Titanic

Education Place
www.eduplace.com
Finding the Titanic

Audiotape
Finding the Titanic
Audiotape for **Journeys**

Lexia Phonics CD-ROM
Intermediate Intervention

PRETEACH

SKILL FOCUS: STRUCTURAL ANALYSIS · 25-30 MINUTES

Syllabication

Warm-Up/Academic Language

Explain that longer words can be divided into parts called **syllables**. Tell students that a syllable is a **word or word part** that has a **single vowel sound**.

Teach

Write the word *cat* on the board and underline the vowel that stands for / ă /. Then write *catnip* and underline the vowels that stand for the sounds / ă / and /ĭ/. Explain that *cat* has one vowel sound and one syllable and that *catnip* has two.

Write the word *boating* on the board. Say the word, pausing between the two syllables. Show how to tap out the two syllables. Then write the word in syllables: *boat / ing*. Have students count the syllables as you say them aloud. Point out the vowel sounds in each syllable. (/ ō /, /ĭ/)

Repeat the procedure using the words *shipwreck* and *explorer*.

Write the following on the board and lead students in tapping out the syllables: p*ort, porthole, survivor*, and *unbreakable*. Read the words aloud.

Write *enormous* on the board, read it aloud, and model decoding:

> **Think Aloud**
>
> *I know that every syllable has a vowel sound. When I look at the word* enormous, *I recognize the word parts* or *and* ous. *Each one has a vowel sound, so they may be syllables. Let me try en/or/mous. That's almost right. The first vowel may stand alone: e/nor/mous. I'll check the dictionary.*

Explain that there are some general guidelines to help students syllabicate words. Display the chart below and review it with students.

Guide students to pronounce the individual syllables of the example words in the chart.

GUIDELINES	EXAMPLES
VC/CV: Divide between two consonants most of the time.	bot/tom, won/der
• VC/V: Often, when a consonant is between two vowels, you can divide after the first vowel sound, making it short.	hov/er, mod/ern
• V/CV: You can try dividing before the consonant, making the first vowel sound long	fe/ver, na/ture
Divide between the two words that form a compound word.	life/boat, ice/berg
Divide between the prefix and the base word.	un/like, pre/view
Divide between the base word and the suffix.	friend/ly, sink/ing

Guided Practice

Display or **distribute** Teaching Master ES1-5 to students, and read the first word with them.

Reread it as students tap out the syllable(s). Remind them to use the number of taps and the number of vowel sounds to help them to identify the number of syllables. Follow the same procedure for *sailing*.

Have students help you to complete entries for the remaining words.

Practice/Apply

Distribute Practice Master ES1-5 to students and go over the directions.

Direct students to complete the Practice Master independently.

Check to ensure students understand syllabication guidelines as they share their answers with the group.

LITERATURE FOCUS: 10-15 MINUTES

Preview *Finding the Titanic*

Segment 1

Refer to the bottom of page 83 in the Teacher's Edition and preview with students Segment 1 of *Finding the Titanic* (pages 82–91). Note suggestions in the Extra Support boxes on Teacher's Edition pages 84, 85, and 90.

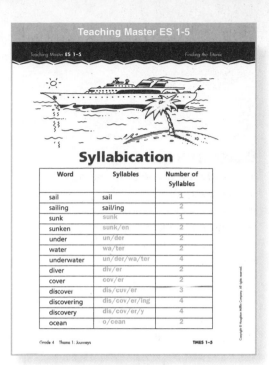

Teaching Master ES 1-5

Teaching Master **ES 1-5**   Finding the Titanic

Syllabication

Word	Syllables	Number of Syllables
sail	sail	1
sailing	sail/ing	2
sunk	sunk	1
sunken	sunk/en	2
under	un/der	2
water	wa/ter	2
underwater	un/der/wa/ter	4
diver	div/er	2
cover	cov/er	2
discover	dis/cov/er	3
discovering	dis/cov/er/ing	4
discovery	dis/cov/er/y	4
ocean	o/cean	2

Grade 4   Theme 1: Journeys   TMES 1-5

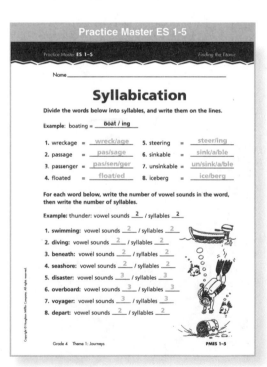

Practice Master ES 1-5

Practice Master **ES 1-5**   Finding the Titanic

Name _____

Syllabication

Divide the words below into syllables, and write them on the lines.

Example: boating = **boat / ing**

1. wreckage = wreck/age
2. passage = pas/sage
3. passenger = pas/sen/ger
4. floated = float/ed
5. steering = steer/ing
6. sinkable = sink/a/ble
7. unsinkable = un/sink/a/ble
8. iceberg = ice/berg

For each word below, write the number of vowel sounds in the word, then write the number of syllables.

Example: thunder: vowel sounds 2 / syllables 2

1. swimming: vowel sounds 2 / syllables 2
2. diving: vowel sounds 2 / syllables 2
3. beneath: vowel sounds 2 / syllables 2
4. seashore: vowel sounds 2 / syllables 2
5. disaster: vowel sounds 3 / syllables 3
6. overboard: vowel sounds 3 / syllables 3
7. voyager: vowel sounds 3 / syllables 3
8. depart: vowel sounds 2 / syllables 2

Grade 4   Theme 1: Journeys   PMES 1-5

Day 2

SKILL FOCUS: COMPREHENSION — 25-30 MINUTES

Text Organization

Warm-Up/Academic Language

Explain that authors **organize** their writing in many ways. They use features such as **titles, text, headings, pictures, labels,** and **captions** to **help readers understand information**.

Teach

Refer students to the Get Set to Read on Anthology pages 80–81 and have them scan the information. Point out these text features—title, text, caption, illustration, sidebar, and labels.

Guide students to observe the purpose of each of these features.

* *Titles* tell what the text will be about.
* *Text* gives most of the information, usually by presenting main ideas and supporting details. (Explain that in this example, important ideas are in boldface type.)
* *Illustrations* show the most important or interesting parts of the text.
* *Labels* tell about parts of the illustration using one or two words.
* *Captions* tell about the illustration using one or two sentences or phrases.
* *Sidebars* give interesting, related information, in a box to the side.

Ask selected students to point to where in the Get Set to Read each of these elements is given. Have each student come up to the front of the room for his or her example.

Guided Practice

Display or **distribute** Teaching Master ES1-6.

Read aloud to students the first description of the various text features in the second column.

Ask all students to help you to complete column one by giving the name of the special feature that fits.

Repeat the same procedure for the remaining features.

Objectives
* identify the purpose of various text features
* use text organization to understand a selection

Materials
* Teaching Master ES1-6
* Practice Master ES1-6
* Anthology: *Finding the Titanic*

Practice/Apply

Distribute Practice Master ES1-6 to students.

Instruct them to read the text and complete the Practice Master independently.

Review the answers with the whole class. Have students read their journal entries aloud and share their artwork.

Check that students can define the main elements of Text Organization.

LITERATURE FOCUS: 10-15 MINUTES

Preview *Finding the Titanic*

Segment 2

Refer to the bottom of page 92 in the Teacher's Edition and preview with students Segment 2 of *Finding the Titanic* (pages 92–101).

Note the suggestions in the Extra Support boxes on Teacher's Edition pages 95 and 100.

Teaching Master ES 1-6

Teaching Master **ES 1–6**   *Finding the Titanic*

Text Organization

Special Features	Description
Titles	Tell what the text is about
Text	A set of main ideas and supporting details
Headings	Tell you what each section is about by breaking the text up into smaller parts
Photos and Illustrations	Present information from the text in a visual way
Labels	Describe an illustration with one or two words
Captions	A longer description of a photo or illustration; may be one or more sentences
Sidebars	Present extra, interesting information about the text; are often on the side of the main text

Grade 4   Theme 1: Journeys   **TMES 1–6**

Practice Master ES 1-6

Practice Master **ES 1–6**   *Finding the Titanic*

Name _____

Text Organization

Read the text below and then write a short journal entry for the next day of the boat trip. Use a heading, text, an illustration, and a caption.

My Sailing Journal

the steering wheel   the anchor

Friday: And we're off!

My friend Sasha's dad has his own sailboat. Today we're all leaving for a three-day sailing trip. I've never slept on a boat before. There's not much room but it's cozy on the boat. The radio says that we can expect great weather. I can't wait to do some star-gazing later tonight.

Saturday: Rough seas!

The weather report was wrong! Today we sailed through a scary storm. Sasha's dad told us to put our life jackets on and stay in the cabin. I was worried that I'd get sick! Luckily, the storm passed quickly. By the time we returned upstairs, the sun was out and there was a big rainbow.

Grade 4   Theme 1: Journeys   **PMES 1–6**

Day 3

Reteach Syllabication

Teach

Remind students that long words can be divided into smaller parts called "syllables." Each syllable has one vowel sound. Breaking words into syllables is another strategy for figuring out a long or unfamiliar word.

Discuss the following generalizations for syllabication.

Objectives
- break long or unfamiliar words into syllables
- use syllabication to decode long words

Materials
- Anthology: *Finding the Titanic*

Breaking Words Into Syllables

1. You can divide between two consonants most of the time.
   bot•tom   swim•ming

2. When a consonant is between two vowels, you can usually divide after the first vowel.
   la•ter

3. When a syllable ends in a vowel, the vowel sound is usually long.
   shi•ny   ho•tel

4. When a syllable ends in a consonant, the vowel sound is usually short.
   vis•its

5. Consonant blends and consonant digraphs are not divided.
   wreck•age   fi•nish•ing

6. A prefix or suffix is also a syllable.
   dis•ap•peared   beau•ti•ful

Practice

Help students break the following story words into syllables:

> **scattered** (scat/tered)
>
> **survivors** (sur/vi/vors)
>
> **elevator** (el/e/va/tor)
>
> **video** (vid/e/o)
>
> **museum** (mu/se/um)

Encourage students to refer to the Phonics/Decoding Strategy poster to help them as they break these words into syllables.

Apply

Have students break the following story words into syllables: *mudslide, passengers, signals, robot.* (mud / slide, pas / sen / gers, sig / nals, ro / bot) Then have pairs of students write sentences with each word.

LITERATURE FOCUS: 10-15 MINUTES

Review *Finding the Titanic*

Guide students through the Comprehension Skill Lesson for **Text Organization** on page 89 of the Teacher's Edition.

Day 4

SKILL FOCUS: GRAMMAR 25-30 MINUTES

Compound Sentences

Teach

Write the following sentences on the chalkboard:

> The Argo took moving pictures, and we watched the pictures on our video screen. We looked for the hole in the ship, but it was covered by mud.

Ask the class to read the sentences aloud with you. Point out that both sentences are *compound*. A compound sentence is made up of two short sentences that are related.

Work together to identify each short sentence within the compound sentences. Emphasize that each sentence has a subject and predicate and could stand on its own. Elicit from students that the two sentences are related because they are very closely connected in meaning.

Draw a single line under each short sentence. Discuss the connecting words *and* and *but*. They link or join the two sentences together. Have a student volunteer point to the connecting words in the two models. Ask students what punctuation is needed before the connecting word in a compound sentence. (a comma)

Objectives

- identify compound sentences
- write compound sentences
- identify the short, related sentences that form a compound sentence
- identify the connecting word that joins the two parts of a compound sentence

Materials

- Reader's Library: *Tommy Thompson's Ship of Gold*

Practice

Write these sentences from *Finding the Titanic* on the chalkboard. Help students identify the parts of each compound sentence: its two short sentences, its comma, and its connecting word.

> Most of the lifeboats had come in, but there was no sign of her family.
>
> We searched the bottom for days, but nothing appeared on the screen.
>
> Ruth found an open cabin door, and she peeked inside.

Apply

Have students work in pairs to examine a current draft of their writing and to locate compound sentences. Ask them to check that those sentences have a comma and a connecting word. Alternatively, ask pairs of students to write some compound sentences together.

LITERATURE FOCUS: 10-15 MINUTES

Preview *Tommy Thompson's Ship of Gold*

Walk students through *Tommy Thompson's Ship of Gold* and discuss the illustrations with them, using words from the story such as *bail*, *valuable*, and *uncover*.

Ask students to flip through the selection and name the various elements of text organization they encounter. Keep a running list on the board.

Reteaching Text Organization

Teach

Have students imagine that one of their textbooks had no chapters, no titles, no pictures or captions. How would they feel? Why? List students' responses on the board.

Explain that the selection *Finding the Titanic* is organized to help readers learn new information, keep track of it, and understand important ideas. Have students look at the pages as you discuss them.

Model using text organization in the selection, using the following:

Think Aloud

By flipping through pages, I see the material is arranged by chapters. Each chapter title is a date. This helps me understand when events are happening. Some are in 1985; some are in 1912; the last happens in 1986. There is an unnumbered section at the very end, the Epilogue, where the author talks to his readers. I see lots of pictures with captions. I have never seen a shipwreck, so I think pictures and captions will help me understand better what is happening.

Objectives
- identify text organization
- use text organization to understand a selection

Materials
- Anthology: *Finding the Titanic*
- Reader's Library: *Tommy Thompson's Ship of Gold*

Practice

Draw the following on the chalkboard:

Chapter Number/Title	Date	Special Features	What the Chapter Talks About

Skim the selection with students and help them complete the chart. Then encourage them to share with the class what features were most helpful and why.

Apply

Have students keep track of text organization by looking for chapters, titles, and other features in the Reader's Library selection *Tommy Thompson's Ship of Gold* by Anne Sibley O'Brien. Ask students to complete the questions and activity on the Responding page.

LITERATURE FOCUS: 10-15 MINUTES

Revisit *Finding the Titanic* and *Tommy Thompson's Ship of Gold*

Guide students through *Finding the Titanic* and *Tommy Thompson's Ship of Gold*, helping them look for multi-syllabic words such as *passengers, Carpathia,* (*Finding the Titanic*, pages 85 and 94) *Discoverer, operated* (*Tommy Thompson's Ship of Gold*, pages 49 and 51). Also compare and contrast the text organization for the two selections.

Day 1

Objectives

- form new words with the roots *tele* and *rupt*
- use the Phonics/Decoding strategy to decode longer words

Materials

- Teaching Master ES1-7
- Practice Master ES1-7
- Anthology: *By the Shores of Silver Lake*

Get Set for Reading CD-ROM

By the Shores of Silver Lake

Education Place

www.eduplace.com
By the Shores of Silver Lake

...diotape

...e Shores of Silver Lake
...pe for **Journeys**

...nics

...ervention

Word Roots *tele* and *rupt*

Warm-Up/Academic Language

Explain to students that today they will be learning about *tele* and *rupt*. Tell students that these are two **roots**, or **word parts**, that have meaning but need a **prefix or suffix** to make a word. Explain that being able to recognize these roots may help them to **decode unfamiliar words.**

Teach

Write *tele* on the board and read it. Tell students that *tele* means "over a distance." Next, write *telephone* and read it with students. Have a volunteer come to the board and underline the root. Ask the group if anyone knows the meaning of the word. If needed, explain that a telephone carries people's voices over a distance.

Write *rupt* on the board and read it. Tell students that *rupt* means "break." Next, write *disrupt* on the board and read it with students. Have a volunteer come to the board and underline the root. Ask the group if anyone knows the meaning of the word. If needed, explain that to *disrupt* means to cause a disturbance or a "break" in the order of things.

Write the words *television* and *telescope* on the board. Have volunteers come up to circle the *tele* root.

Guide students to use their knowledge of the root's meaning to define the words.

Ask students to offer sentences using each word. Write selected sentences on the board.

Repeat the procedure for *rupt*, using *interrupt* and *erupt*.

Guided Practice

Display or **distribute** Teaching Master ES1-7 to students.

Review how to decode *telephone* using the illustration, the definition of the root, and the definition of the whole word.

Guide students to write the meanings of the remaining words using picture clues and what they have learned about the roots.

Practice/Apply

Distribute Practice Master ES1-7 to students, and review the directions.

Instruct students to complete the practice master independently.

Check student understanding of *rupt* and *tele* by having them read their answers aloud.

LITERATURE FOCUS: 10-15 MINUTES

Preview *By the Shores of Silver Lake* Segment 1

Refer to the bottom of page 111 in the Teacher's Edition and preview with students Segment 1 of *By the Shores of Silver Lake* (pages 110–117).

Note the suggestions in the Extra Support boxes on Teacher's Edition pages 112 and 116.

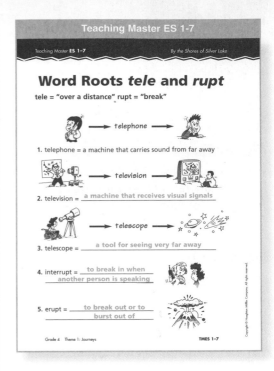

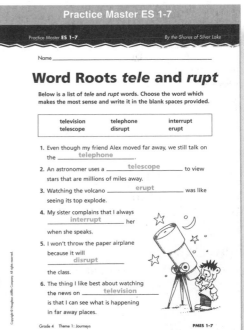

Day 2

Objectives

- identify details that explain, give information, or convey feelings
- distinguish important from less important details

Materials

- Teaching Master ES1–8
- Practice Master ES1–8
- Anthology: *By the Shores of Silver Lake*

PRETEACH

SKILL FOCUS: COMPREHENSION   25-30 MINUTES

Comprehension: Noting Details

Warm-Up/Academic Language

Inform students that authors use **details** for many purposes. A detail may **explain ideas**, **give key information**, or **convey feelings**. These kinds of details are **more important** than details that only help to give **background information**.

Teach

Guide students to choose the three or four most important details.

Read Aloud

Hi, I'm José. Last weekend I played a soccer game. It was a very hot day. I wore a red sweatband that matched my team's colors. The game was fun, but we lost. The other team's goal won them the game at the very last minute. I felt badly about losing. After the game I ate a candy bar.

Ask students to name details from the story. Then copy their answers on the board until you have the following list:

- played soccer
- wore a red sweatband
- lost the game
- it was hot
- other team won at the last minute
- felt badly about losing
- ate candy bar

Use the Think Aloud to model detail selection. Guide students to choose the most important details.

Think Aloud

José played soccer and lost. He described how he felt about losing. These are important details because they tell what game José played, the outcome, and how he felt about it. The other details, the hot day, the sweatband, and the candy bar, help describe the day, and how José looked during the game and what he ate afterwards. They do not add to the main idea of the story, so they are less important.

Display a chart like the one shown below on the board, leaving the entries for the 2nd and 3rd columns blank. Call on students to give you the answers.

DETAIL	IMPORTANT	WHY?
It was hot.	No	Gives background information
José played soccer.	Yes	Tells what José did
The opponent won the game.	Yes	Tells the outcome of game
José ate candy.	No	Gives background information
José felt badly about losing.	Yes	Tells how José felt

Guided Practice

Display or **distribute** Teaching Master ES1-8 and read the introduction with students.

Ask them to follow along as you read the details aloud.

Help students to complete the chart.

Practice/Apply

Distribute Practice Master ES1-8, and discuss the illustration.

Have students read the story and fill out the charts independently.

Check that they are able to differentiate between important and less important details as they share their answers with the class.

LITERATURE FOCUS: 10-15 MINUTES

Preview *By the Shores of Silver Lake* Segment 2

Refer to page 118 in the Teacher's Edition and preview with students Segment 2 of *By the Shores of Silver Lake* (pages 118–127).

Note the suggestions in the Extra Support boxes on Teacher's Edition pages 119, 124, and 126.

Teaching Master ES 1-8

Teaching Master ES 1-8   By the Shores of Silver Lake

Noting Details

- A detail can give important information which explains an idea, or tells about a character's feelings.
- A detail can give less important information for background or just to set the scene.

Detail 1: I am so upset with my sister Rosa today!
Detail 2: Her snoring kept me awake last night, and today I am tired.
Detail 3: I overslept and will be late for school!
Detail 4: We are having cereal and juice for breakfast.
Detail 5: I am not speaking to Rosa this morning.
Detail 6: I am wearing a blue sweater today.

Detail	Is the detail important?	Why or why not?
1	yes	Tells us what the character feels
2	yes	Tells us why the character is upset
3	yes	Tells us why the character is upset
4	no	Detail gives background
5	yes	Shows that the character is upset
6	no	Detail gives background

Grade 4   Theme 1: Journeys   TMES 1-8

Practice Master ES 1-8

Practice Master ES 1-8   By the Shores of Silver Lake

Name _____

Noting Details

Read the story and fill in the charts below.

Later that day, when Mrs. Keating called on me, I was so tired from not sleeping last night that I didn't even answer! At recess, the kids played kickball. I sat down to rest with my friend Mark under the big oak tree. It was a cool, sunny day. The leaves were turning orange. Mark told me the story of a movie he saw but I fell asleep. "Sara!" shouted Mark. "Wake up! You slept through the best part of the story!" I said I was sorry. Then we all went inside.

Sample answers:

Important Detail # 1	Sara feels so tired, she doesn't answer the teacher.
Important Detail # 2	Sara sits under the tree instead of playing kickball.
Important Detail # 3	Sara falls asleep while Mark is telling a story.
Background Detail # 1	It was a cool, sunny day.
Background Detail # 2	The leaves were starting to turn orange.
Background Detail # 3	The story was about a movie Mark saw.

Grade 4   Theme 1: Journeys   PMES 1-8

Day 3

Objectives
- decode words with *tele* and *rupt*
- identify the meaning of words with *tele* and *rupt*

Materials
- Anthology: *By the Shores of Silver Lake*
- index cards

SKILL FOCUS: STRUCTURAL ANALYSIS   25-30 MINUTES

Word Roots *tele* and *rupt*

Teach

Explain that a word root is a word part that has meaning. When it is put together with another word part it makes a whole word.

Write the following on chart paper:

> tele + phone = telephone
>
> inter + rupt = interupt

Explain that the root *tele* means "over a long distance." Ask students why this would make sense knowing what they know about a telephone. (The telephone lets people talk to each other over long distances.) Next, point to *rupt* in *interrupt* and explain that it means "break." Point to *inter* and explain that it means "between." Tell students that *interrupt* means "to break into the middle of someone's conversation." Now ask two volunteers to act out the word *interrupt*.

Practice

Write the roots *tele* and *rupt* on separate index cards. Then write each of the following word parts on separate index cards: *dis, bank, inter, phone, scope, vision, cast*. Work with students to create words by putting the word parts together. Have volunteers tell what the word is and what it means.

Apply

Ask students to write sentences using words from the Practice section.

Review *By the Shores of Silver Lake*

Guide students through the Comprehension Skill Lesson **Noting Details** on page 121 of the Teacher's Edition.

Day 4

Objective

• identify common nouns

Materials

• Anthology: *By the Shores of Silver Lake*
• Reader's Library: *Race of the River Runner*

Common Nouns

Teach

Write the following common nouns on the chalkboard:

People	Places	Things
child	school	bicycle

Remind students that *child*, *school*, and *bicycle* are called nouns. Since these nouns don't name a particular person, place, or thing, they are called *common nouns*.

Direct students to find common nouns in the last paragraph on page 121 of the story. Have students explain why the nouns they selected are common. Then add the common nouns to the chart.

Practice

Have pairs of students create their own charts and list common nouns found on one of the following story pages: 115, 119, or 124. Remind students to select carefully so that they record only words that name *any* person, place, or thing.

Apply

Ask students to choose five common nouns from their charts. Have them write some sentences for a story using these common nouns. You may want students to exchange stories and underline the common nouns.

LITERATURE FOCUS: 10-15 MINUTES

Preview *Race of the River Runner*

Walk students through *Race of the River Runner* and discuss the illustrations, using words from the story, such as *steamboat* and *engine*.

Ask students to flip through the illustrations and list details they notice that tell about story. Keep a running list on the board.

Day 5

Objectives
- identify important details
- use details to visualize characters, places, and events

Materials
- Anthology: *By the Shores of Silver Lake*
- Reader's Library: *Race of the River Runner*

SKILL FOCUS: COMPREHENSION   25-30 MINUTES

Noting Details

Teach

Write this sentence on the board: *Grace sat still in her little starched white lawn dress and bonnet, her feet in small new shoes sticking straight out.*

Discuss how important details help readers picture characters, setting, and actions in their minds.

Use the following to model noting details in the main selection.

Think Aloud

From the writer's details about Grace on page 111 of the selection from By the Shores of Silver Lake, *I can "see" her in my mind, without looking at the illustration on the next page. Grace is wearing a white dress, bonnet, and new shoes. From the details "little… dress," "small… shoes," "feet… sticking straight out," I know she's a very young child. Also the detail that Laura kept an eye on Grace leads me to think that she was very young and in need of supervision.*

Help students put together a set of tips for noting details. For example:

> To find important details I could ask myself:
>
> 1. What do I think this person/place/thing is like?
>
> 2. What details gave me this idea?
>
> 3. Do these details "add up"?

Practice

Have students work in groups to locate important story details that support the following statements:

- The train seemed like a huge, scary monster. (Skim p. 115 to the top of p. 116.)

- Laura thinks the car is wonderful. (Skim from the middle of p. 121 to the top of p. 124.)

Apply

Have students keep track of details in the Reader's Library selection *Race of the River Runner* by Geoff Smith. Ask students to complete the questions and activity on the Responding page.

LITERATURE FOCUS: 10-15 MINUTES

Revisit *By the Shores of Silver Lake* and *Race of the River Runner*

Have students turn to page 119 of *By the Shores of Silver Lake* and look for the word with a *tele* root. (telegraph, first paragraph) Write the word on the board and circle the root, explaining that a *telegraph* is an old machine that sent written messages over a distance. Also have students note several important details in each selection.

Theme 2

American Stories

Selections

1 Tomás and the Library Lady

2 Tanya's Reunion

3 Boss of the Plains

4 A Very Important Day

Day 1

Objective

• read contractions and identify their meanings

Materials

• Teaching Master ES2-1
• Practice Masters ES2-1
• Anthology: *Tomás and the Library Lady*

Technology

Get Set for Reading CD-ROM

Tomás and the Library Lady

Education Place

www.eduplace.com
Tomás and the Library Lady

Audiotape

Tomás and the Library Lady
Audiotape for **American Stories**

Lexia Phonics CD-ROM

Intermediate Intervention

PRETEACH
SKILL FOCUS: STRUCTURAL ANALYSIS   25–30 MINUTES

Contractions

Warm-Up/Academic Language

Inform students that **two words** can sometimes be **shortened by removing** one or more **letters** and **replacing** the missing letters **with an apostrophe**. Next, the two words are joined together to **form one word—a contraction.**

Teach.

Ask students "Are we sixth graders?" Respond by writing this sentence on the board: *We are not.* Then suggest another way of answering the question that has the same meaning but uses a contraction. Write *We aren't* on the board. Explain that *aren't* is a contraction, which is really two words that together form one word meaning the same thing.

Model how the contraction *aren't* is formed by crossing out the *o* in *not* in the first sentence. Next, close up the space between the two words and underline *aren't* in the second sentence. Guide students to see that the apostrophe replaced the missing letter *o*. Circle the apostrophe.

Ask "Is today Saturday?" Write two responses on the board, one on top of the other: *No, today is not Saturday. No, today isn't Saturday.* Underline *it is* and *isn't*, and read the Think Aloud.

Think Aloud

I can see that the two words is *and* not *were combined into one word. I also see that new word has an apostrophe. The apostrophe is where the* o *in* not *was removed. The word* isn't *must be a contraction. Since* isn't *and* is not *mean the same thing, these two sentences have exactly the same meaning.*

Write the following phrases on the board: "he is," "I am," and "have not." Guide students through the process of changing "he is" to "he's." Have students tell you which letter to omit and where to place the apostrophe. Write *he's* on the board. Repeat the process for the subsequent phrases.

Explain that certain words can be shortened to form contractions. On the board, list some common examples in a chart like the following one.

Word	Contraction	Examples
1. not	1. n't	1. (wasn't, couldn't)
2. is	2. 's	2. (it's, what's)
3. am	3. 'm	3. (I'm)
4. are	4. 're	4. (you're, we're)
5. will	5. 'll	5. (she'll, he'll)
6. have	6. 've	6. (we've, should've)

Ask students to use each example word in a sentence in the contraction and non-contraction forms. Write sentences on the board. Point out that numbers five and six are special examples because two letters (*wi*, *ha*) are removed instead of one.

Guided Practice

Display or **distribute** Teaching Master ES2-1 and discuss the pictures.

Have students read the first five sentence pairs.

Have students explain each step needed to form the contraction.

Help students to write the contraction forms for the remaining sentences.

Practice/Apply

Distribute Practice Master ES2-1 to students and go over the directions.

Have students complete the Practice Master independently.

Check students' responses to be sure they can form contractions.

Preview *Tomás and the Library Lady* Segment 1

Refer to the bottom of page 159 in the Teacher's Edition and preview with students Segment 1 of *Tomás and the Library Lady* (pages 159–169).

Note the suggestion in the Extra Support boxes on Teacher's Edition pages 165, 167, and 168.

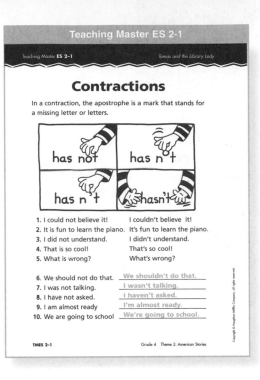

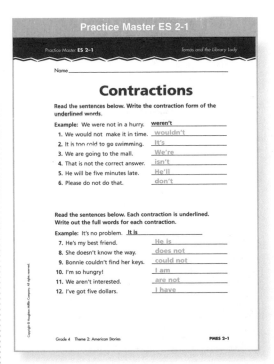

Day 2

Sequence of Events

Warm-Up / Academic Language

Explain that stories contain a **series of events** that the author presents in a **certain order**, or **sequence**. Point out that authors often use particular words, known as **signal words**, to help readers understand the order of events.

Teach

Tell students that you are going to act out a sequence of events. Instruct them to pay close attention to what you do. Tell them that later, they will have to retell these events in sequence, or order.

Act out the following steps:

* Walk over to a corner and stand facing it for a few seconds.

* Go to the board and write the word *boom*.

* Turn to the class and say *boom* in a normal voice as you throw your hands up.

* Cover your ears.

Ask students to tell you the events in order. Then have them write the sequence of events, numbering each event. Check to make sure their final lists reflect the actual events. Their lists should roughly resemble the one shown below.

---

1. Our teacher walked to the corner and stood there for a while.
2. She went to the board and wrote *boom*.
3. She said *boom* and raised her hands.
4. She covered up her ears.

Explain that rather than using numbers to show the order of each event, students can use signal words to tell when each event occurred.

Write these words on the board: *before, first, second, finally, then, next, while, as, after.*

Have students cross out the numbers on their papers and use some of the listed words instead.

Objectives

* identify order of story events
* identify words that signal sequence

Materials

* Teaching Master ES2-2
* Practice Master ES2-2
* Anthology: *Tomás and the Library Lady*

Guided Practiace

Display or **distribute** Teaching Master ES2-2.

Read the category titles and the signal words in the box with students.

Guide students to sort each word in the box as a *before*, *during*, or *after* word.

Have students use the signal words in sentences.

Practice/Apply

Distribute Practice Master ES2-2 and go over the directions with students before they begin.

Have students work independently to complete the Practice Master.

Check students' understanding of sequence of events as they share their answers with the group.

LITERATURE FOCUS: 10–15 MINUTES

Preview *Tomás and the Library Lady* Segment 2

Refer to the bottom of page 170 in the Teacher's Edition and preview with students Segment 2 of *Tomás and the Library Lady* (pages 170–175).

Note the suggestions in the Extra Support boxes on Teacher's Edition page 174.

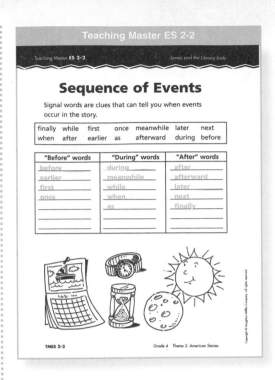

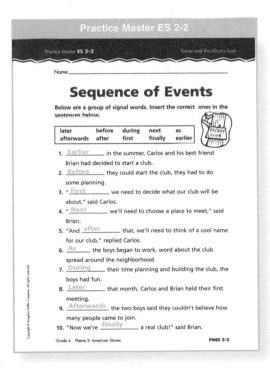

Day 3

Objectives
- decode contractions
- identify the two words from which contractions are formed

Materials
- Anthology: *Tomás and the Library Lady*

RETEACH

SKILL FOCUS: STRUCTURAL ANALYSIS   25–30 MINUTES

Contractions

Teach

Review that a contraction is a shortened form of two words and that an apostrophe shows where one or more letters have been left out.

Display the following sentences:

> Tomás <u>could not</u> move.
>
> Tomás <u>couldn't</u> move.

Have students identify the word(s) in each sentence that are different. (*could not* and *couldn't*) Then review these concepts:

1. *Couldn't* is a contraction. It is a combination of two words, *could* and *not*.

2. The apostrophe (') takes the place of one or more letters.

3. A contraction has the same meaning as the two words that were combined.

Display the following chart. Walk students through the structure of each contraction, showing how each word is two words that are combined. Read each row aloud together and use the words in a sentence.

Contraction	Two Words
I'm	I am
you're	you are
it's	it is
I've	I have
he'd	he would
you've	you have

Practice

Write these contractions on the board: *we're, she'll, don't, doesn't*. Have volunteers name the two words used to form each contraction. Have each volunteer use the contraction in a sentence.

Apply

Write these sentences on the board and ask students to underline the contractions. Then have students rewrite the sentences using the two words which formed each contraction.

- *It's a hot day.*

- *What's your name?*

- *I can't read this word.*

- *I'm going out for a walk.*

- *Jackie couldn't hear the whistle.*

- *Mona and I aren't speaking.*

- *The day just isn't long enough.*

LITERATURE FOCUS: 10–15 MINUTES

Review *Tomás and the Library Lady*

Guide students through the Comprehension Skill Lesson for **Sequence of Events** on page 167 in the Teacher's Edition.

Day 4

Proper Nouns

Teach

Review with students that common nouns name any person (*teacher*), place (*school*), or thing (*car*).

Ask volunteers to write their name, name of their town, and name of this day on the board. Explain that the words they wrote are *proper nouns*. Each proper noun names a particular person, place, or thing and begins with a capital letter. Use the chart to further distinguish common nouns from proper nouns.

	Common Nouns	Proper Nouns
Persons	girl	Maria
	uncle	Uncle Edward
	queen	Queen Elizabeth
Places	state	Arizona
	country	Canada
	bay	Bay of Fundy
	park	Glacier National Park
Things	pet	Patches
	day	Saturday
	holiday	Fourth of July

Explain to students that the first letter of each important word in a proper noun must be capitalized. Ask volunteers to point out which proper nouns in the chart are more than one word. Ask others to tell which two proper nouns demonstrate that only the important words should be capitalized. (Bay of Fundy, Fourth of July)

Objectives

- identify proper nouns
- categorize proper nouns
- distinguish between common and proper nouns
- capitalize proper nouns correctly

Materials

- Reader's Library: *The Math Bee*

Practice

Write these sentences on the board:

> The family is in _____ in the winter. (Texas)
>
> They go to _____ in the summer. (Iowa)
>
> The boys listen to _____ tell stories. (Papá Grande)
>
> The library lady speaks to _____. (Tomás)
>
> He teaches her some words in _____. (Spanish)

Have students find proper nouns in the story to fill in the blanks. Ask students to write the proper nouns in the blanks. Work together to check for capitalization. You may want to ask students to identify the common nouns in these sentences, as practice in distinguishing common nouns from proper. (family, winter, summer, boys, stories, lady, words)

Apply

Have students work in pairs to find other proper nouns from the story. Have students categorize them into groups of names of people and places or any other categories that fit. Be sure to have them check on each other's capitalization.

LITERATURE FOCUS: 10–15 MINUTES

Preview *The Math Bee*

Walk students through *The Math Bee*. Discuss illustrations using words such as *controllers*, *bee*, *teammates* and *chemistry*.

Ask students to preview the sequence of story events by scanning through the illustrations.

Day 5

SKILL FOCUS: COMPREHENSION   25–30 MINUTES

Sequence of Events

Objectives
- identify sequence of events in a story
- identify time-order words

Materials
- Anthology: *Tomás and the Library Lady*
- Reader's Library: *The Math Bee*
- index Cards

Teach

Write the following list of time-order words on the chalkboard.

first	second	next	then
before	after	finally	

Have volunteers use these words to tell what they did this morning from the time they woke up to when they arrived at school. You might want to start things off by recounting your morning. Have a volunteer point to each word as it is used.

Explain that authors sometimes use these words to help readers follow the events in a story in the proper order, or sequence. Explain also that these words aren't always in a story, in which case readers have to be even more alert to the correct sequence.

Use the following sentences from the story to model figuring out the sequence of events:

"'¡Qué tigre tan grande!' Tomás said first in Spanish and then in English, 'What a big tiger!'"

Think Aloud

The author uses the words first *and* then *to show that Tomás read in Spanish before he read in English. This helps me understand that Papá Grande's first language is Spanish and that he is learning English.*

Practice

Write the following events from the story on index cards: *Tomás walked around the library. Tomás peeked in the front door. Tomás climbed the steps. Tomás walked downtown.* Then have students put the events in order. Students can then use time-order words such as the ones listed on the board to retell these events in a summary.

Apply

Have students keep track of the sequence of events, with an eye to identifying time-order words in the Reader's Library selection *The Math Bee* by Delores Lowe Friedman. Ask students to complete the questions and activity on the Responding page.

LITERATURE FOCUS: 10–15 MINUTES

Revisit *Tomás and the Library Lady* and *The Math Bee*

Review with students the sequence of events in *Tomás and the Library Lady* and *The Math Bee*. Also, help them to look for contractions such as *couldn't, what's,* (*Tomás and the Library Lady*, pages 165 and 166) *they're,* and *I'm* (*The Math Bee*, pages 8 and 12).

Day 1

Objectives
- read words that have word roots *sign* and *spect*
- use the Phonics/Decoding strategy to decode longer words

Materials
- Teaching Master ES2-3
- Practice Masters ES2-3
- Anthology: *Tayna's Reunion*

**Get Set for Reading
CD-ROM**
Tayna's Reunion

Education Place
www.eduplace.com
Tayna's Reunion

Audiotape
Tayna's Reunion
Audiotape for **American Stories**

**Lexia Phonics
CD-ROM**
Intermediate Intervention

PRETEACH

SKILL FOCUS: STRUCTURAL ANALYSIS   25–30 MINUTES

Word Roots *sign* and *spect*

Warm-Up / Academic Language

Explain to students that they will learn about **spect** and **sign** — two **word roots**. Explain that word roots **have meaning** but that they need to have **a prefix or suffix** added to them to make a word. Explain that being able to recognize these roots may **help them to read unfamiliar words.**

Teach

Draw a tree on the board that includes a root system. Draw six branches—three on one side and three on the other.

Write *inspect*, *spectacle*, and *spectator* on the left branches. Tell students that all these words share the same five letters, which spell out a word root. Have students study the three words. Ask them what each of the words has in common. (spect)

Write *spect* in the left portion of the root system of the tree, and underline *spect* in each of the three words in the tree branches. Explain that *spect* means "to look." Write this meaning under *spect*.

Repeat the same procedure for *sign* (meaning "a mark or pattern"), labeling the branches and roots on the right side of the tree. Use the words *sign*, *signature*, and *design* on the three branches.

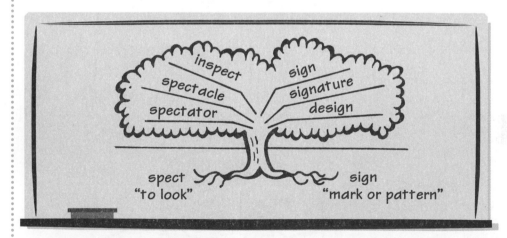

Explain to students that knowing the meaning of word roots can often help them read unfamiliar words.

Copy the following chart onto the board. Fill in the first two columns only, leaving column 3 blank.

Word	Context	Sentence Meaning
in**spect**	Let's closely *inspect* this book.	to look carefully at something
spectacle	The circus act was quite a *spectacle*.	something interesting or amazing to look at
spectator	The *spectator* clapped when the show was over.	someone who looks at something
sign	The *sign* said STOP.	something with marks on it that gives a message
signature	Write your *signature* here.	a group of marks that forms a name
de**sign**	She made a pretty *design*.	a group of marks that makes a pattern

Complete column 3 for the word *inspect*. Guide students to help you to fill in the remainder of column 3. You may wish to have students look up the words in a dictionary to compare the dictionary definitions with their own.

Guided Practice

Display or **distribute** Teaching Master ES2-3 and review the meanings of *sign* and *spect*.

Read the story with students and have them underline and sort *spect* and *sign* words under the correct heading.

Practice/Apply

Distribute Practice Master ES2-3 and read the instructions with students.

Have students complete the Practice Master independently.

Check students' understanding of the word roots *sign* and *spect* by having them read their answers aloud.

Preview *Tanya's Reunion*

Segment 1

Refer to the bottom of page 187 in the Teacher's Edition and preview with students Segment 1 of *Tanya's Reunion* (pages 187–195).

Note the suggestion in the Extra Support boxes on Teacher's Edition pages 191 and 194.

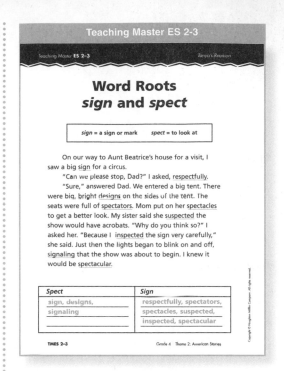

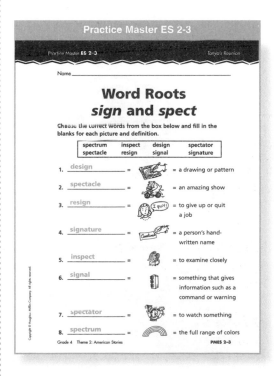

Day 2

Objective

- use evidence from the story and life experiences to make inferences about characters and their feelings.

Materials

- Teaching Master ES2-4
- Practice Master ES2-4
- Anthology: *Tanya's Reunion*

Making Inferences

Warm-Up / Academic Language

Explain that when authors write stories, they often give the reader **clues about characters and their feelings**. Sometimes authors leave information out, so readers use these **clues and their own experiences** to figure some things out for themselves. This is called **making inferences.**

Teach

Read Aloud

> I was working on my science project after school when my friend Leanne called. She wanted me to go see an early movie with her. It was this great movie we'd both been wanting to see for weeks. "Hmmm. I'd like to go, but I can't," I told her. "My project is due in three days. Sorry."
>
> "Three whole days?" she said. "So just work on it tomorrow."
>
> "Can we go this weekend instead?" I asked. "I want to do the project right and not at the last minute. I'm working on a cool model of the solar system."
>
> "OK, Laura," said Leanne. "Good luck with your project."

Model how to make inferences about Laura's feelings by using the Think Aloud.

Think Aloud

> *I can tell that Laura really wants to see the movie, but she says no. I know it can be hard to say no to having fun sometimes. I once had to skip a birthday party because I had to look after my sister for a while. I think that Laura feels responsible and serious about her schoolwork. It's also easy to see that she enjoys science because she's so excited about her model.*

Guided Practice

Display or **distribute** Teaching Master ES2-4 and preview the headings of the chart with students.

Read the first story event with students and model making inferences using the entries in columns 2 and 3.

Ask students to respond to your inference. Does it makes sense to them? Do they have anything they want to add?

Have students read the second story event in the chart. Have them work in pairs to generate responses for columns 2 and 3. Discuss responses as a group.

Practice / Apply

Distribute Practice Master ES2-4 to students.

Preview the format, noting that students are expected to fill in two responses in each block of the second and third columns. Have students complete the Practice Master independently.

Check all students' understanding of making inferences by discussing individual responses.

LITERATURE FOCUS: ⏐0–15 MINUTES

Preview *Tanya's Reunion*

Segment 2

Refer to the bottom of page 196 in the Teacher's Edition and preview with students Segment 2 of *Tanya's Reunion* (pages 196–211).

Note the suggestions in the Extra Support boxes on Teacher's Edition pages 199, 204, and 210.

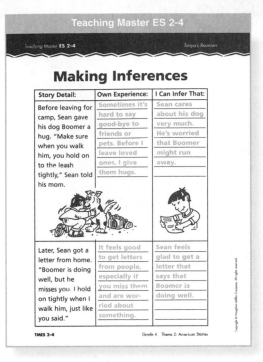

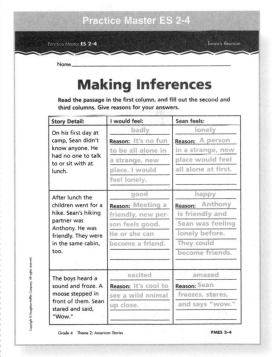

Word Roots: *sign* and *spect*

Objectives

- recognize the root word *sign* in words
- recognize the root word *spect* in words

Materials

- Anthology: *Tanya's Reunion*

Teach

Remind students what a word root is. (a word part that has meaning and can not stand alone) Tell students that many English words contain word roots from the ancient Latin language.

Write these two sentences on the board and underline the two words as shown:

> The <u>signal</u> at the train crossing was flashing.
>
> Eleanor helped her mother <u>inspect</u> the quilts for holes.

Read the sentences out loud and ask volunteers to give the meanings of each underlined word. Circle the roots *sign* and *spect* and review that these are root words from the Latin. Write each root separately on the board with its meaning next to it: *sign* = "a sign or a mark" and *spect* = "to look at."

Use the following Think Aloud to model decoding the word *inspect* in the sentence: *Eleanor helped her mother <u>inspect</u> the quilts for holes.*

Think Aloud

First I look for a root. I draw a line between in and spect because I know spect is a root that means "look at." When I blend sounds, I get / in SPEKT /. I try this word in the sentence, and it sort of makes sense. I know the meaning of the root and I know what in means. Together, they seem to mean "to look at in or in at," but that doesn't seem quite right. In this sentence, it must mean "to look at carefully." That would make sense. I'll look up the meaning in the dictionary just to be sure.

Practice

Write these sentences on the board, leaving blank spaces as shown:

• A letter needs a _____ from the person who writes it. (signature)

• We're planning Maria's surprise party, and she does not _____ a thing. (suspect)

• Felix knows how to _____ t-shirts. (design)

• Even if you don't play a sport, you can still enjoy being a _____ at a sports event. (spectator)

Write the following roots and words:

<u>sign</u>	<u>spect</u>
design	spectator
signature	suspect

Discuss what each word means and have volunteers identify and underline the roots. Invite volunteers to write the correct words in the blanks in the sentences. Discuss how the meaning of each word relates to the meaning of each root and how it makes sense in the sentence.

Apply

Have students use the Practice words in sentences of their own.

LITERATURE FOCUS: 10–15 MINUTES

Review *Tanya's Reunion*

Guide students through the Comprehension Skill Lesson for **Making Inferences** on page 191 in the Teacher's Edition.

Day 4

SKILL FOCUS: GRAMMAR   25–30 MINUTES

Singular and Plural Nouns

Teach

Write *grandmother*, *farm*, and *bus* on the board. Have a volunteer tell what kind of words they are. (nouns) Elicit from students that each of these nouns names just one person, place, or thing. Explain that a noun that names one person, place, or thing is called a *singular noun*. Ask them for more examples, and list their suggestions.

Explain to students that a noun that names more than one person, place, or thing is called a *plural noun*. Use the following chart to illustrate which plurals are formed by simply adding *s* and which plurals are formed by adding *es*.

Objectives

- identify singular and plural nouns
- form the plural of most nouns by adding *s*
- form the plural of nouns that end in *s*, *x*, *ch*, or *sh*, adding *es*
- distinguish between singular and plural nouns

Materials

- Reader's Library: *A Breath of Fresh Air*

How to Form Plurals		
Rules	**Singular**	**Plural**
Add *s* to most singular nouns.	one boy one puddle a rose	two boys both puddles ten roses
Add *es* to a singular noun that ends with *s*, *x*, or *sh*.	one bus this box one bunch a wish	three buses some boxes six bunches many wishes

Practice

Write *grandmothers*, *farms*, and *buses* on the board near the singular nouns *grandmother*, *farm*, and *bus*. Invite a volunteer to give the definition of a plural noun. (A plural noun is a noun that names more than one person, place, or thing.)

Ask students to identify the three plural nouns. Have them tell which plural nouns were formed by adding *s* (grandmothers, farms) and by adding *es*. (buses) Have students add the words to the chart. Invite pairs of students to work together to look for singular nouns in the story. Tell students also to write the nouns in their plural form.

Apply

Have students write the plural nouns they find on page 196 of the story and then write their singular forms.

Ask students to write the plural forms of the following singular nouns: *brush*, *prize*, *circus*, *fox*, *inch*, and *tax*.

LITERATURE FOCUS: 10–15 MINUTES

Preview *A Breath of Fresh Air*

Walk students through *A Breath of Fresh Air*. Discuss illustrations using words such as *program*, *several*, *scowled*, and *accepted*.

Ask students to infer how Javi may be feeling throughout the story by scanning through the illustrations.

Day 5

SKILL FOCUS: COMPREHENSION
25–30 MINUTES

Objective
- learn to use story details and their own knowledge to make inferences

Materials
- Anthology: *Tanya's Reunion*
- Reader's Library: *A Breath of Fresh Air*

Making Inferences

Teach

Instruct a volunteer to come to the front of the room and smile. Explain that this student has just won a new bicycle. Ask students to tell how the volunteer is feeling and why. (happy he or she has won a bicycle) Point out that they used what they knew about getting something new and the expression on the volunteer's face to make an inference.

Explain that good readers use details along with their own personal knowledge to make inferences.

Write the following sentences from the story on the board and use the Think Aloud to model making inferences: *"A trip with Grandma! Just the two of them. Tanya couldn't believe her ears."*

> **Think Aloud**
>
> *The author tells me Tanya's thoughts and uses an exclamation mark which I know can show excitement. I know "couldn't believe her ars" shows surprise. Tanya must love her Grandma and want to be with her—I know that's how I feel about some of my friends and relatives. I can infer that Tanya feels excited, surprised, and happy.*

Practice

Work with students as they use details on page 207 and personal knowledge to infer how Grandma feels about the farm. Have students complete a web for each inference.

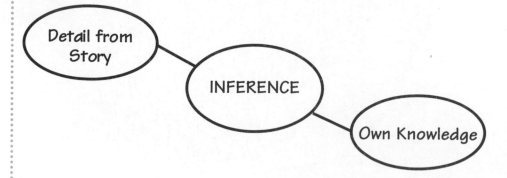

Apply

Have students make inferences with an eye to using story clues and their own experiences in the Reader's Library selection *A Breath of Fresh Air* by Rhonda Rodriguez. Ask students to complete the activity on the Responding page.

LITERATURE FOCUS:	10–15 MINUTES

Revisit *Tanya's Reunion* and *A Breath of Fresh Air*

Review with students inferences about the main characters' feelings in *Tanya's Reunion* and *A Breath of Fresh Air*. Also, help them look for words using the roots *sign* and *spect* such as *suspect*, and *designs* (*Tanya's Reunion*, pages 190 and 200).

Day 1

Objectives
- read words with the suffixes -er, -or, and -ist
- use the Phonics/Decoding strategy to read longer words

Materials
- Teaching Master ES2-5
- Practice Masters ES2-5
- Anthology: *Boss of the Plains*

Technology

Get Set for Reading
CD-ROM
Boss of the Plains

Education Place
www.eduplace.com
Boss of the Plains

Audiotape
Boss of the Plains
Audiotape for **American Stories**

Lexia Phonics
CD-ROM
Intermediate Intervention

PRETEACH

SKILL FOCUS: STRUCTURAL ANALYSIS   25–30 MINUTES

Suffixes -er, -or, and -ist

Warm-Up / Academic Language

Remind students that a **base word** is a word that can have its meaning changed by **adding different beginnings and endings.** Explain that students will learn about three endings, or **suffixes: -er, -or,** and **-ist**. List them on the board, and explain that these suffixes mean **"someone who."** Explain that **these endings are added to a base word to show what a person does.**

Teach

Write these sentences on the board, circling the *-ist, -er,* and *-or* words:

> A performer is someone who _____.
>
> A visitor is someone who _____.
>
> A violinist is someone who _____.

Tell students that if they don't know what the three circled words mean, they should start by finding a base word they recognize. Explain that this will give them an important clue about each word's meaning. Remind them that each of the suffixes means *someone who.*

Ask a volunteer to come to the board and underline the base word in *performer.* Explain that the definition of *performer* will have something to do with the base word *perform.* Explain that an *s* will need to be added to the base word so that it agrees with the verb in the sentence. Guide the student to write *performs* in the blank.

Repeat the procedure for *visitor* (visits) and *violinist* (plays the violin).

List these professions on the board: *actor, dancer, singer, sculptor, guitarist, painter, conductor, writer, drummer.* Under the word list, write this sentence pair:

I want to be a(n)_____. I want to be someone who _____.

Demonstrate how to fill in the blanks, using *actor.* (actor), (acts) Next, have students go to the board and erase *actor* and *acts.* Instruct them to fill in the blanks for the next word on the list.

Repeat this procedure until all words have been addressed.

Explain that when a suffix is added to a base word, the spelling of the base word may change.

List these words on the board: *dancer, drummer, flutist, rapper.*

Ask students to name the base word for each of the words. List them on the board. For each word, discuss how the base words changed by applying these rules:

- Drop the final *e* of a base word before adding *-er, -or, -ist (dancer, flutist)*

- If a one-syllable base word ends in a short vowel and a consonant, double the consonant before adding *-er, -or, -ist (drummer, rapper).*

Guided Practice

Display or **distribute** Teaching Master ES2-5 and review the meaning of *-er, -or,* and *-ist.*

Read the first five sentences with students and demonstrate the relationship between the two underlined words in each sentence pair.

Help students to fill in the missing words for the remaining sentence pairs and to identify the base words that needed spelling changes when the suffix was added. (*survivor, writer, scientist,* and *operator*)

Practice/Apply

Distribute Practice Master ES2-5 to students and have them complete it independently.

Check students' understading of of *-er, -or,* and *-ist* by having them read and explain their answers.

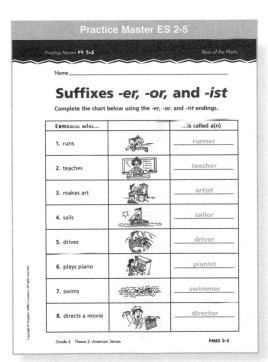

LITERATURE FOCUS: 10–15 MINUTES

Preview *Boss of the Plains*

Segment 1

Refer to the bottom of page 219 in the Teacher's Edition and preview with students Segment 1 of *Boss of the Plains* (pages 219–231).

Note the suggestion in the Extra Support boxes on Teacher's Edition pages 221, 228, and 230.

Day 2

Objective
- use story details to make generalizations

Materials
- Teaching Master ES2-6
- Practice Masters ES2-6
- Anthology: *Boss of the Plains*

SKILL FOCUS: COMPREHENSION   25–30 MINUTES

Making Generalizations

Warm-Up / Academic Language

Explain to students that sometimes people make statements that are true most, but not all, of the time. Explain that these statements are called **generalizations**. Point out that when people make generalizations, they often include words such as *all, most, usually, often, many, few, never, always,* and *some*.

Teach

Tell students that they are going to use some facts to make a generalization about baseball. Write these three sentences on the board and read them with students:

- Baseball is known as our "national pastime." (Explain that "pastime" is a hobby or fun activity.)
- The number of teams in the American and National Leagues has grown over the years.
- Millions of Americans (but not all) watch the World Series on TV.

Model making a generalization based on these facts.

Think Aloud

If baseball is known as our "national pastime," people must like it. If there are more and more teams added, then there must be lots of people going to see baseball games. The fact that millions of Americans watch the World Series also tells me that lots of people like baseball. So I can generalize by saying this: Many Americans love baseball.

Discuss why this is a "fair" generalization that fits the facts. Explain that students need to be careful not to create unfair generalizations.

Write these sentences on the board: *Ed's cat is mean. All cats are mean.*

Tell students that the second sentence is a generalization but it is unfair. Explain that just because one cat is mean, that doesn't prove all cats are mean. Stress that a generalization must be supported by facts.

Guided Practice

Display or **distribute** Teaching Master ES2-6. Read the introduction.

Model scanning the passage to look for details that will help students to make a generalization. Point to these details as you mention them.

Think Aloud

The first sentence says rain forests get lots of rain. The second sentence is still about rain, so it's important. The next two sentences tell how warm rain forests are, so I'll include warm. *It says rain forests are always green and that tall trees block out light. Finally, I see there are many kinds of plants and animals in rain forests. These details all describe what most rain forests are like.*

Help students to complete the chart.

Practice/Apply

Distribute Practice Master ES2-6 to students. Have them read the passage.

Go over the directions with students and have them complete the Practice Maser independently.

Check students' responses to be sure they can make generalizations.

LITERATURE FOCUS: 10–15 MINUTES

Preview *Boss of the Plains*

Segment 2

Refer to the bottom of page 232 in the Teacher's Edition and preview with students Segment 2 of *Boss of the Plains* (pages 232–239).

Note the suggestions in the Extra Support boxes on Teacher's Edition pages 236 and 238.

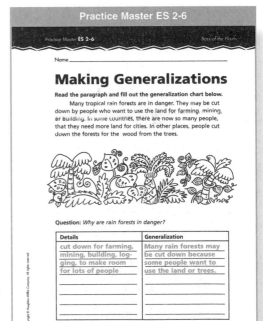

Teaching Master ES 2-6

Teaching Master **ES 2-6**   *Boss of the Plains*

Making Generalizations

A generalization is a statement that is true most of the time. It often uses words such as *all, few, often, some, rarely, never, always, many,* or *most.*

A tropical rain forest is a forest of tall trees that gets a lot of rain. Some rain forests get over 250 inches of rain in one year! Rain forests are always warm. The temperature rarely goes over 93 degrees or drops below 68 degrees. Rain forests remain green all year long. The tallest trees block out much of the light below. Most rain forests are near the equator. Tropical rain forests have more species, or types, of plants and animals in them than any other places in the world.

Question: *What are most rain forests like?*

Details	Generalization
lots of rain, always warm, tall trees, blocked light, more types of wildlife than any other places in the world	Most rain forests are hot, dark, green, and wet with lots of wildlife.

TMES 2–6   Grade 4   Theme 2: American Stories

Practice Master ES 2-6

Practice Master **ES 2-6**   *Boss of the Plains*

Name _____

Making Generalizations

Read the paragraph and fill out the generalization chart below.

Many tropical rain forests are in danger. They may be cut down by people who want to use the land for farming, mining, or building. In some countries, there are now so many people, that they need more land for cities. In other places, people cut down the forests for the wood from the trees.

Question: *Why are rain forests in danger?*

Details	Generalization
cut down for farming, mining, building, logging, to make room for lots of people	Many rain forests may be cut down because some people want to use the land or trees.

Grade 4   Theme 2: American Stories   PMES 2–6

SKILL FOCUS: STRUCTURAL ANALYSIS   25–30 MINUTES

Suffixes *er, or, ist*

Teach

Display the following word equations and sentences.

travel + er = ?

sail + or = ?

biolog + ist = ?

Other <u>miners</u> teased John about his funny hat.

There was only one <u>sailor</u> on the ship.

Objectives

- decode words with the suffixes *-er, -or, -ist*
- identify the meaning of words with suffixes *-er, -or, -ist*

Materials

- Anthology: *Boss of the Plains*

Call on a volunteer to complete each equation with the words *traveler*, *sailor*, and *biologist*. Underline *-er* in *traveler* and explain that in this word, *-er* is a suffix, or a word part added to the end of a base word. Have students read aloud the base word, suffix, and new word. Continue this process for the other two word equations.

Use the Think Aloud to model decoding the word *miners* in the sentence:

Other <u>miners</u> teased John about his funny hat.

Think Aloud

First I take away the ending -s. *Then I see the suffix* -er. *I don't think* min *is the base word, but I know sometimes* e *is dropped from a base word before a suffix is added. I think the base word is* mine. Mine + er = miner, *and* miners *makes sense in the sentence.*

Practice

Encourage students to decode words with the suffixes *-or* and *-ist*: *John was a visitor in the town of St. Joseph. John was a specialist in making hats.*

Apply

Have students find, decode, and define seven words with suffixes in the story. Ask students to check their definitions in a dictionary.

LITERATURE FOCUS: 10–15 MINUTES

Review *Boss of the Plains*

Guide students through the Comprehension Skill Lesson for **Making Generalizations** on page 235 in the Teacher's Edition.

Day 4

Objectives

* identify plural nouns (including those ending in *y*)
* form the plural of nouns ending in *y*
* form the plural of irregular nouns

Materials

* Reader's Library: *Two Cold Ears*

More Plural Nouns

Teach

Remind students that a *plural noun* is a noun that names more than one person, place, or thing.

Write *caps* and *boxes* on the board, and have volunteers tell how these plural nouns are formed. (Add *s*; add *es*.) Explain to students that the plurals of some nouns are not always formed by simply adding *s* or *es*. Tell them that nouns that end in *y* follow special rules for forming the plural.

How to Form Plurals for Nouns Ending in y		
Rules	Singular	Plural
If the noun ends with a vowel and y, add *s*	one toy a monkey	many toy*s* five monkey*s*
If the noun ends with a consonant and y, change the y to *i* and add *es*	one family this city a baby	some famili*es* six citi*es* two babi*es*

Elicit from students the changes that occurred to form the plural *families*. (Change the final *y* to *i*. Add *es*.)

Explain that other nouns have special plural forms too. They are words that do not follow a specific spelling pattern or rule. The chart will help students remember some of them.

Singular	Plural	Singular	Plural
one child	two children	each tooth	five teeth
a man	many men	one goose	both geese
this woman	three women	an ox	nine oxen
that foot	these feet	a mouse	some mice

Familiarize the class with the nouns in the chart by reading, speaking, and dissecting the contents systematically together. Tell students that still other nouns are the same in both the singular and the plural forms.

Singular	Plural
One deer nibbled the bark.	Several deer ate quietly.
Did you see a moose?	Two moose crossed a stream.
I have a pet sheep.	These sheep have soft wool.

Practice

Have students write the plural forms of these nouns: *cowboy, day, decoy, derby, huckleberry, chimney, sheep, sky, supply, moose.*

Apply

Have students write sentences for each of the plural nouns found in the Practice activity.

LITERATURE FOCUS: 10–15 MINUTES

Preview *Two Cold Ears*

Walk students through *Two Cold Ears*. Discuss illustrations using words such as *ached, mufflers, throbbing,* and *protectors.*

Ask students to make some generalizations about the story setting by previewing the illustrations.

Day 5

Objectives

- use story details to recognize generalizations
- use information from the story to make generalizations

Materials

- Anthology: *Boss of the Plains*
- Reader's Library: *Two Cold Ears*

SKILL FOCUS: COMPREHENSION   25–30 MINUTES

Making Generalizations

Teach

Have several students tell the kind of shoes they're wearing. Ask if this statement is true: *Most fourth-grade students wear sneakers.* Explain this is a *generalization*—a statement that is true about most of the items or people in a group most of the time. Generalizations are based on facts and usually contain signal words: *all, few, generally, many, most, usually.*

Use the following Think Aloud to model making a generalization about the hat in the story *Boss of the Plains.*

> **Think Aloud**
>
> *I read that Westerners liked John's hat. They said "you can smell it across a room" and "you just can't wear it out." I can make this generalization: Westerners wore John's hat almost all the time.*

Practice

Help students use story facts to form generalizations.

Story Fact	Generalization
The dampness and steam of the hat shop caused John to become sick with tuberculosis.	All workers in the hat shop got tuberculosis.
John made a felt tent.	All tents are made of felt.

Apply

Have students make generalizations with an eye to identifying signal words, in the Reader's Library selection *Two Cold Ears* by Kitty Colton. Ask students to complete the questions and activity on the Responding page.

LITERATURE FOCUS: 10–15 MINUTES

Revisit *Boss of the Plains* and *Two Cold Ears*

Review with students the process of making generalizations about the settings of *Boss of the Plains* and *Two Cold Ears.* Also, help them look for words with suffixes *-er*, *-or*, and *-ist* such as *explorers*, *hatmakers*, (*Boss of the Plains*, page 222), and *inventor* (*Two Cold Ears*, page 56).

A Very Important Day

SKILL FOCUS: STRUCTURAL ANALYSIS   25–30 MINUTES

Possessives

Warm-Up / Academic Language

Explain that a **possessive noun** shows that **a person owns something**. Tell students that an **apostrophe s** is usually **added to a person's and/or people's names** to **show that something belongs to them**.

Teach

Write this formula on the board: *'s = belongs to.*

Point to a student's desk and say, "This desk belongs to the student. This is the student's desk."

Write these sentences on the board, underlining *belongs to the student* and *student's*. Identify the apostrophe and tell students that adding *'s* to a singular noun is the same as saying "belongs to." Guide students to understand that each sentence has the same meaning.

Write the following sentences on the board:

> The pencil that belongs to Ian broke.
>
> Molly borrowed the CD that belongs to Erin.

Direct students to come to the board to rewrite each sentence, using the possessive form. (Ian's pencil broke; Molly borrowed Erin's CD.)

Point to several of the students' chairs and say "These chairs belong to the students. These are the students' chairs." Write these sentences on the board, underlining *belong to* and *students'*.

Discuss how the possessive form of most plural nouns is made by adding an apostrophe after the plural. (The Cohens' home is next door.)

Write the following question and phrases on the board, leaving out the *(')* or *('s)* for each. Read each phrase aloud.

Objective
- read possessive nouns

Materials
- Teaching Master ES2-7
- Practice Masters ES2-7
- Anthology: *A Very Important Day*

Technology

**Get Set for Reading
CD-ROM**

A Very Important Day

Education Place
www.eduplace.com
A Very Important Day

Audiotape
A Very Important Day
Audiotape for **American Stories**

**Lexia Phonics
CD-ROM**
Intermediate Intervention

Teaching Master ES 2-7

> **Where does the apostrophe go?**
>
> one kitten('s) toy   Jess(') game
>
> two boys(') sneakers   the children('s) homework
>
> my mother('s) purse   both my grandparents(') gifts
>
> the men('s) shirts   Ben('s) book

Ask volunteers to insert the *apostrophe* or *apostrophe s* in its correct place for each phrase.

Guided Practice

Display or **distribute** Teaching Master ES2-7.

Discuss the concept of a lost-and-found department. Explain that the paragraphs are the words said by three different people who are talking about something each has lost.

Read the passage with students.

Help students to underline the possessive and to tell you who owns each item. For example, ask, "Who owns the hat?" (the woman's sister) **Ask** students to tell you if each possessive is plural or singular.

Practice/Apply

Distribute Practice Master ES2-7 to students. Read the instructions as students follow along.

Have students complete the Practice Master independently.

Check student responses to be sure they understand the forms of the possessive.

Practice Master ES 2-7

LITERATURE FOCUS: 10–15 MINUTES

Preview *A Very Important Day*

Segment 1

Refer to the bottom of page 249 in the Teacher's Edition and preview with students Segment 1 of *A Very Important Day* (pages 249–259).

Note the suggestion in the Extra Support boxes on Teacher's Edition pages 257 and 258.

Day 2

Objectives
- arrange like items into groups
- find a name to describe all members of a group

Materials
- Teaching Master ES2-8
- Practice Masters ES2-8
- Anthology: *A Very Important Day*

PRETEACH

SKILL FOCUS: COMPREHENSION   25–30 MINUTES

Categorize and Classify

Warm-Up / Academic Language

Explain that a **category** is a name given to a **group of related items.** Explain that when students **arrange items into a group**, they are **classifying**, or sorting. Tell students that this is a helpful way of **organizing information** so that it is easier to understand.

Teach

List these categories on the board: *Sports, Foods, Colors*. Have students volunteer items that would fit in each of these categories.

List these animal names on the board: *snake, bear, crow, fish, lizard, owl, dog, seagull, cat*. Read aloud each item. Model how to begin to categorize and classify these animals.

Think Aloud

I've looked through all the items, and I think I have a way to classify them into categories. The first item is a snake. I know that a snake is covered with scales. Are there any other animals like that listed? A fish and a lizard are also covered with scales. So my first category is Animals Covered with Scales.

Write this category on the board and list *snake, fish,* and *lizard,* crossing them off the list of animals.

Help students to create two similar categories for the remaining six animals, listing the appropriate animals beneath each heading.

ANIMALS WITH:		
SCALES	FUR	FEATHERS
snake	bear	crow
fish	dog	owl
lizard	cat	robin.

Guided Practice

Display or **distribute** Teaching Master ES2-8

Read the passage with students and discuss the illustration.

Have students look at the circle labeled "Florida Cousins," connecting the names in the circle (Robbie, Ricky) to the passage. Identify *Florida Cousins* as the category and note that Robbie and Ricky are classified here because they live in Florida.

Discuss the next two circles with students.

Help students fill out the remaining entries for the last two circles.

Practice/Apply

Distribute Practice Master ES2-8 to students.

Read aloud the directions and make sure students understand that the list contains what Cheryl does each day of the week. Point out that each numbered item is a category. Students should review Cheryl's weekly schedule to see which activities can be classified in each category.

Have students read the list and complete the Practice Master independently.

Check all students' ability to categorize and classify.

LITERATURE FOCUS: 10–15 MINUTES

Preview *A Very Important Day*

Segment 2

Refer to the bottom of page 260 in the Teacher's Edition and preview with students Segment 2 of *A Very Important Day* (pages 260–269).

Note the suggestions in the Extra Support boxes on Teacher's Edition pages 266 and 268.

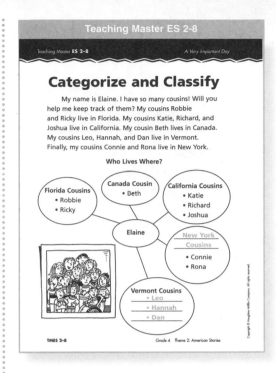

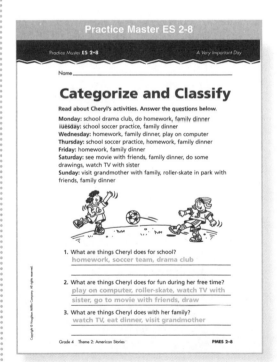

Day 3

Objectives
- identify possessive nouns
- identify the possessive form of singular nouns
- identify the possessive form of plural nouns

Materials
- Anthology: *A Very Important Day*

RETEACH

SKILL FOCUS: STRUCTURAL ANALYSIS   25–30 MINUTES

Possessives

Teach

Display the following sentence:

These books belong to the student.

Ask volunteers if they can say the same thing in a different way, using a possessive noun. (These are the student's books.) Write the answer on the board. Ask students to explain how these two sentences are different. Point out that by adding an apostrophe and *s* to a noun, it turns the noun into a possessive form. Review that possessive nouns show that someone or something owns or has something.

Display a different version of the sentence:

These are the students' books.

Ask a volunteer to explain how the meaning of the sentence has changed. Point out that in this sentence, the apostrophe in the word *students'* has come after the *s*, which means it is a possessive plural.

Have a volunteer underline each possessive noun and circle the apostrophes in each sentence.

Review the ways possessives are formed:

- Add *'s* to a singular noun.

- Add *'* to most plural nouns.

- Add *'s* to plural nouns not ending in *s*.

Display this sentence: *These are the children's books.* Use the Think Aloud to model decoding the possessive noun *children's*.

> **Think Aloud**
>
> *I see an apostrophe in this word, so I know the word is probably a possessive noun. I know the word* children, *so this is the possessive form of* children. *I try* children's *and find that this possessive noun makes sense:* the books belong to the children.

Practice

Work with students to identify the possessives on pages 234–235 of the story. Have volunteers tell whether or not the possessive is singular or plural, and how they know this. Then, ask students to write out the sentences in which the possessives appear and to rewrite them to make plural possessives singular and singular possessives plural.

Apply

Encourage students to identify other possessives in the Anthology selection.

LITERATURE FOCUS: 10–15 MINUTES

Review *A Very Important Day*

Guide students through the Comprehension Skill Lesson for **Categorize and Classify** on page 265 in the Teacher's Edition.

SKILL FOCUS: GRAMMAR 25–30 MINUTES

Singular and Plural Possessive Nouns

Teach

Remind students that a possessive noun shows that someone or something owns or has something.

Write *daughter*, *neighbors*, and *grandchildren* on the board, and have volunteers tell whether the nouns are singular or plural. Explain the rules for forming possessives of singular nouns, using the graphic below.

Singular Nouns	Singular Possessive Nouns
This football belongs to Bob. ⟶	This is Bob's football.
The bike the girl owns is new. ⟶	The girl's bike is new.
These poems by Leo are funny. ⟶	Leo's poems are funny.
The tail of the beaver is flat. ⟶	The beaver's tail is flat.

Elicit from students that to form the possessive of a singular noun, you add an apostrophe and *s* (*'s*). Then explain the rules for forming possessives of plural nouns. Tell students to use plural possessive nouns when you want to show ownership by more than one person or thing.

Present these two rules:

1. When a plural noun ends with *s*, add an apostrophe (').

   pumpkins owned by the boys ⟶ the boys' pumpkins

   eyes of the puppies ⟶ the puppies' eyes

2. When a plural noun does not end with *s*, add an apostrophe and *s* (*'s*).

   antlers of both deer ⟶ both deer's antlers

   reports by these men ⟶ these men's reports

Objectives

- identify singular and plural possessive nouns
- form singular possessive nouns
- form plural possessive nouns

Materials

- Reader's Library: *Two Star Day*

Practice

Have students write the possessive forms of these nouns: *driver, people, Eugenia, waitress, Leonovs, parents*.

Provide students with the sentences below. Ask them to identify all the possessive nouns. Ask them to tell if each is a singular or plural possessive noun.

1. Nelia is the head of the radio station's disk jockeys. (singular possessive)

2. The Zengs' trip to town was slow. (plural possessive)

3. The children's friends were happy. (plural possessive)

Apply

Ask students to work in pairs to search through the story for possessive nouns. If they are unable to find enough examples, ask them to take nouns from the story and create the missing possessive forms.

LITERATURE FOCUS: 10–15 MINUTES

Preview *Two Star Day*

Walk students through *Two Star Day*. Discuss illustrations using words such as *citizen*, *ceremony*, *oath*, and *jury*.

Guide students in categorizing and classifying the subjects of the illustrations throughout the selection. (objects vs. people, historical figures vs. present day people)

Day 5

Objectives

- identify similarities among a group of objects
- categorize and classify similar objects by their common attributes

Materials

- Anthology: *A Very Important Day*
- Reader's Library: *Two Star Day*
- pencil, catalog, marker, newspaper, book, pen, chalk, magazine, crayon, workbook

RETEACH

SKILL FOCUS: COMPREHENSION   25–30 MINUTES

Categorize and Classify

Teach

Write the following on the chalkboard:

> Things you write with.
>
> Things you read.

Explain that these two phrases are titles of categories. Point out that there are certain things in the classroom that can be grouped, or classified, in each of these categories.

Ask volunteers to name examples of things from each category.

Display these objects: a pencil, a catalog, a felt marker, a newspaper, a book, a pen, a piece of chalk, a magazine, a crayon, a workbook. Ask volunteers to come up and place each object in one of the two categories. Tell students that by putting these similar items into a like group, they are *classifying* them into these two groups, or *categories*: *things you write with* and *things you read*.

Use the Think Aloud to model classifying the characters in the story into two categories: *male* and *female*.

Think Aloud

I'm going to classify the people into two categories: "females" and "males." I will reread parts of the story to help me sort some names.

Practice

Have partners list all the names of the characters in the story. Then, have them classify each character into one of two categories: *U. S. citizen* and *Soon to be a citizen*.

Apply

Have students categorize and classify the characters in the Reader's Library selection *Two Star Day* by Veronica Freeman Ellis. Ask students to complete the questions and activity on the Responding page.

Revisit *A Very Important Day* and *Two Star Day*

Help students to categorize and classify elements from *A Very Important Day* and *Two Star Day*. Also, help them look for possessives such as *Nelia's*, *Jorge's*, (*A Very Important Day*, pages 250 and 256) *Tonieh's*, and *Citizen's* (*Two Star Day* pages 65 and 69).

Theme 3

That's Amazing!

Selections

1 The Stranger

2 Cendrillon

3 Heat Wave!

Day 1

Objectives
- identify and read compound words
- use the Phonics/Decoding strategy to decode longer words

Materials
- Teaching Master ES3-1
- Practice Master ES3-1
- Anthology: *The Stranger*

Technology

Get Set for Reading CD-ROM
The Stranger

Education Place
www.eduplace.com
The Stranger

Audiotape
The Stranger
Audiotape for **That's Amazing!**

Lexia Phonics CD-ROM
Intermediate Intervention

PRETEACH

SKILL FOCUS: STRUCTURAL ANALYSIS   25–30 MINUTES

Compound Words

Warm-Up/Academic Language

Remind students that **two smaller words can be put together** to form a **larger word.** Explain that the larger word is called a **compound word** and that the words within a compound word are sometimes separated by a hyphen, but often, they are not. Tell students that **recognizing the smaller words within a compound word** can help them to read and understand **unfamiliar compound words**.

Teach

Write the word *classroom* on the board and ask students to tell you which smaller, familiar words they can find within the compound word. (*class* and *room*)

Circle each smaller word within *classroom* and write *class + room =* in front of *classroom*. Elicit that recognizing one or both words made it easier to decode the longer word.

Guide students to explain why the compound word *classroom* makes sense. (it is a *room* with a *class* of students in it.)

Point out that in the compound word *classroom*, the shorter words, *class* and *room* run together. Explain that many compound words may also be formed by joining the shorter words with a hyphen (*good-bye*).

Repeat the above process for the following words: *first-born, firefighter, greenhouse, playground, haircut, car-pool.*

Guided Practice

Display or **distribute** Teaching Master ES3-1 and discuss the illustration with students.

Read the sentences with students, and underline the compound words.

Help students write the compound words, separating them into smaller words with a slash.

Practice/Apply

Distribute Practice Master ES3-1 and go over the directions with students.

Have them complete the Practice Master independently.

Check students' responses to make sure they can decode compound words.

LITERATURE FOCUS: 10–15 MINUTES

Preview *The Stranger* Segment 1

Refer to the bottom of page 301 in the Teacher's Edition and preview with students Segment 1 of *The Stranger* (pages 300–309).

Note the suggestions in the Extra Support boxes on Teacher's Edition pages 303 and 308.

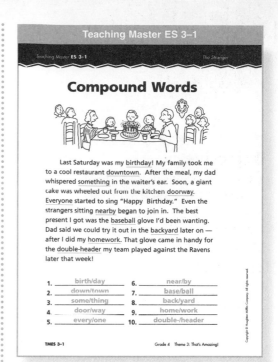

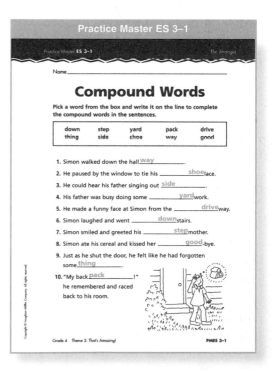

Day 2

PRETEACH

SKILL FOCUS: COMPREHENSION   25–30 MINUTES

Noting Details

Objective

- note important details about story characters, events, and setting

Materials

- Teaching Master ES3-2
- Practice Master ES3-2
- Anthology: *The Stranger*

Warm-Up/Academic Language

Explain that authors use **details** to help readers understand more about a story's **characters, events,** and **setting**. Stress that **some details are more important than others**. Being able to tell which details are the **most important** can help readers better **understand the author's meaning.**

Teach

Tell students that you will read a story to them. Instruct them to listen carefully for important details that tell about the story events. Also have them listen for less important, descriptive details.

Read the story below to students.

> **Read Aloud**
>
> "Uh-oh," thought Amy as she looked inside her purple lunchbox. She had remembered to take her lunchbox but forgotten to pack a lunch!
>
> For breakfast, Amy had eaten a big bowl of oatmeal. But Amy worried she might be hungry by the end of the day without a lunch. She needed to have energy for soccer practice after school.
>
> At lunch, she sat down beside her new friend Graham, who had just moved here from Chicago. Amy thought about her hunger and sighed. Graham asked what was wrong and she told him about her problem.
>
> Graham smiled and said, "No problem. I'll share my lunch with you."

Help students fill in a chart similar to the one that follows. Lead them to note details about story events and to classify them as less important or more important. Guide students as needed to tell why a given detail is important.

Important Details	Unimportant Details
Amy forgot her lunch.	Amy's lunchbox is purple.
Why: Shows the story problem.	**Why:** Describes lunchbox but isn't key story event
Graham offers to share.	Graham lived in Chicago.
Why: Shows story solution.	**Why:** Gives background; doesn't show kind of person he is.

Add details not listed above to the chart and discuss as time allows.

Guided Practice

Display or **distribute** Teaching Master ES3-2 and read the story.

Guide students to fill out the chart and discuss why the details that you recorded are important.

Ask students to point out less important details and discuss. (Jean hums; it's a bright, chilly day; a cloud passes by.)

Practice/Apply

Distribute Practice Master ES3-2 and read the passage with students.

Go over the directions and point out that students will be looking for details that describe the setting of the story.

Have students complete the Practice Master independently.

Check students' responses to make sure they can distinguish important details from less important details.

LITERATURE FOCUS: 10–15 MINUTES

Preview *The Stranger* Segment 2

Refer to the bottom of page 310 in the Teacher's Edition and preview with students Segment 2 of *The Stranger* (pages 310–317).

Note the suggestions in the Extra Support boxes on Teacher's Edition pages 312, 314, and 316.

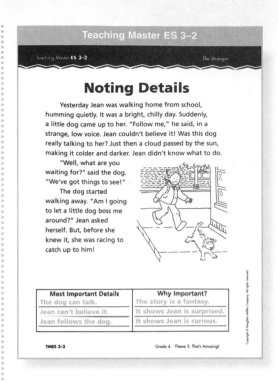

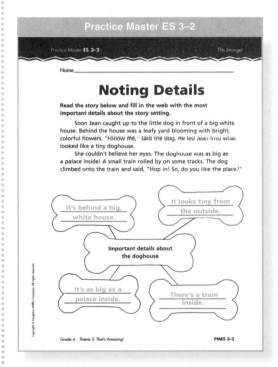

Day 3

Objectives
- read words that are compound words
- identify the two words that make up a compound word
- identify the meaning of compound words

Materials
- Anthology: *The Stranger*
- index cards
- scissors

SKILL FOCUS: STRUCTURAL ANALYSIS   25–30 MINUTES

Compound Words

Teach

Write the following sentence on the board: *Katy watched from her bedroom window*.

Ask students to read the underlined word. Explain that two base words have been combined to form a new word. Draw a line between the two base words so that students can see its parts.

Write another sentence on the board: *He left his skateboard in the driveway this afternoon*.

Draw a line under the three compound words and then discuss the following steps for decoding compound words:

- Find the two small words.

- Think about the meaning of each small word.

- Put the two small words together.

Have students refer to the Phonics/Decoding Strategy Poster for more tips.

Practice

Help students practice identifying visual patterns of compound words. Display the following list, and read each word aloud with students.

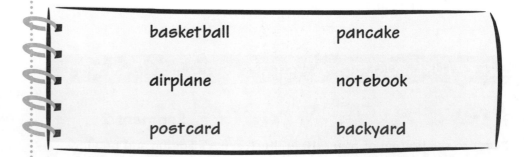

basketball	pancake
airplane	notebook
postcard	backyard

Discuss the meaning of each word. Ask students to draw a line between the two base words, say each one, and then say the whole word and use it in a sentence.

Apply

Display the following compound words:

downstairs	toothbrush
flashlight	rowboat
newspaper	popcorn

Write the compound words from the list on index cards. Cut the cards into two parts. Have students work together to match parts. Ask pairs to write a sentence using the compound word formed from their word parts. Have students read their sentences aloud.

LITERATURE FOCUS: 10–15 MINUTES

Review *The Stranger*

Guide students through the Comprehension Skill Lesson for **Noting Details** on page 307 in the Teacher's Edition.

Day 4

Objectives

• identify action verbs
• use action verbs in sentences

Materials

• Reader's Library: *One Day in May*

Action Verbs

Teach

Write the following sentences about *The Stranger* on the chalkboard:

> Mr. Bailey drove home.
> The man fell down.
> Katy peeked into the room.

Remind students that most verbs are words that show action. Ask students to identify the verb in each sentence on the board. (drove, fell, peeked)

Help students identify some of the action verbs that appear on the first page of the story, for example, *liked, whistled, blew, jammed*. Then ask students to read the sentences in which those verbs appear.

Practice

Work with students to identify some more action verbs from page 304: *found, knelt, opened, looked, jumped, tried, fell, took*. Write these words on the board. Ask students to read the sentences in which those verbs appear.

Encourage students to add words to the list: *run, walk, hop, skip, lift, clap, shake, nod*.

Have volunteers come up and mime actions for their classmates to identify. Add those action verbs to the list. Have students use each verb in a sentence.

Apply

Ask students to think about how they would respond to this stranger, if he had visited them. Have students work in small groups to write sentences describing what might happen. Each sentence should include an action verb. Have each group share their sentences with the class.

Preview *One Day in May*

Walk students through *One Day in May,* and discuss illustrations using words such as *buds, mass, sprouted,* and *falcon.*

Ask students to flip through the illustrations and note descriptive details about the characters and setting.

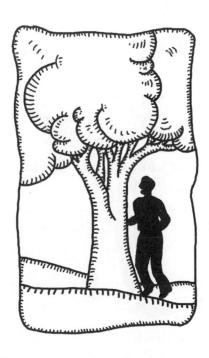

Day 5

Objectives

- use details to explain a character's feelings
- use details to visualize events
- use details to infer important ideas

Materials

- Anthology: *The Stranger*
- Reader's Library: *One Day in May*

Noting Details

Teach

Write the following sentence on the board: *This place has a bed, a dresser, and a closet with clothes.*

Ask students, *What place usually has these things?*

Ask students to identify the place and to explain how they knew. Encourage students to use the following strategy for noting details as they read.

1. Notice important details.

2. Think about what they mean.

3. Use details to visualize events.

Practice

Have students follow in their books as you read aloud pages 306–308. Work with students to select the details that can be used to learn who the stranger is. Model the thinking.

Think Aloud

Who is this stranger? On page 306 I learn that the mercury is stuck at the bottom when the doctor takes the stranger's temperature.

On page 308 I read that when the man eats with the Baileys, he is fascinated by the steam that rises from the hot food. Also, Mrs. Bailey shivers. So somehow, this man is connected to things being cold. I have some good clues, but I'll have to read more before I can figure out who the stranger is.

Skim the rest of the story with students. Help them identify other details that might help solve the mystery. (p. 310, fascinated by geese flying south; p. 312, seasons don't change; p. 314, stranger departs and weather gets cold, leaves turn; p. 316, every autumn, "See you next fall" appears on farmhouse window.)

Remind students that these details describe what happens when autumn comes. Help them see that the author provided details to help readers identify the stranger as Autumn.

Apply

Have students keep track of details and use them to understand the story better as they read the Reader's Library selection *One Day in May* by Kitty Colton. Have students complete the questions and activity on the Responding page.

LITERATURE FOCUS: 10–15 MINUTES

Revisit *The Stranger* and *One Day in May*

Review with students the process for noting key character details in *The Stranger* and *One Day in May*. Also, help them to look for compound words, such as *buttonholes, bedroom, pitchfork, something,* (*The Stranger*, pages 308, 308, 309, and 314) *everything, outside, anyone,* and *doorway* (*One Day in May*, pages 5, 7, 8, and 19).

Day 1

Objectives
- read words with the suffix *-able*
- use the Phonics/Decoding strategy to decode longer words

Materials
- Teaching Master ES3-3
- Practice Master ES3-3
- Anthology: *Cendrillon*

Technology

Get Set for Reading CD-ROM
Cendrillon

Education Place
www.eduplace.com
Cendrillon

Audiotape
Cendrillon
Audiotape for **That's Amazing!**

Lexia Phonics CD-ROM
Intermediate Intervention

Words with the Suffix *-able*

Warm-Up/Academic Language

Remind students that a **suffix** is a **word part added to the end of a base word.** Explain that the addition of a suffix may **change a base word's meaning or its part of speech.** Tell students that the suffix *-able* means **"able to be."** Being able to recognize suffixes such as *-able* can help them to decode longer, unfamiliar words.

Teach

Inform students that the suffix *-able* means "able to be." Write *use* and *useable* on the board. Read each word aloud. Elicit that something that is *useable* is "able to be used."

Write this equation on the board: *use + able = useable*. Circle *use* and explain that it is the base word. Underline the suffix *-able* and remind students that it means "able to be." Then write the following word equations on the board:

> do + able = doable
> teach + able = teachable
> refund + able = refundable
> adore + able = adorable

Have students identify the base word and suffix in each equation. Then ask them to read the new word aloud. Ask them to tell you the meaning of each new word. (able to be done; able to be taught; able to be refunded; able to be adored)

Explain to students that each of the base words is a verb that becomes an adjective when *-able* is added to it.

Ask students to identify the base word that changed its spelling when the suffix was added. (adore) Explain that if a base word contains a silent *e*, the *e* may be dropped when adding *-able*.

Display the following sentence. Read it aloud, and model how to decode *unbelievable: Judy's excuse that the dog ate her homework was unbelievable.*

Think Aloud

I see the suffix -able *at the end of this word. The suffix has two syllables,* uh *and* bull. *I go to the beginning of the word and see the prefix* un-. *If I cover the prefix and suffix, I see a word that looks almost like* believe. *I think the final* e *was dropped when the suffix was added. Now I sound out the whole word, from beginning to end.* Uhn bee LEEV uh buhl. Unbelievable. *That makes sense in the sentence.*

Teaching Master ES 3–3

Teaching Master **ES 3–3**   *Cendrillon*

Words with the Suffix -able

1. Glass vases are **breakable**.

2. Kay's dress is **washable**.

3. My father gave me some **valuable** baseball cards.

4. Juan's birthday party was **enjoyable**.

5. Leslie's new puppy is **lovable**.

6. Dominick tried to get **comfortable**.

7. Tyrone's riddle is not **solvable**.

8. Is that old CD **playable**?

TMES 3–3   Grade 4   Theme 3: That's Amazing!

Guided Practice

Display or **distribute** Teaching Master ES3-3.

Read the sentences with students and discuss the corresponding illustrations.

Help students to tell the meaning of the boldfaced words, using the sentence context, the illustration, and their knowledge of the suffix *-able*.

Discuss words which required spelling changes in order to add *-able*. *(valuable, lovable, solvable)*

Practice/Apply

Distribute Practice Master ES3-3 and review the directions with students.

Have students complete the Practice Master independently.

Check student's responses to make sure they can decode words with *-able*.

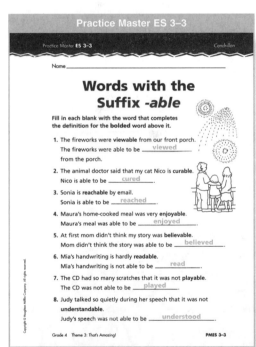

Practice Master ES 3–3

Practice Master **ES 3–3**   *Cendrillon*

Name _____

Words with the Suffix -able

Fill in each blank with the word that completes the definition for the **bolded** word above it.

1. The fireworks were **viewable** from our front porch. The fireworks were able to be ___viewed___ from the porch.

2. The animal doctor said that my cat Nico is **curable**. Nico is able to be ___cured___.

3. Sonia is **reachable** by email. Sonia is able to be ___reached___.

4. Maura's home-cooked meal was very **enjoyable**. Maura's meal was able to be ___enjoyed___.

5. At first mom didn't think my story was **believable**. Mom didn't think the story was able to be ___believed___.

6. Mia's handwriting is hardly **readable**. Mia's handwriting is not able to be ___read___.

7. The CD had so many scratches that it was not **playable**. The CD was not able to be ___played___.

8. Judy talked so quietly during her speech that it was not **understandable**. Judy's speech was not able to be ___understood___.

Grade 4   Theme 3: That's Amazing!   PMES 3–3

LITERATURE FOCUS: 10–15 MINUTES

Preview *Cendrillon* **Segment 1**

Refer to the bottom of page 329 in the Teacher's Edition and preview with students Segment 1 of *Cendrillon* (pages 328–339).

Note the suggestions in the Extra Support boxes on Teacher's Edition pages 331 and 338.

Day 2

PRETEACH

SKILL FOCUS: COMPREHENSION   25–30 MINUTES

Compare and Contrast

Warm-Up/Academic Language

Explain that to **compare** two things, we **show how they are alike,** and to **contrast** two things, we **show how they are different.** Point out that recognizing **likenesses and differences** helps readers to **organize and remember information.**

Teach

Demonstrate how to compare and contrast using a banana and an apple as examples. Ask students to tell how they are alike. (Each can be eaten, is a fruit, grows on trees) Then have students contrast the fruits by telling how they differ. (The apple is red, the banana is yellow. A banana must be peeled. An apple is round, a banana is long.)

Point out that readers can also compare and contrast story characters and events to see how they are alike and how they differ.

Read the following paragraph aloud.

Objectives

- compare details to see how characters and events are alike
- contrast details to see how characters and events differ

Materials

- Teaching Master ES3-4
- Practice Master ES3-4
- Anthology: *Cendrillon*
- apple and banana or picture of each

Read Aloud

> Sid and Chloe are both dogs. Sid is a golden retriever, and Chloe is a fox terrier. Sid likes to chew furniture. Chloe likes to chew shoes. When they entered a dog show, Sid won first prize and Chloe came in last. She barked too much.

Ask students to listen carefully for similarities and differences between Sid and Chloe. Reread the paragraph and display a Venn diagram on the board similar to the one shown. Have students guide you to complete the diagram.

Sid: golden retriever, chews furniture, won first prize at a dog show

Sid and Chloe: dogs, like to chew, went to a dog show

Chloe: fox terrier, chews shoes, came in last at dog show

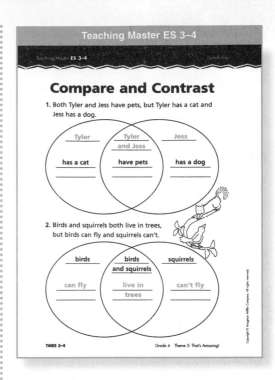

Teaching Master ES 3–4

Compare and Contrast

1. Both Tyler and Jess have pets, but Tyler has a cat and Jess has a dog.

Tyler — has a cat
Tyler and Jess — have pets
Jess — has a dog

2. Birds and squirrels both live in trees, but birds can fly and squirrels can't.

birds — can fly
birds and squirrels — live in trees
squirrels — can't fly

TMES 3–4   Grade 4 · Theme 3: That's Amazing!

Guided Practice

Display or **distribute** Teaching Master ES3-4 and read the first sentence with students.

Help them to compare and contrast the characters and fill out the missing information in the first Venn diagram.

Repeat this procedure for the second Venn diagram.

Practice/Apply

Distribute Practice Master ES3-4 and read the directions with students.

Instruct them to complete the Practice Master independently.

Review the answers as a group. Guide students to identify text from the passage that helped them identify likenesses and differences.

Check students' ability to compare and contrast.

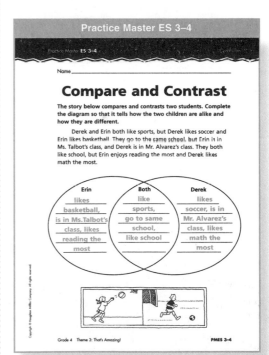

Practice Master ES 3–4

Name _____

Compare and Contrast

The story below compares and contrasts two students. Complete the diagram so that it tells how the two children are alike and how they are different.

Derek and Erin both like sports, but Derek likes soccer and Erin likes basketball. They go to the same school, but Erin is in Ms. Talbot's class, and Derek is in Mr. Alvarez's class. They both like school, but Erin enjoys reading the most and Derek likes math the most.

Erin — likes basketball, is in Ms. Talbot's class, likes reading the most
Both — like sports, go to same school, like school
Derek — likes soccer, is in Mr. Alvarez's class, likes math the most

Grade 4 · Theme 3: That's Amazing!   PMES 3–4

LITERATURE FOCUS: 10–15 MINUTES

Preview *Cendrillon* Segment 2

Refer to the bottom of page 340 in the Teacher's Edition and preview with students Segment 2 of *Cendrillon* (pages 340–353).

Note the suggestions in the Extra Support boxes on Teacher's Edition pages 343, 345, and 352.

Day 3

Objectives
- recognize when words have the suffix *-able*
- decode words with the suffix *-able*

Materials
- Anthology: *The Stranger*

SKILL FOCUS: STRUCTURAL ANALYSIS   25–30 MINUTES

The Suffix *-able*

Teach

Write the following sentences on the board:

> The shoe was small, and Vitaline's large toes were <u>breakable.</u>
>
> Her new dress was <u>washable.</u>

Ask students what is similar about the underlined words. Call attention to the suffix *-able*. Explain that it means "having the ability to do something."

Model how you would decode words with the suffix *-able* by reading the following Think Aloud.

Think Aloud

I start to read this sentence, "The shoe was small, and Vitaline's large toes were _____ ." I can't read this word right away. Sometimes it helps to break a word into parts. Do I recognize any parts of this word? Yes. Here is the suffix -able. *The first part of this word is* break. *When I put the parts together, I get* breakable. *It makes sense in this sentence.*

Review the following strategy for decoding words with suffixes.

1. Divide the word into a base word and a suffix.

2. Think about the meaning of the base word.

3. Think about the suffix and its meaning.

4. Put the base word and suffix together and say the word.

5. Check that it makes sense in the sentence.

Refer students to the Phonics/Decoding Strategy Poster for more tips.

Practice

Display the following words with the suffix *-able*:

- curable
- reachable
- likable
- manageable

Read each word aloud with students. Then have a volunteer draw a slash between the base word and the suffix. Invite students to read each part aloud, then read the whole word and use it in a sentence.

Have students identify the base words that dropped final *e* before adding *-able*. *(cure, like)*

Apply

Display more words with *-able: believable, imaginable, available, portable*. Have students draw a slash between the suffix and the rest of the word, read each word part, and then read the entire word.

LITERATURE FOCUS: 10–15 MINUTES

Review *Cendrillon*

Guide students through the Comprehension Skill Lesson for **Compare and Contrast** on page 333 in the Teacher's Edition.

Day 4

Objectives

- identify main verbs and helping verbs
- give examples of main verbs and helping verbs

Materials

- Reader's Library: *Tattercoat*

SKILL FOCUS: GRAMMAR　25–30 MINUTES

Main Verbs and Helping Verbs

Teach

Display the following sentences:

I <u>live</u> on a green island.

I <u>have lived</u> on a green island.

Ask students to compare the two sets of underlined words. (One is in the present; the other, in the past. One verb has one word; the other, two.) Put a double line under the main verb, and circle the helping verb in the second sentence above. Then review these concepts:

- When a verb has more than one word, the main verb shows the action.

- A helping verb works with the main verb. The verbs *am, is,* and *are* help other verbs show action that is happening now. Display this example: *Cendrillon <u>is going</u> to the ball.*

- The verbs *was, were, have, has,* and *had* help other verbs show action that happened in the past. Display these examples:

The Prince <u>has looked</u> everywhere for the slipper's owner.

Madame and Vitaline <u>have acted</u> rudely.

Practice

Help students underline main verbs and circle helping verbs in sentences about the story:

> Paul is dancing with Cendrillon.
> I have found a way to help Cendrillon.
> Paul has placed the slipper on her foot.
> We had found ourselves on the dusty road beside a smashed breadfruit.

Ask students to supply some original, story-based sentences, using main and helping verbs. Continue to underline main verbs and circle helping verbs.

Apply

Have students suggest a list of ten action verbs that act as main verbs. Tell students to get into small groups that have an even number of members. Ask half the group to name one of the action verbs, and the other half to add a helping verb. Then the group as a whole creates an original sentence, using the main verb and helping verb.

LITERATURE FOCUS: 10–15 MINUTES

Preview *Tattercoat*

Walk students through *Tattercoat* and discuss illustrations using words such as *lord, battlefield, servants, graceful,* and *lagged*.

Ask students to flip through the illustrations to compare and contrast the portrayal of the characters and setting against similar depictions from *Cendrillon*.

Day 5

Objectives

- distinguish between comparison and contrast
- infer comparison and contrast
- compare and contrast details, characters, and events in a story

Materials

- Anthology: *Cendrillon*
- Reader's Library: *Tattercoat*
- pen and pencil

Compare and Contrast

Teach

Draw a Venn diagram, such as the one shown here, on the chalkboard.

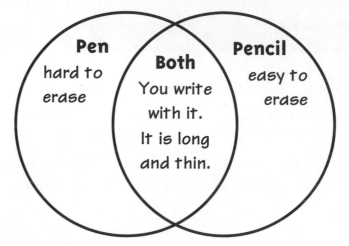

Show students a pen and a pencil. Ask how the two items are alike. Write students' responses in the overlapping section of the two circles. Explain to students that they have just made a comparison.

Ask students how a pen and a pencil are different. Write responses in the appropriate outer sections of the Venn diagram. Explain to students that when they think about how two people, places, things, or events are different, they are contrasting them.

Practice

Go through *Cendrillon* with students and identify differences between characters and events. (p. 335, Mamma and Vitaline eat well, while Cendrillon does not; Vitaline and Mamma can go to the ball, but Cendrillon cannot; p. 339, Cendrillon's "poor calico dress" becomes a fancy gown; p. 340, the narrator's "shift" becomes "a fine red dress"; p. 350, Cendrillon's clothes change from poor to rich to poor again.)

Go through the story looking for examples of things that are similar. (p. 331, Cendrillon and the narrator are both loving and kind; p. 345, Cendrillon and the narrator are both happy; p. 347, Cendrillon and the narrator are both dressed like washerwomen; p. 349, Mamma and Vitaline both say Cendrillon is lazy.)

Write student responses on a Venn diagram or other graphic organizer.

Apply

Have students compare and contrast the characters in the Reader's Library selection *Tattercoat* by Susan Delaney. Ask students to complete the questions and activity on the Responding page.

Revisit *Cendrillon* and *Tattercoat*

Review with students the process for comparing and contrasting selected story elements from *Cendrillon* and *Tattercoat*. Also, help them to look for words ending with the suffix *-able*, such as *miserable* (*Cendrillon*, page 335).

Day 1

Objectives

- read words with *-ed* or *-ing* endings
- use the Phonics/Decoding strategy to decode longer words

Materials

- Teaching Master ES3-5
- Practice Master ES3-5
- Anthology: *Heat Wave!*

Technology

Get Set for Reading CD-ROM
Heat Wave!

Education Place
www.eduplace.com
Heat Wave!

Audiotape
Heat Wave!
Audiotape for **That's Amazing!**

Lexia Phonics CD-ROM
Intermediate Intervention

PRETEACH

SKILL FOCUS: STRUCTURAL ANALYSIS   25–30 MINUTES

Words Ending in *-ed* or *-ing*

Warm-Up/Academic Language

Inform students that the **endings *-ed* and *-ing*** are used with verbs, or action words. Remind them that **verbs ending in *-ed*** usually describe an **action that was done in the past,** and **verbs ending in *-ing*** usually describe **an action that is in the present and continuing.**

Teach

Write *jumped* and *jumping* on the board. Have students read both words aloud.

Emphasize the *-ed* ending in *jumped* by circling it. Cover the ending to show the base word *jump*. Have students say the base word aloud together. Explain that the meaning changes when you add an *-ed* or *-ing* ending. The *-ed* ending means that something happened in the past. (The students jumped.)

Repeat the procedure for *jumping*, explaining that the *-ing* ending means that something is continuing in the present. (The students are jumping.)

Write the words *taste, tasted,* and *tasting* on the board. Circle the *-ed* and *-ing* endings. Use this example to explain that when *-ed* or *-ing* is added to a base word that ends in *e*, the *e* is dropped before the ending is added.

Write *mop, mopped,* and *mopping.* Circle the *-ed* and *-ing* endings. Use this example to explain that when *-ed* or *-ing* is added to a one-syllable base word that ends with one vowel followed by a single consonant, the consonant is usually doubled.

taste – e = tast + ed = tasted	mop + p + ed = mopped
taste – e = tast + ing = tasting	mop + p + ing = mopping

Guided Practice

Display or **distribute** Teaching Master ES4-5 to students.

Read the sentences with them and go over the first sentence pair.

Help them to underline the correct form of the verb, pointing out the time words *right now* and *last weekend*, which set the sentences in the present or past.

Follow a similar procedure for the remaining sentence pairs.

Practice/Apply

Distribute Practice Master ES3-5 to students and go over the directions.

Have students complete the Practice Master independently.

Check to make sure students understand the difference between the *-ed* and *-ing* endings as they share their sentences.

LITERATURE FOCUS: 10–15 MINUTES

Preview *Heat Wave!* Segment 1

Refer to the bottom of page 361 in the Teacher's Edition and preview with students Segment 1 of *Heat Wave!* (pages 360–367).

Note the suggestions in the Extra Support boxes on Teacher's Edition pages 363 and 366.

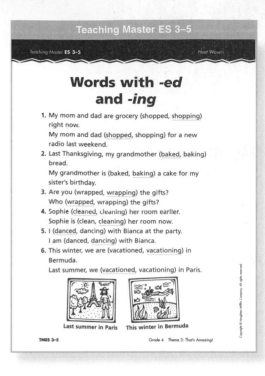

Teaching Master ES 3–5

Teaching Master **ES 3-5**   *Heat Wave!*

Words with *-ed* and *-ing*

1. My mom and dad are grocery (shopped, shopping) right now.
   My mom and dad (shopped, shopping) for a new radio last weekend.
2. Last Thanksgiving, my grandmother (baked, baking) bread.
   My grandmother is (baked, baking) a cake for my sister's birthday.
3. Are you (wrapped, wrapping) the gifts?
   Who (wrapped, wrapping) the gifts?
4. Sophie (cleaned, cleaning) her room earlier.
   Sophie is (clean, cleaning) her room now.
5. I (danced, dancing) with Bianca at the party.
   I am (danced, dancing) with Bianca.
6. This winter, we are (vacationed, vacationing) in Bermuda.
   Last summer, we (vacationed, vacationing) in Paris.

Last summer in Paris   This winter in Bermuda

TMES 3-5   Grade 4   Theme 3: That's Amazing!

Practice Master ES 3–5

Practice Master **ES 3-5**   *Heat Wave!*

Name _____

Words with *-ed* or *-ing*

Write the base word for each of the following words.
Then use the word with *-ed* or *-ing* in a short sentence.

1. hopped
   Base word: ___hop___
   Sentences will vary.
2. racing
   Base word: ___race___
3. laughing
   Base word: ___laugh___
4. pulled
   Base word: ___pull___
5. saving
   Base word: ___save___
6. dragging
   Base word: ___drag___
7. scored
   Base word: ___score___
8. mixed
   Base word: ___mix___

Grade 4   Theme 3: That's Amazing!   **PMES 3-5**

Day 2

Objectives

- identify fantastic and realistic story elements
- decide how well the author uses fantasy and realism

Materials

- Teaching Master ES3-6
- Practice Master ES3-6
- Anthology: *Heat Wave!*

PRETEACH

SKILL FOCUS: COMPREHENSION   25–30 MINUTES

Fantasy and Realism

Warm-Up/Academic Language

Remind students that a **realistic** story tells about **characters and events that can happen in real life.** Point out that when a story has events or situations that **could not occur in real life,** the story is a **fantasy.**

Teach

Explain that in order to tell the difference between fantasy and realism, students should ask themselves, "Could this really happen in everyday life? Is this something I've ever experienced?"

Ask students to tell you whether or not the following descriptions are fantasy or realism:

- an elephant driving a car (fantasy)

- a bear doing a trick at the circus (realism)

- a girl has a conversation with a scarecrow (fantasy)

- a girl helps a grown-up fly a plane (realism)

Read this story aloud:

Read Aloud

Sandra quickly drank a glass of orange juice, gulped a carton of yogurt, and headed for school. She was running late.

"Oh no," Sandra said, stopping her bike at the train tracks. A very long train was approaching. It could take 20 minutes to pass by!

"No problem," said a voice that came from her bike.

Sandra held on tightly as her bicycle rose high over the tracks and glided easily over the roaring train. She landed right in front of the school.

"Uh, thanks!" said Sandra. She felt strange speaking to a bike, but she had to be polite. Sandra looked around. What if someone heard?

Display the chart below on the board. Have students guide you to complete the chart by writing an F for *fantasy*, or an R for *realism* in the second column to show what can and what can't happen in real life.

Event	Fantasy or Realism?
Sandra eats breakfast quickly because she is late	R
Long train blocks Sandra's way	R
Bike talks	F
Sandra and bike take a short cut in the air	F
Sandra feels odd speaking to a bike	R

Guided Practice

Display or **distribute** Teaching Master ES3-6 and read the first sentence pair with students. Discuss the illustration.

Prompt students to explain what makes the first sentence realism and the second sentence fantasy.

Help students read the remaining sentence pairs and identify each sentence as fantasy or realism.

Practice/Apply

Distribute Practice Master ES3-6 and read the directions with students.

Have students complete the Practice Master independently.

Check students' work to make sure they can differentiate between fantasy and realism in their reading.

LITERATURE FOCUS: 10–15 MINUTES

Preview *Heat Wave!* Segment 2

Refer to the bottom of page 368 in the Teacher's Edition and preview with students Segment 2 of *Heat Wave!* (pages 368–377).

Note the suggestions in the Extra Support boxes on Teacher's Edition pages 372 and 376.

Teaching Master ES 3–6

Teaching Master **ES 3–6**   *Heat Wave!*

Fantasy and Realism

1. The corn grew until it was taller than I was. **Realism**
   The corn grew taller than a skyscraper. **Fantasy**

2. It was so cold that the cows were giving ice cream instead of milk. _Fantasy_
   It was cold, but we went to the barn and milked the cows anyway. _Realism_

3. The farmer down the road wasn't very friendly. _Realism_
   The farmer down the road was so mean, he once stopped a tornado just by yelling at it. _Fantasy_

4. The tomatoes we put on our sandwiches were so juicy that they made the bread soggy. _Realism_
   We had to wear raincoats to eat our tomatoes because they squirted so much juice. _Fantasy_

5. The dog growled and said, "Don't even think about petting me right now!" _Fantasy_
   The look on the dog's face told me not to pet her. _Realism_

TMES 3–6   Grade 4   Theme 3: That's Amazing!

Practice Master ES 3–6

Practice Master **ES 3–6**   *Heat Wave!*

Name_____

Fantasy and Realism

Tell whether each of the short passages below uses fantasy or realism. Give a reason for your answer.

1. When I got up this morning, I went into the bathroom. I looked into the mirror and said, "Boy, am I tired!"
   "Better wake up!" my reflection replied. "You've got a long day ahead."
   Fantasy or realism? _fantasy_
   Why? _Reflections in the mirror can't talk._

2. I was trying to watch a video, but my brother wouldn't stop talking. So I pointed the remote control at him and pressed "pause." He froze. Finally, I watched the movie in peace.
   Fantasy or realism? _fantasy_
   Why? _A remote control doesn't work on a person._

Grade 4   Theme 3: That's Amazing!   PMES 3–6

Day 3

Objectives
- identify the suffixes *-ed* and *-ing*
- read words with the suffixes *-ed* and *-ing*

Materials
- Anthology: *Heat Wave*

RETEACH

SKILL FOCUS: STRUCTURAL ANALYSIS   25–30 MINUTES

Words Ending in *-ed* or *-ing*

Teach

Display the following sentences and ask students to read them aloud with you:

> He <u>changed</u> his tune that day.
>
> I <u>looked</u> out across the horizon.
>
> The geese were <u>plucked</u>, <u>stuffed</u>, and <u>roasted</u>.
>
> I was <u>feeding</u> the chickens.
>
> The Heat Wave came <u>rolling</u> across the sky.

Ask students what is similar about each set of underlined words. Mask the first half of each word to help students focus on the suffixes.

Model for students how to decode *crinkled* in this story sentence: *I looked out across the horizon and saw a big old clump of crinkled, yellow air rolling across the sky.*

Think Aloud

"I looked out across the horizon and saw a big old clump of _____ ." I can't read this word right away. But I'll look for a part I know. Do I recognize any parts of this word? Yes. Here is the suffix, -ed. The first part of this word is crinkle. *When I put the parts together, I get* crinkled. *It makes sense in this sentence.*

Remind students that sometimes when *-ed* is added to a word, the first part of the word drops an *e*: *change + ed = changed.* Sometimes when *-ing* is added to a word, an extra letter is added: *pop + ing = popping.*

Practice

Display the following sets of base words and inflected forms, and read the words aloud with students.

holler	hollered	hollering
pop	popped	popping
blast	blasted	blasting
pull	pulled	pulling

Read each word aloud with students.

Have students refer to the Phonics/Decoding Strategy Poster for more tips.

Apply

Have pairs of students choose four of the words ending in *-ed* or *-ing* from the Practice list. Ask them to use the words in sentences. Have partners exchange papers and take turns reading the sentences aloud.

LITERATURE FOCUS: 10–15 MINUTES

Review *Heat Wave*

Guide students through the Comprehension Skill Lesson for **Fantasy and Realism** on page 365 in the Teacher's Edition.

Day 4

Present, Past, and Future Tenses

Objective
- identify the tense of a verb as present, past, or future

Materials
- Reader's Library: *The Big Gust*

Teach

Display the following sentences:

> I <u>look</u> at the chart.
> I <u>looked</u> at the chart.
> I <u>will look</u> at the chart.

Remind students that the tense of a verb tells when something happens.

- *Present tense* shows action that is happening now.

- *Past tense* shows action that has already happened.

- *Future tense* shows action that is going to happen.

Discuss the examples.

Practice

Write the following sentences on the board. Ask students to identify the tenses.

> I take my sister to school. (present)
> She dropped her books. (past)
> We will find a new backpack for her. (future)

Write the following words on the board: *look, help, crawl.* Have students write the past and future tenses of each word.

Apply

Have students look back at the story *Heat Wave!* and choose three verbs. Ask them to write the present and future tenses of each word.

Preview *The Big Gust*

Walk students through *The Big Gust* and discuss illustrations using words such as *gust, polo, thicket,* and *hailstorm*.

Ask students to flip through the illustrations to identify elements of both fantasy and realism.

Day 5

Objectives
- recognize the difference between fantasy and realism in a fantasy story
- identify fantastic and realistic details in a fantasy story

Materials
- Anthology: *Heat Wave!*
- Reader's Library: *The Big Gust*

Fantasy and Realism

Teach

Tell students the following stories:

Story 1   *Today, I got to school, took off my coat, and sat down at my desk. Then the principal came into the room and began to talk to me.*

Story 2   *Today, I rode my dinosaur to get to school. I took off my coat and stood on the ceiling, waiting for the class to arrive. Then a glowing, green giant started to talk to me.*

Ask students how the stories are alike and how they are different. Help students see that the second story is a *fantasy*, even though it has some elements of reality. On a chart, make two lists: *Fantasy* and *Realism*. Have students identify the different types of details in the two stories.

Story 1	**Realism** went to school principle talked
Story 2	**Fantasy** rode a dinosaur a giant talked **Realism** went to school

Point out that in *Heat Wave!* the author mixes fantastic and realistic details. Good readers need to keep them sorted out. Read the second paragraph on page 361 aloud with students. Then model distinguishing between fantasy and reality:

Think Aloud

The narrator is feeding the chickens—that's something she could really do. But then she sees "a big old clump of crinkled, yellow air rolling across the sky." That's not real! You can't see air like that! I can see that this author is mixing fantasy and realism in this fantasy story.

Practice

Go through *Heat Wave!* with students and list details under *Fantasy* or *Realism*.

Fantasy	cows hop
Realism	cows get hot

Apply

Have students keep track of fantasy and realism in the Reader's Library selection *The Big Gust* by Andrew Clements. Ask students to complete the questions and activity on the Responding page.

Revisit *Heat Wave!* and *The Big Gust*

Review with students elements of fantasy and realism presented in *Heat Wave!* and *The Big Gust*. Also, help them to look for words ending with *-ed* and *-ing*, such as *changed, hollered, looking, popping,* (*Heat Wave!*, pages 361, 363, 363, and 365) *doing, flying, looped,* and *turned* (*The Big Gust*, pages 41, 42, 45, and 46).

Theme 4

Problem Solvers

Selections

Day 1

Objective
- to read words with the suffix *-ible*

Materials
- Teaching Master ES4-1
- Practice Masters ES4-1
- Anthology: *My Name Is María Isabel*

Technology

Get Set for Reading CD-ROM
My Name Is María Isabel

Education Place
www.eduplace.com
My Name Is María Isabel

Audiotape
My Name Is María Isabel
Audiotape for **Problem Solvers**

Lexia Phonics CD-ROM
Intermediate Intervention

PRETEACH

SKILL FOCUS: STRUCTURAL ANALYSIS   25–30 MINUTES

Words with the Suffix *-ible*

Warm-Up/Academic Language

Remind students that **suffixes are endings** that can be **added** to a **word root** or **base word**. Explain that knowing how suffixes are spelled and what they mean **can help readers figure out longer words**. Tell students that they will learn about the **suffix *-ible*,** which means **"can" or "able to be."**

Teach

Write the following sentences on the board and ask students to listen as you say them aloud:

> - This writing is visible.
> - This eraser is not edible.

Repeat the last word in each sentence (*visible, edible*). Ask students what suffix these words have in common. (All end in *-ible*.) Underline the suffix in each word.

Explain that the suffix *-ible* means "can" or "able to be."

Write the following on the board:

> - vis<u>ible</u> = able to be seen
> - ed<u>ible</u> = able to be eaten

Point out that *-ible* may be added to base words (word parts that can stand alone, such as *collect*) or word roots (word parts that cannot stand alone, such as *vis*).

Write *collectible* on the board and read this sentence aloud: *Some dolls are popular, collectible toys.* Then write *audible*, and read this sentence aloud: *The sound of my voice is audible.*

Have students define *collectible* (able to be collected) and *audible* (able to be heard).

Guided Practice

Display or **distribute** Teaching Master ES4-1.

Read the first question and answer aloud with students.

Help students to underline the base word with *-ible* in the answer (sensible), and to develop a definition for it. (able to make sense of something)

Follow a similar procedure for the next five questions and answers.

Practice/Apply

Distribute Practice Master ES4-1 and read the directions with students.

Have students work independently to complete the Practice Master.

Check students' understanding of *-ible* by having them read their answers.

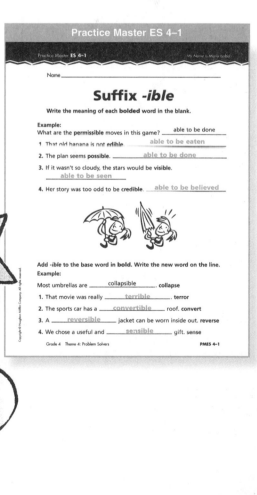

LITERATURE FOCUS: 10–15 MINUTES

Preview *My Name Is María Isabel* Segment 1

Refer to the bottom of page 393 in the Teacher's Edition and preview with students Segment 1 of *My Name Is María Isabel* (pages 393–401).

Note the suggestion in the Extra Support boxes on Teacher's Edition pages 395, 398, and 400.

Day 2

PRETEACH

SKILL FOCUS: COMPREHENSION   25–30 MINUTES

Predicting Outcomes

Warm-Up/Academic Language

Explain that when readers think about **what may happen next in a story,** they are **predicting outcomes.** Point out that readers must **use clues in the story** and **their own experiences** of how similar things happen in real life to predict an outcome in a story.

Teach

Ask students to watch what you do and to predict what you will do next. Go over to the board, pick up a piece of chalk, and look as if you're about to write something. Freeze, and ask students to write down what they think you will do next.

Have students hold up their papers as you write on the board. Turn around to see if students predicted correctly. Discuss with students how they knew what you would do.

Guide students to see that it was possible to predict what you would do by noting details of your actions such as picking up chalk and going to the board and by thinking about experiences from their own lives. Explain that students can ask themselves "What would I do if I were in the same situation?"

Write the following formula on the board: *Story Details + Personal Experiences = Predicting Outcomes*

Read the following passage aloud:

Objective
- use story details and personal knowledge to predict outcomes in different situations

Materials
- Teaching Master ES4-2
- Practice Masters ES4-2
- Anthology: *My Name Is María Isabel*

Read Aloud

Maya and Gwen are best friends. When they spend time together, they always have fun. The last time Maya slept over Gwen's house, they stayed up late giggling and telling stories. They played games and watched a funny movie. They even let Gwen's younger brother Nate join in while they played computer games. Tonight Maya is going to sleep over Gwen's house again….

Instruct students to write down the answer to this question: *Do you think Gwen and Maya will have fun?* Review answers as a group and discuss how and why each student arrived at his or her outcome. (Possible response: I think Maya and Gwen will have fun because they did before and they are best friends. I always have fun when I sleep over a friend's house.)

Guided Practice

Display or **distribute** Teaching Master ES4-2 to students.

Read the story with students and discuss the illustrations with them.

Ask students, "What will happen next?"

Tell students to write down their predictions. When they are done, have them hold up their papers. Use students' work to write a prediction on the board.

Discuss what story clues and personal experiences led students to make their predictions.

Practice/Apply

Distribute Practice Master ES4-2 to students.

Have students read the story and predict an outcome independently.

Check students' responses as they share their predictions to assess their understanding of the skill.

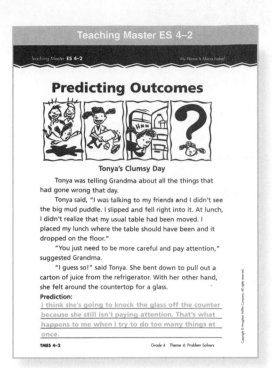

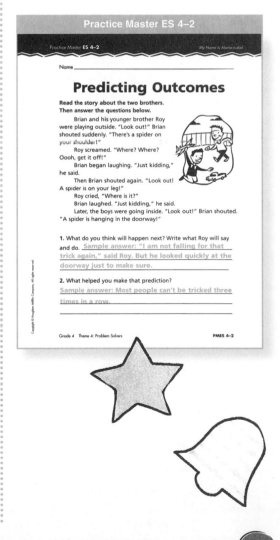

LITERATURE FOCUS: 10–15 MINUTES

Preview *My Name Is María Isabel* Segment 2

Refer to the bottom of page 402 in the Teacher's Edition and preview with students Segment 2 of *My Name Is María Isabel* (pages 402–407).

Note the suggestions in the Extra Support boxes on Teacher's Edition pages 405 and 406.

Day 3

SKILL FOCUS: STRUCTURAL ANALYSIS   25–30 MINUTES

Suffix -*ible*

Teach

Objectives
- decode words with the suffix -*ible*
- identify the meaning of words with the suffix -*ible*

Materials
- Anthology: *My Name Is María Isabel*

Write the following words on the board: *reversible, sensible.* Ask students if they can see anything alike in the two words. Underline the suffix -*ible* in each word.

Tell students that these letters form the suffix -*ible*, a word part added to the end of a base word that changes the base word's meaning. Point out that the suffix -*ible* usually means "able to."

Clarify that when the suffix -*ible* is added to a base word ending in *e*, the *e* is dropped before the suffix is added.

Explain that recognizing this suffix can help students decode new words as well as understand their meaning.

Use a Think Aloud to model the process for decoding the underlined word and understanding its meaning. Display the following sentence and ask students to read it.

At first María Isabel isn't allowed to be part of the Winter Pageant, but this situation is <u>reversible</u>.

Think Aloud

I can separate the suffix -ible from the base word so that I can pronounce each part. When I add back the e that has been dropped from the base word, I see that the base word is reverse. *I know what* reverse *means— "a change to the opposite, go back to." So I can figure out that* reversible *means "able to be changed to the opposite." Oh, so María Isabel's situation could be changed so that she would be in the pageant.*

Display the following sentence and help students use the strategy to decode the word *sensible*.

María Isabel's wish to be called María Isabel Salazar López is <u>sensible</u> *because that is her real name.*

Practice

Display the sentences below. Have students copy the underlined words and circle the suffix in each word. Have students work in pairs to decode the words and give the meanings. Ask students to read the whole sentence aloud.

1. The stage sets are <u>collapsible</u> and can be stored in a closet.

2. Family objects are <u>collectible</u> items.

3. María Isabel is wearing a <u>convertible</u> jacket.

Apply

Have students look up the underlined words in a dictionary to check their meanings. Then ask students to write a sentence using each word. Have them exchange their papers with a partner and take turns reading these original sentences.

LITERATURE FOCUS: 10–15 MINUTES

Review *My Name Is María Isabel*

Guide students through the Comprehension Skill Lesson **Predicting Outcomes** on page 405 in the Teacher's Edition.

Day 4

Objectives

- identify forms of the irregular verb *be*
- use correct forms of the irregular verb *be* with singular and plural nouns and pronouns

Materials

- Reader's Library: *The Best Fish Ever*

The Irregular Verb *Be*

Teach

Write the following sentences on the board. Invite volunteers to read the sentences aloud and fill in the blanks.

> I <u>am</u> a _____ person.
>
> You <u>are</u> a _____ person.
>
> Today the weather <u>is</u> _____ .
>
> Yesterday the weather <u>was</u> _____ .
>
> This year my wishes <u>are</u> for _____ .
>
> Last year my wishes <u>were</u> for _____ .

Point out that the underlined words are all forms of the verb *be*. Help students use sentence context to understand that *am, is*, and *are* are present-tense forms and *was* and *were* are past-tense forms.

Help students identify which forms are used with singular nouns and pronouns and which forms are used with plural nouns and pronouns. Display and review the following chart.

Form	Tense	Use With
am	present	Pronoun *I*
is	present	singular nouns, pronouns *he, she, it*
are	present	plural nouns, pronouns *we, they, you*
was	past	singular nouns, pronouns *I, he, she, it*
were	past	plural nouns, pronouns *we, they, you*

Practice

Write these sentences on the board:

> 1. María Isabel (was, were) too shy to say anything.
> 2. She wrote, "My name (is, are) María Isabel."
> 3. Two days (was, were) left until the pageant.
> 4. The barrettes (is, are) shiny.

Have partners take turns choosing the correct form of the verb *be* and explaining how they knew which form was correct.

Apply

Direct students to look for forms of the verb *be* on page 398 and to copy the sentences containing these forms. Next to each sentence, have students identify the verb form and its use by writing *present* or *past* and *singular* or *plural*.

Preview *The Best Fish Ever*

Walk students through *The Best Fish Ever.* Discuss the illustrations using words such as *tryouts, grants, performance,* and *success.*

Ask students to predict the outcome of the story by scanning through the illustrations.

Day 5

Objectives

- use story details combined with personal knowledge and thinking to make predictions
- confirm or revise predictions

Materials

- Anthology: *My Name Is María Isabel*
- Reader's Library: *The Best Fish Ever*

RETEACH

SKILL FOCUS: COMPREHENSION   25–30 MINUTES

Predicting Outcomes

Teach

Walk over to your classroom door. If it is open, put your hand on it. If it is closed, take hold of the doorknob.

Ask students to predict, or make a guess about, what they think you will do next. Perform the motion.

Point out to students that they used the details they saw and their own personal experience and knowledge to predict what you would do.

Tell students that making predictions about characters in stories is done in the same way as in real life. Explain the process:

- Look at the details the author gives.

- Think about your own knowledge and life experiences.

- Put details and experience together to predict an outcome.

Direct students' attention to the first paragraph on page 398 and have them read it. Use a Think Aloud to model the process of predicting an outcome.

Think Aloud

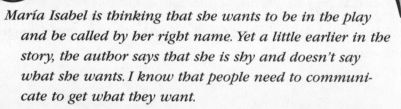

María Isabel is thinking that she wants to be in the play and be called by her right name. Yet a little earlier in the story, the author says that she is shy and doesn't say what she wants. I know that people need to communicate to get what they want.

Putting together the author's details and my own knowledge at this point in the story, I predict that María Isabel is not going to get to be in the play or get her teacher to call her by her right name. When I read on, I will be able to confirm my prediction—see if I am correct—or see what else happens and then revise—change—my prediction when I get more information.

Ask students if your prediction makes sense.

Practice

Display this chart for students to copy and fill out:

Story Details	My Knowledge and Experience	Prediction

Have partners first read María Isabel's essay on page 403 and predict an outcome about María Isabel based on this new information. Then have partners make a prediction about how María Isabel will act the next time something new happens in her classroom. For this last prediction, tell students to think about how María Isabel changed in the story and what she accomplished. Encourage students to share and compare their charts.

Apply

Have students keep track of predicting outcomes, with an eye to using details and their own personal experience, in the Reader's Library selection *The Best Fish Ever* by Julio Varela. Then have them complete the questions and activity on the Responding page.

LITERATURE FOCUS: 10–15 MINUTES

Revisit *My Name Is María Isabel* and *The Best Fish Ever*

Guide students to predict the outcomes for *My Name is María Isabel* and *The Best Fish Ever*. Also, help them to look for words with the suffix *-ible*, such as *impossible* (*My Name is María Isabel*, page 402).

Day 1

Objective

- read words with the prefixes *re-*, *mis-*, and *ex-*

Materials

- Teaching Master ES4-3
- Practice Masters ES4-3
- Anthology: *Marven of the Great North Woods*

Technology

Get Set for Reading
CD-ROM
Marven of the Great North Woods

Education Place
www.eduplace.com
Marven of the Great North Woods

Audiotape
Marven of the Great North Woods
Audiotape for **Problem Solvers**

Lexia Phonics
CD-ROM
Intermediate Intervention

PRETEACH

SKILL FOCUS: STRUCTURAL ANALYSIS   25–30 MINUTES

Prefixes *re-*, *mis-*, and *ex-*

Warm-Up/Academic Language

Remind students that a **prefix** is a **word part** that comes **at the beginning of a base word or word root.** Explain that knowing a prefix can help **with reading longer words.** Tell students that they will be learning about three different prefixes: *re-*, *mis-*, and *ex-*.

Teach

Write *re-*, *mis-*, and *ex-* on the board and identify them as common prefixes. Ask students to listen for words that contain one of the prefixes as you read the following sentences. After each sentence, ask a volunteer to identify the word with a prefix and then write it on the board.

> 1. I don't want to <u>mislead</u> you.
> 2. The piñata will <u>explode</u> with candy.
> 3. Many people <u>mispronounce</u> Sean's name.
> 4. Please <u>refill</u> my glass.
> 5. Let's <u>explore</u> this cave.
> 6. <u>Remind</u> me to feed the cat.

Explain that when a prefix is added to a base word or root, it changes its meaning. Write the following on the board: re- = *again*; mis- = *badly* or *wrongly*; ex- = *out* or *out of.*

Guide students to define the words on the board. Help them to see that *refill* means to "fill again," *mislead* means to "lead wrongly," and that *explode* means to "blow out."

Guided Practice

Display or **distribute** Teaching Master ES4-3 and read it with students.

Ask them to listen as you read the dialogue, raising their hands if they hear a word beginning with *re-*, *mis-*, or *ex-*.

Help students to underline, read, and define the words with suffixes *re-*, *mis-*, and *ex-*.

Practice/Apply

Distribute Practice Master ES4-3 and discuss the illustration and speech balloon with students.

Go over the directions with them.

Have students independently complete the Practice Master.

Check students' responses to be sure that they can read words with *re-*, *mis-*, and *ex-*.

Prefixes *re-*, *mis-*, *ex-*

Bess: Your story was <u>exciting</u>! I liked the part where the robot made the ship <u>explode</u>. I didn't <u>expect</u> that to happen.
Phil: Are there any parts I should <u>rewrite</u>?
Bess: You <u>repeated</u> the word *very* in these sentences. Maybe you should <u>replace</u> one or two.
Phil: OK. I'll <u>revise</u> this part. Did you <u>misunderstand</u> any parts? Are there any <u>misspelled</u> words?
Bess: I didn't see any other <u>mistakes</u>. It's a great story. I'd like to <u>reread</u> it.

LITERATURE FOCUS:	10–15 MINUTES

Preview *Marven of the Great North Woods* Segment 1

Refer to the bottom of page 417 in the Teacher's Edition and preview with students Segment 1 of *Marven of the Great North Woods* (pages 416–427).

Note the suggestion in the Extra Support boxes on Teacher's Edition pages 423 and 426.

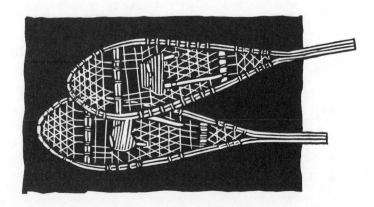

Name _____

Prefixes *re-*, *mis-*, *ex-*

Read each sentence. Find the word in the box that has the same meaning as the **bolded** word or words. Write the word on the line.

review	misprint	extreme
retold	except	misbehave

Let me **explain** my **mistake**, and **redo** the job.

1. The book has a **printing mistake** on page 2. <u>misprint</u>
2. Everyone is here **but** Kerry. <u>except</u>
3. Please **look again** at your notes. <u>review</u>
4. Even a trained dog may **behave badly**. <u>misbehave</u>
5. The tale was **told again** by a new storyteller. <u>retold</u>
6. Polar bears stay warm in the **very great** cold. <u>extreme</u>

Underline the word that fits in the sentence. Write it on the line.

1. What is the <u>exact</u> amount? (<u>exact</u>, react)
2. Mom <u>misplaced</u> her glasses and can't find them. (<u>misplaced</u>, replaced)
3. Think back to <u>recall</u> the events. (miscall, <u>recall</u>)
4. Try not to <u>misuse</u> the radio. (excuse, <u>misuse</u>)

Day 2

Objectives
- identify multiple solutions to one problem
- decide which solution is best
- see how different characters solve the same problem

Materials
- Teaching Master ES4-4
- Practice Masters ES4-4
- Anthology: *Marven of the Great North Woods*

Problem Solving

Warm-Up/Academic Language

Explain that **story characters**, like people in real life, **face problems that they try to solve.** Point out that characters often **consider many solutions** before **deciding on one.** Tell students that sometimes they decide on a good solution and sometimes they don't — just like people in real life.

Teach

Remind students of a familiar fairy tale, *The Three Little Pigs.* Invite students to retell the story. Be sure that students explain that

- three pigs were afraid that a wolf would eat them if they didn't protect themselves.

- each one built a house.

- the first house was made of straw, the second of sticks, and the third of bricks.

- each pig hoped the wolf would not be able to blow down his house.

Model how to identify a problem and a solution.

Think Aloud

The problem the pigs face is that the wolf wants to eat them. Their solution is to build a house that will be strong enough to keep them safe. The first pig's solution is to build a house of straw. That's not a very good solution. Straw is too weak to keep the wolf out.

Lead students to evaluate the other solutions, settling on the third pig's solution as the best of the three. Ask students to suggest other building materials strong enough to keep out a wolf. (possible responses: stone, adobe, strong wood, steel)

Guided Practice

Display or **distribute** Teaching Master ES4-4 and read the story with students.

Ask students to identify the problem that Lee faced.

Help students identify Lee's solution and break it down into steps by filling out the chart.

Practice/Apply

Distribute Practice Master ES4-4 to students and go over the directions with them.

Have students read the story and complete the Practice Master independently.

Check students' responses to be sure that they understand the skill.

LITERATURE FOCUS: 10–15 MINUTES

Preview *Marven of the Great North Woods* Segment 2

Refer to the bottom of page 428 in the Teacher's Edition, and preview with students Segment 2 of *Marven of the Great North Woods* (pages 428–443).

Note the suggestions in the Extra Support boxes on Teacher's Edition pages 429, 430, and 442.

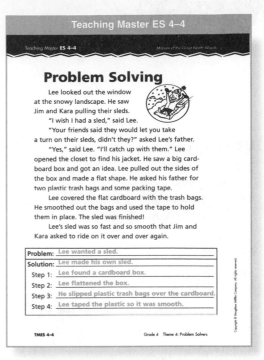

Teaching Master ES 4–4

Teaching Master **ES 4–4**   *Marven of the Great North Woods*

Problem Solving

Lee looked out the window at the snowy landscape. He saw Jim and Kara pulling their sleds.

"I wish I had a sled," said Lee.

"Your friends said they would let you take a turn on their sleds, didn't they?" asked Lee's father.

"Yes," said Lee. "I'll catch up with them." Lee opened the closet to find his jacket. He saw a big cardboard box and got an idea. Lee pulled out the sides of the box and made a flat shape. He asked his father for two plastic trash bags and some packing tape.

Lee covered the flat cardboard with the trash bags. He smoothed out the bags and used the tape to hold them in place. The sled was finished!

Lee's sled was so fast and so smooth that Jim and Kara asked to ride on it over and over again.

Problem:	Lee wanted a sled.
Solution:	Lee made his own sled.
Step 1:	Lee found a cardboard box.
Step 2:	Lee flattened the box.
Step 3:	He slipped plastic trash bags over the cardboard.
Step 4:	Lee taped the plastic so it was smooth.

TMES 4–4   Grade 4   Theme 4: Problem Solvers

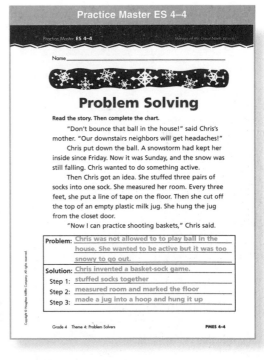

Practice Master ES 4–4

Practice Master **ES 4–4**   *Marven of the Great North Woods*

Name _____

Problem Solving

Read the story. Then complete the chart.

"Don't bounce that ball in the house!" said Chris's mother. "Our downstairs neighbors will get headaches!"

Chris put down the ball. A snowstorm had kept her inside since Friday. Now it was Sunday, and the snow was still falling. Chris wanted to do something active.

Then Chris got an idea. She stuffed three pairs of socks into one sock. She measured her room. Every three feet, she put a line of tape on the floor. Then she cut off the top of an empty plastic milk jug. She hung the jug from the closet door.

"Now I can practice shooting baskets," Chris said.

Problem:	Chris was not allowed to to play ball in the house. She wanted to be active but it was too snowy to go out.
Solution:	Chris invented a basket-sock game.
Step 1:	stuffed socks together
Step 2:	measured room and marked the floor
Step 3:	made a jug into a hoop and hung it up

Grade 4   Theme 4: Problem Solvers   **PMES 4–4**

Day 3

Objectives
- decode words with the prefix *re-*, *mis-*, or *ex-*
- identify the meaning of words with the prefixes *re-*, *mis-*, and *ex-*

Materials
- Anthology: *Marven of the Great North Woods*

RETEACH

SKILL FOCUS: STRUCTURAL ANALYSIS   25–30 MINUTES

Prefixes *re-*, *mis-*, and *ex-*

Teach

Write the following on the board:

> Marven needed to <u>restore</u> order to Mr. Murray's books.
>
> Marven was not the kind of boy to <u>misbehave</u> while he was working.
>
> After taking a deep breath, Marven <u>exhaled</u> the cold winter air.

Ask students to read the sentences. Point out that each underlined word has a prefix. Review that a prefix is a word part added to the beginning of a base word or another word part called a root. A prefix is usually a syllable.

Circle the prefix in each word. Remind students that knowing when words have prefixes can help them decode words more quickly.

Use the following sentence to model decoding words with prefixes: *If Marven wasn't careful, he might miscount the amounts he listed in the book.*

Think Aloud

I read, If Marven wasn't careful, he might _____ *... If I didn't recognize the next word, I would look carefully for a part I know, like a base word, and cover the rest of the word. I know* count. *Now I'm going to look at the other part of this word. I know the prefix* mis-; *it means "bad or wrong." So I can read* mis- *and* count. *When I read the parts together, I get the word* miscount, *meaning "count wrongly." I check and it makes sense in the sentence.*

Repeat the process using the first three sentences you have written on the board. Make sure that students understand that *re-* means "again" and *ex-* can mean "out of or from."

Practice

Help students practice identifying words with prefixes. Display the following:

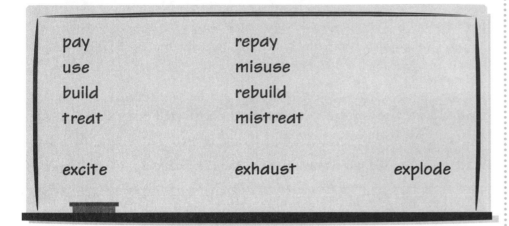

pay	repay
use	misuse
build	rebuild
treat	mistreat
excite	exhaust explode

Discuss each word pair using *re-* and *mis-*. Then discuss the words using the prefix *ex-*.

Apply

Have students write a sentence using each prefixed word in the Practice section. Allow time for students to share sentences and identify the prefixed words.

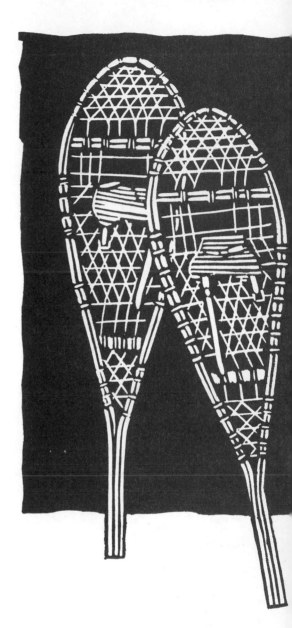

LITERATURE FOCUS: 10–15 MINUTES

Review *Marven of the Great North Woods*

Guide students through the Comprehension Skill Lesson **Problem Solving** on page 419 in the Teacher's Edition.

Other Irregular Verbs

Teach

Write this sentence on the board: *Marven ate his first latke when the train stopped in Floodwood.*

Have volunteers underline each past-tense verb (*ate, stopped*). Then discuss how *stopped* was formed, helping students recall that most verbs form the past tense by adding *-ed* at the end.

Ask students if *-ed* was added to *eat* to form the past tense. Point out that *eated* is not the correct form. Remind students that other verbs, called irregular verbs, have special past-tense forms.

Read aloud the second paragraph on page 421 and identify the irregular verbs *stood, ran, met, felt, went, thought*. Ask students to tell the present-tense form of these verbs. If necessary, identify them: *stand, run, meet, feel, go, think*.

Create a chart on the board to record the present- and past-tense verb forms of all the verbs discussed above.

Present Tense	Past Tense
eat	ate
stand	stood
run	ran
meet	met
feel	felt
go	went
think	thought

Practice

Write the following present-tense verbs on the board: *begin, keep, say, make, hold, come, grow*. Have partners list the words and then write the past-tense form of each one. Students can make their own charts to list the verbs. Then ask students to choose three past-tense verbs and to write sentences using them.

Objectives

- identify forms of irregular verbs
- use forms of irregular verbs in sentences

Materials

- Reader's Library: *Cora at Camp Blue Waters*

Apply

Direct students to find three irregular past-tense verbs in the first paragraph on page 434. Have them write each verb and its present-tense form. (heard, hear; fell, fall; came, come)

LITERATURE FOCUS: — 10–15 MINUTES

Preview *Cora at Camp Blue Waters*

Walk students through *Cora at Camp Blue Waters*. Discuss illustrations using words such as *homebody, encouraged, especially,* and *patterns*.

Ask students to preview possible problems (pages 25, 28–29, 31) and possible solutions (pages 34–35, 36–37) by scanning through the illustrations.

Day 5

Objectives
- identify a character's problem(s)
- analyze possible solutions to the problem(s)
- analyze a character's problem-solving abilities

Materials
- Anthology: *Marven of the Great North Woods*
- Reader's Library: *Cora at Camp Blue Waters*

SKILL FOCUS: COMPREHENSION   25–30 MINUTES

Problem Solving

Teach

Have students meet in small groups, and give each group the following problem to solve: *You have never been away from home for a long time. Now you are at summer camp for the very first time. It is too far away to go home each night. You miss your family and your friends. You feel terribly homesick. What should you do?*

Give students five minutes to come up with a solution. Then bring the groups together to share their problem-solving process and their final solution.

Use the discussion to help students identify the five steps of the problem-solving process:

1. Define the problem.

2. Consider possible solutions.

3. Evaluate possible solutions.

4. Decide on a solution.

5. Carry out the solution.

Remind students that characters in stories often have to solve problems just as people do in real life. The time and place in which characters live often creates problems for them, as when Marven is sent to the logging camp.

Review with students the first problems Marven faced: He was alone and actually had to ski to get to the camp; he didn't know anyone there; he didn't speak French except for a few words.

Record the details on a chart such as the following:

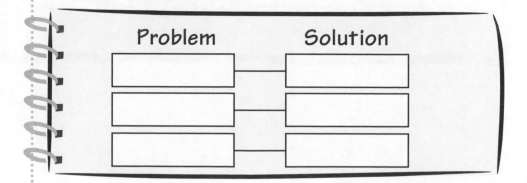

Use the Think Aloud to help students identify Marven's problems and his solutions.

Think Aloud

On page 429, Marven has to wake up the big loggers. He uses the few French words he knows and doesn't give up even when he has trouble waking Jean Louis. I think this shows that Marven is determined and brave.

Practice

Have small groups read page 433, identifying Marven's problem and his solution. Students can copy the Problem/Solution chart and add their information. Have groups share their thoughts.

Apply

Have students keep track of problems and solutions, with an eye to identifying characters' problem-solving processes, in the Reader's Library selection *Cora at Camp Blue Waters* by Philemon Sturges. Then have them complete the questions and activity on the Responding page.

LITERATURE FOCUS: **10–15 MINUTES**

Revisit *Marven of the Great North Woods* and *Cora at Camp Blue Waters*

Review with students the problems and solutions presented in *Marven of the Great North Woods* and *Cora at Camp Blue Waters*. Also, help them to look for words with the prefixes *re-*, *mis-*, and *ex-*, such as *repeated, explore, (Marven of the Great North Woods*, pages 419 and 433) *except,* and *excited (Cora at Camp Blue Waters*, pages 24 and 26).

Day 1

Objectives

- read words that have prefixes *pre-*, *con-*, and *com-*
- use the Phonics/Decoding strategy to decode longer words

Materials

- Teaching Master ES4-5
- Practice Masters ES4-5
- Anthology: *The Last Dragon*

Get Set for Reading
CD-ROM

The Last Dragon

Education Place

www.eduplace.com
The Last Dragon

Audiotape

The Last Dragon
Audiotape for **Problem Solvers**

Lexia Phonics
CD-ROM

Intermediate Intervention

PRETEACH

SKILL FOCUS: STRUCTURAL ANALYSIS   25–30 MINUTES

Prefixes *pre-*, *con-*, and *com-*

Warm-Up/Academic Language

Remind students that a **prefix** is a **word part** that is **added before a base word or word root** to **form a new word**. Explain that knowing common prefixes and their meanings can **help students read new words** and give them **clues about their meaning**. Tell students that they will learn about the following three prefixes: *pre-*, *con-*, and *com-*.

Teach

Write the prefixes *pre-*, *con-*, and *com-* on the board. Then write the following sentences. Ask students to come to the board and underline each prefix within the sentences.

- We are ready to *preview* the story.

- Sheila's dog Ernie makes a fine *companion*.

- We all met to *confer* about the project.

Explain that a prefix is a word part that is placed before a base or root word to create a new word. Point out that the word *preview* was made by placing the prefix *pre-* before the base word *view*. Ask students what the prefix *pre-* might mean. (before) Beside *pre-*, write = *before*.

Model how to use the meaning of *pre-* to define *preview*.

> **Think Aloud**
>
> *When I look at the word* preview, *I see the prefix* pre- *and the word* view. *I know that* view *means to look at something. The prefix* pre- *usually means* before. *So when I preview a chapter, I'm looking over the content of the chapter before I actually begin to read and study it.*

Follow a similar procedure with *com-* and *con-*, related prefixes that both usually mean "with" or "together." List the meaning *with* or *together* beside the prefixes *com-* and *con-*.

Write *companion* and *confer* on the board. Then read the word *companion* for students, defining it as "a person who spends time with another person in a friendly way." Then read *confer*, defining it as "to discuss something together."

Guided Practice

Display or **distribute** Teaching Master ES4–5 and discuss the illustrations with students.

Help them to see that the products are pictured with labels that tell about them.

Read labels with students, and have them underline words with the prefix *pre-, com-,* or *con-*.

Help students to break each word into syllables, pronouncing each one separately and then combining them to decode the word.

Discuss with students whether the meanings of the prefixes help them with the meanings of the words.

Practice/Apply

Distribute Practice Master ES4-5 to students and discuss how the art shows what a prefix is.

Read the directions to make sure students understand what to do. Then have them complete the Practice Master independently.

Check students' understanding of *pre-, con-,* and *com-* by having them share their answers.

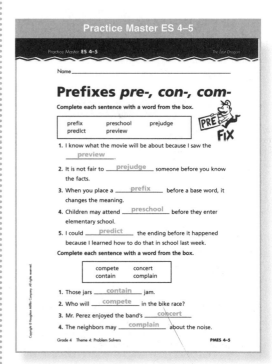

LITERATURE FOCUS: 10–15 MINUTES

Preview *The Last Dragon* Segment 1

Refer to the bottom of page 453 in the Teacher's Edition and preview with students Segment 1 of *The Last Dragon* (pages 453–465).

Note the suggestion in the Extra Support boxes on Teacher's Edition pages 454 and 464.

Day 2

PRETEACH

SKILL FOCUS: COMPREHENSION   25–30 MINUTES

Drawing Conclusions

Warm-Up/Academic Language

Explain that **good readers are like "story detectives."** They pay attention to **clues** in the story to help them **figure out** information about **a story character or event.** Tell students that this is called **drawing conclusions.**

Teach

Explain that drawing conclusions can be like answering a riddle. Read the riddle shown below to students. Have them raise their hands when they think they know the answer, and have them write their answers.

Read Aloud

> I'm all around you, but you can't see or touch me.
>
> You need me to live, and I am everyplace where people can be.
>
> Without me, birds would have no place to fly.
>
> You use me all day long and never have to buy.
>
> What am I?

Write the following details from the riddle on the board and discuss each one:

- Detail 1:   *invisible*
- Detail 2:   *need it to live*
- Detail 3:   *everywhere people are*
- Detail 4:   *used all the time, free*

Point out that each additional detail/clue in the riddle gave new information and that putting all the clues together helped to answer the riddle. (air)

Objectives

- use story details to draw conclusions
- see how different conclusions can be drawn from the same details

Materials

- Teaching Master ES4-6
- Practice Masters ES4-6
- Anthology: *The Last Dragon*

Guided Practice

Display or **distribute** Teaching Master ES4-6 and read the story with students.

Ask students to think about who or what Oro is as you reread the passage, sentence by sentence.

Tell students to raise their hands whenever you come to a detail that they think is a clue to Oro's identity.

Help students to add each detail to the graphic organizer and have students help you identify Oro.

Practice/Apply

Distribute Practice Master ES4-6 to students and go over the directions with them.

Direct students to read the story independently and complete the Practice Master.

Check students' responses by having them share their details and conclusions.

LITERATURE FOCUS: 10–15 MINUTES

Preview *The Last Dragon*

Segment 2

Refer to the bottom of page 466 in the Teacher's Edition and preview with students Segment 2 of *The Last Dragon* (pages 466–479).

Note the suggestions in the Extra Support boxes on Teacher's Edition pages 468 and 478.

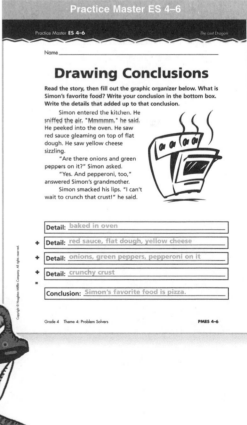

Teaching Master ES 4–6

Teaching Master **ES 4-6**   *The Last Dragon*

Drawing Conclusions

Who is Oro?

Something awakened Manny. He sat up in bed suddenly, and his eyes flew open. Then he heard the gentle groan of floorboards—*creak, creak, creak.* Manny opened his eyes wider. The room was completely dark. For just a moment, Manny saw two yellow circles glowing near the floor. Then he saw a leaping shadow. He felt something flop at the foot of the bed. Soon he heard a soft, purring sound. He sighed, "Oh, it's just Oro." Manny went back to sleep.

Detail: two yellow, glowing circles
+ **Detail:** leaping shadow
+ **Detail:** Oro flops at foot of bed and purrs
+ **Detail:** Manny is not scared when he recognizes Oro.
= **Conclusion:** Oro is Manny's cat.

TMES 4–6   Grade 4   Theme 4: Problem Solvers

Practice Master ES 4–6

Practice Master **ES 4-6**   *The Last Dragon*

Name _____

Drawing Conclusions

Read the story, then fill out the graphic organizer below. What is Simon's favorite food? Write your conclusion in the bottom box. Write the details that added up to that conclusion.

Simon entered the kitchen. He sniffed the air. "Mmmmm," he said. He peeked into the oven. He saw red sauce gleaming on top of flat dough. He saw yellow cheese sizzling.

"Are there onions and green peppers on it?" Simon asked.

"Yes. And pepperoni, too," answered Simon's grandmother.

Simon smacked his lips. "I can't wait to crunch that crust!" he said.

Detail: baked in oven
+ **Detail:** red sauce, flat dough, yellow cheese
+ **Detail:** onions, green peppers, pepperoni on it
+ **Detail:** crunchy crust
= **Conclusion:** Simon's favorite food is pizza.

Grade 4   Theme 4: Problem Solvers   PMES 4–6

Day 3

RETEACH

SKILL FOCUS: STRUCTURAL ANALYSIS   25–30 MINUTES

Prefixes *pre-*, *com-*, and *con-*

Objectives
- decode words with the prefixes *pre-*, *com-*, or *con-*
- identify the meaning of words with the prefixes *pre-*, *com-*, or *con-*

Materials
- Anthology: *The Last Dragon*

Teach

Write the following lists on the board.

Pre-	Com-	Con-
preview	company	construction
prepaid	community	concentrate
predict	commotion	conclusion

Have students read the first column of words. Circle the letters *pre-* and explain that *pre-* is a prefix, a word part that is added to the beginning of a word and changes its meaning. The prefix *pre-* means "before;" so, for example, the word *preview* means "see something before or ahead of seeing the whole thing."

Encourage students to use the meaning of *pre-* to tell the meanings of the next two words in the first column. If necessary, tell students that *prepaid* means "paid beforehand, or in advance."

Help students read the words in the second list. Follow the same procedure as above and explain that the prefix *com-* means "join or bring together." Explain that knowing this prefix can help them decode new words and get a clue to their meaning. Help students realize that all three words have to do with a getting together, or gathering, of people.

Help students read the words in the third list. Repeat the procedure used above and explain that the prefix *con-* is very similar in meaning to *com-*. Help students realize that *construct* means "bringing together of parts to build something;" *concentrate* has to do with gathering one's thoughts and attention on something; and *conclusion* has to do with the bringing together of ideas to decide something.

Practice

List the following words: *predate, prearrange, combine, committee, conference, connection.* Have partners copy the words, circle the prefix in each one, and use the meaning of the prefix to help them understand each word's meaning. Ask students to check meanings in the dictionary.

Apply

Have students locate the following words in the story and use the prefixes and sentence context to help them write the meaning of each word.

companions (p. 455)

complained (p. 460)

concluded (p. 467)

LITERATURE FOCUS: 10–15 MINUTES

Review *The Last Dragon*

Guide students through the Comprehension Skill Lesson **Drawing Conclusions** on page 461 in the Teacher's Edition.

Day 4

Objectives
- identify adjectives that tell what kind, how many
- identify articles
- use adjectives in sentences

Materials
- Reader's Library: *Murals for Joy*

SKILL FOCUS: GRAMMAR 25–30 MINUTES

Adjectives

Teach

Write this sentence on the board:

The dragon now had bold eyebrows, red cheeks, and lots of sharp teeth.

Ask students to tell you what kind of eyebrows the dragon had. As they respond, underline *bold*. Repeat the procedure for the adjectives describing *cheeks* and *teeth*. (red, sharp)

Point out that *bold, red,* and *sharp* are adjectives. Remind students that an adjective describes a noun and can tell *what kind* or *how many*.

Explain that the words *a, an,* and *the* are special adjectives called articles.

Write these sentences on the board and have students underline the articles.

> A man stood on the sidewalk and painted
> a new sign on a restaurant window.
> "I need an artist," thought Peter.

Remind students that articles are used before nouns. Review the rules for using each article. Discuss the rules as they apply to the sample sentences.

1. Use *a* before a noun that begins with a consonant. Use *a* before a noun to mean "any" or "one."
2. Use *an* before a noun that begins with a vowel. Use *an* before a noun to mean "any" or "one."
3. Use *the* before a noun that begins with either a consonant or a vowel. Use *the* before a particular person, thing, or group.

Practice

Have partners read the first paragraph of the story on page 455. Ask them to list the adjectives they find, including the articles. Ask them to label each adjective appropriately as *what kind* or *how many*.

Tell students to skim page 459. Ask the following question: *What was the dragon like?* Ask pairs of students to fill in the blanks in the following sentence with two adjectives that describe the dragon:

The dragon was _____ and _____ .

Have students share their sentences. Write some of their sentences on the board, underlining the adjectives.

Apply

Direct partners to see how many adjectives, including articles, they can find on pages 459 and 460. Ask partners to list the words next to the appropriate adjectives, and to label them *what kind* or *how many*.

Have students look over a recent draft of their writing to see if there are places where they could add adjectives.

LITERATURE FOCUS: 10–15 MINUTES

Preview *Murals for Joy*

Walk students through *Murals for Joy*. Discuss illustrations using words such as *center, auditorium*, and *mural*.

Ask students to scan through the illustrations in order to draw conclusions about Joy's time in the city.

Day 5

Objectives

- use story clues to draw conclusions
- identify details in a story that can be used to draw conclusions

Materials

- Anthology: *The Last Dragon*
- Reader's Library: *Murals for Joy*

Drawing Conclusions

Teach

Ask students to think about a mystery they have read or seen on TV. Discuss what the detective(s) did to solve the case. (followed clues, put facts and evidence together to figure out "whodunnit")

Have students read aloud the last paragraph on page 459, continue on page 460, and stop after the paragraph in which Great Aunt says, *"Humph. Couldn't have his mouth hanging open like a fool."*

Point out that the author doesn't directly tell readers who combed the dragon's whiskers and polished the pearl. Instead, she gives details that readers use to *draw* their own *conclusions*.

Help students understand the process of drawing a conclusion by using a Think Aloud.

Think Aloud

I know that Great Aunt says the dragons of her childhood were royal in appearance and were respected. That's one fact the author gives. Great Aunt also complains that the dragon is in bad shape and is a very "sorry dragon." These are more facts. She also says, "Couldn't have his mouth hanging open like a fool." All these facts lead me to think that Great Aunt cares about the dragon and she is the one who combed the whiskers and polished the pearl. This is my conclusion.

Place the following graphic organizer on the board and fill in the details to give students a visual representation.

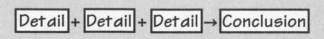

Detail + Detail + Detail → Conclusion

Ask students why they agree or disagree with your conclusion.

Help students put the strategy into their own words:

> 1. Notice story clues.
> 2. Think about what they mean.
> 3. Add the clues up to draw conclusions.

Practice

Have partners read paragraphs 7–10 on page 463 and use the details given to draw a conclusion about who made the dragon's new crest. Partners can fill in their own graphic organizer.

Apply

Have students keep track of drawing conclusions, with an eye to identifying story clues, in the Reader's Library selection *Murals for Joy* by Veronica Freeman Ellis. Have students complete the questions and activity on the Responding page.

LITERATURE FOCUS: 10–15 MINUTES

Revisit *The Last Dragon* and *Murals for Joy.*

Review with students the conclusions drawn about events and characters for *The Last Dragon* and *Murals for Joy*. Also, help them to look for words with the prefixes *pre-, con-* and *com-*, such as *companions, community, concluded, and concentrated* (*The Last Dragon*, pages 455, 465, 467, and 471).

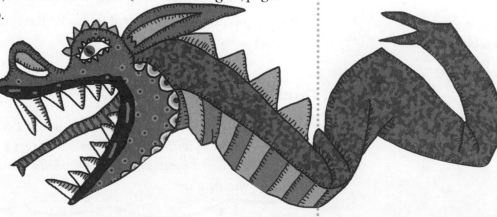

Day 1

Objectives
- read words that follow the VCCV pattern
- use the Phonics/Decoding strategy to decode longer words

Materials
- Teaching Master ES4-7
- Practice Masters ES4-7
- Anthology: *Sing to the Stars*

Get Set for Reading CD-ROM

Sing to the Stars

Education Place

www.eduplace.com
Sing to the Stars

Audiotape

Sing to the Stars
Audiotape for **Problem Solvers**

Lexia Phonics CD-ROM

Intermediate Intervention

PRETEACH

SKILL FOCUS: STRUCTURAL ANALYSIS — 25–30 MINUTES

VCCV Pattern

Warm-Up/Academic Language

Remind students that a good way to read a long, unfamiliar word is to **break it into syllables**. Review that a **syllable is a word part** with just **one vowel sound.** Tell students that they can use the **pattern of vowels and consonants** to help them figure out how to **divide a word into syllables**. Point out that words with the **vowel-consonant-consonant-vowel (VCCV) pattern,** can be **divided between the two consonants.**

Teach

Tell students that they will learn a way to divide two-syllable words that have the vowel-consonant-consonant-vowel pattern. Copy the following words on the board and underline the VCCV pattern in each of the words:

wi**ndo**w	e**ffo**rt
VCCV	VCCV
ca**rpe**t	fo**rge**t
VCCV	VCCV

Tell students that each of the words contains a vowel-consonant-consonant-vowel pattern. Write VCCV under the underlined letters in *window*.

Follow the same procedure with the remaining words.

Use the following Think Aloud to model the syllabication of VCCV pattern words.

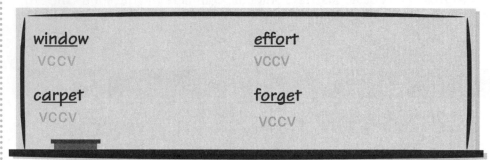

Think Aloud

> *When I look inside the word* window, *I see two consonants,* n *and* d, *with vowels on either side,* i *and* o. *So I'll break the word between the consonants. That leaves me with* win *and* dow.

Display the following words: *pencil, master, problem, costume,* and *party*. Guide students to identify the VCCV pattern in each word. Ask volunteers to insert a slash mark between the central consonants and label the VCCV pattern.

(pen/cil, mas/ter, prob/lem, cos/tume, par/ty).
VC CV   VC CV   VC CV   VC CV   VC CV

Guided Practice

Display or **distribute** Teaching Master ES4–7 to students.

Read the haiku with students.

Help them to underline the words with the VCCV pattern in each haiku.

Have them mark VCCV patterns and use slash marks to indicate syllables. Have students pronounce the VCCV pattern words and then reread each haiku.

Practice/Apply

Distribute Practice Master ES4-7 to students and discuss the illustration.

Go over the directions with students and have them complete the Practice Master independently.

Check student responses to be sure they can use the VCCV pattern to pronounce long, unfamiliar words.

LITERATURE FOCUS: 10–15 MINUTES

Preview *Sing to the Stars* Segment 1

Refer to the bottom of page 489 in the Teacher's Edition and preview with students Segment 1 of *Sing to the Stars* (pages 489–499).

Note the suggestion in the Extra Support boxes on Teacher's Edition pages 494, 497, and 498.

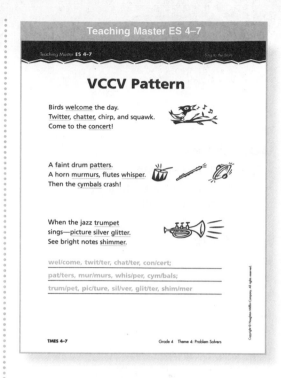

Teaching Master ES 4–7

VCCV Pattern

Birds welcome the day.
Twitter, chatter, chirp, and squawk.
Come to the concert!

A faint drum patters.
A horn murmurs, flutes whisper.
Then the cymbals crash!

When the jazz trumpet
sings—picture silver glitter.
See bright notes shimmer.

wel/come, twit/ter, chat/ter, con/cert;

pat/ters, mur/murs, whis/per, cym/bals;

trum/pet, pic/ture, sil/ver, glit/ter, shim/mer

Copyright © Houghton Mifflin Company. All rights reserved.

TMES 4–7   Grade 4 Theme 4: Problem Solvers

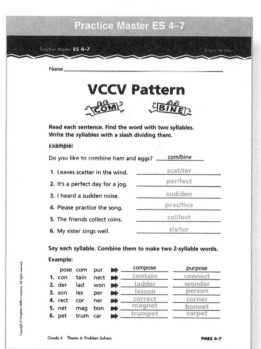

Practice Master ES 4–7

Name_____

VCCV Pattern

Read each sentence. Find the word with two syllables.
Write the syllables with a slash dividing them.
Example:
Do you like to combine ham and eggs? ____com/bine____

1. Leaves scatter in the wind.   scat/ter
2. It's a perfect day for a jog.   per/fect
3. I heard a sudden noise.   sud/den
4. Please practice the song.   prac/tice
5. The friends collect coins.   col/lect
6. My sister sings well.   sis/ter

Say each syllable. Combine them to make two 2-syllable words.
Example:

				compose	purpose
pose	com	pur	➡		
1. con	tain	nect	➡	contain	connect
2. der	lad	won	➡	ladder	wonder
3. son	les	per	➡	lesson	person
4. rect	cor	ner	➡	correct	corner
5. net	mag	bon	➡	magnet	bonnet
6. pet	trum	car	➡	trumpet	carpet

Grade 4 Theme 4: Problem Solvers   PMES 4–7

Story Structure

Warm-Up/Academic Language

Explain that all stories have a **story structure** and that most stories include **characters**, a **setting**, and a **plot**. Define **characters** as the **people or animals in a story**. Point out that **setting** is the **time and place** of the story. Explain that **plot** describes: 1. the **problem** the characters face; 2. the **events that happen** as they try to **solve the problem**; and 3. the ending that tells **how the problem is solved**.

Teach

Revisit with students a familiar story, such as *The Tortoise and the Hare.*

Use a story map like the one below to define the key elements of story structure.

<u>Characters</u>	<u>Setting</u>
<u>Who</u> is in the story? The Tortoise and the Hare	<u>When</u> did the story happen? not mentioned <u>Where</u> did the story happen? the forest

<u>Plot</u>

What <u>problem</u> do the characters face? Who will win the race?

What <u>events</u> happen as the characters try to solve the problem?

Hare stops to rest because he thinks he'll win and Tortoise passes him.

<u>How</u> is the problem solved? Tortoise wins the race.

Use this Think Aloud to model the story and its structure:

Objectives
- identify story elements
- differentiate between major and minor story elements

Materials
- Teaching Master ES4-8
- Practice Masters ES4-8
- Anthology: *Sing to the Stars*

Think Aloud

In The Tortoise and the Hare, *the characters are Tortoise and Hare. The story happens in the forest. That's the* setting. *Tortoise and Hare are in a race. The* problem *is that we don't know who will win. Hare is so sure that he will win that he stops to rest. Tortoise continues to move along slowly and steadily. These are some key* story events. *Finally, he surprises everyone by winning the race. That's the ending, or* solution.

Guide students as they help you to fill in the story map with details from *The Tortoise and the Hare.*

Guided Practice

Display or **distribute** Teaching Master ES4–7 to students.

Read the story with students.

Help students to fill out the story map.

Discuss completed story maps with students.

Practice/Apply

Distribute Practice Master ES4-8 to students and go over the directions with them.

Have students read the story and complete the Practice Master independently.

Check students' story maps during a group discussion about their answers.

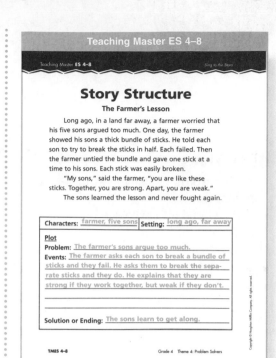

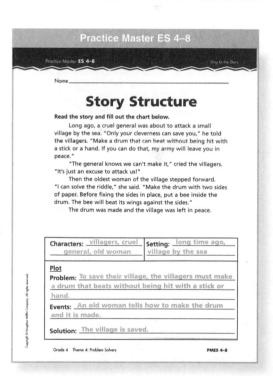

LITERATURE FOCUS: 10–15 MINUTES

Preview *Sing to the Stars*

Segment 2

Refer to the bottom of page 500 in the Teacher's Edition and preview with students Segment 2 of *Sing to the Stars* (pages 500–507).

Note the suggestions in the Extra Support boxes on Teacher's Edition pages 504 and 506.

Day 3

VCCV Pattern

Objectives

- decode words by using a syllable generalization
- divide words into syllables using VCCV pattern

Materials

- Anthology: *Sing to the Stars*

Teach

Remind students that a good way to decode a word they don't know is to break it into syllables. Review that a syllable is a word part with just one vowel sound.

Display the following sentence: *He was <u>supposed</u> to practice for an hour today.*

Have students read the sentence. Then write the following:

V C C V

s u p p o s e d

Point out that there are some patterns of vowels and consonants that help us to recognize how to divide a word into syllables. One pattern is called the VCCV pattern. It stands for vowel-consonant-consonant-vowel.

Help students to understand the VCCV pattern by using the Think Aloud.

> **Think Aloud**
>
> *I know that when two consonants fall between two vowels, the first vowel sound usually is short; and when the first vowel sound is short, the word usually is divided between the consonants. So I can divide the word on the board between the* p *and the* p. *Now I have two syllables: sup / posed. I know from the VCCV pattern the first vowel is short. I know the word* posed *is the second syllable. I read* supposed. *I check, and it makes sense.*

Practice

Have pairs of students copy the following:

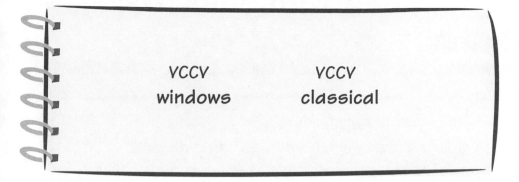

VCCV	VCCV
windows	classical

Tell students to use a slash to break the words into syllables. Ask students to explain how they knew how to pronounce the syllables.

Give additional practice with the following story-based words: *across, practice, hubbub, murmur, fingers, harness.*

Apply

Have the same pairs look through the selection. Ask them to jot down words that follow the VCCV pattern, break them into syllables, and use them in original sentences.

LITERATURE FOCUS: 10–15 MINUTES

Review *Sing to the Stars*

Guide students through the Comprehension Skill **Story Structure** on page 491 in the Teacher's Edition.

Day 4

Objectives

- identify comparative and superlative forms of adjectives
- use comparative and superlative forms of adjectives in sentences

Materials

- Reader's Library: *Ruthie's Perfect Poem*

Comparing with Adjectives

Teach

Write these sentences on the board and underline the words as shown:

> A violin makes <u>sweet</u> sounds.
>
> A violin makes <u>sweeter</u> sounds than a drum.
>
> Ephram's playing is the <u>sweetest</u> music at the concert.

Remind students that adjectives can be used to compare two or more things.

Have students read the sentences. Then ask them what they notice about the endings added to the underlined words in the second and third sentences. Explain that the ending *-er* is added to an adjective to compare two things; the ending *-est* is added to an adjective to compare more than two things.

Display a chart such as the one below and review each set of examples.

Adjective	Compare Two Things	Compare More Than Two Things
sweet	sweeter	sweetest
hot	hotter	hottest
important	more important	most important
good	better	best
bad	worse	worst

- For some adjectives, the consonant is doubled before the *-er* or *-est* is added.

- For adjectives of more than two syllables, the word *more* is used to compare two things and the word *most* is used to compare more than two things.

- For some adjectives such as *good* and *bad*, the adjective itself changes.

Practice

Write these sentences.

1. The rock group thinks the guitar is a <u>better</u> instrument than a violin.

2. Ephram feels practicing is <u>more important</u> than eating.

3. Music is one of the <u>most important</u> things in his life.

4. That night had the <u>worst</u> heat of the summer.

Have partners work together to determine whether the underlined adjective compares two things or more than two things.

Apply

Have students write three sentences using adjectives that compare two things and three sentences using adjectives that compare more than two things. They can use the adjectives on the chart or ones of their own choosing.

<table>
<tr><td>LITERATURE FOCUS:</td><td>10–15 MINUTES</td></tr>
</table>

Preview *Ruthie's Perfect Poem*

Walk students through *Ruthie's Perfect Poem*. Discuss illustrations using words such as *poem, nervous, assembly,* and *caravans*.

Ask students to scan through the illustrations in order to draw conclusions about how the characters may feel about their community.

Day 5

Objectives
- identify story structure: characters, setting, plot
- analyze how story elements affect a story

Materials
- Anthology: *Sing to the Stars*
- Reader's Library: *Ruthie's Perfect Poem*

Story Structure

Teach

Read the following story:

Long ago in Tune City, there once lived twins who loved music very much. Ahmed played the flute. Kira played the clarinet. The big concert was in one hour, and the twins were excited. They ran out of the house and hopped into the car.

Just as they arrived on the stage, Ahmed said to Kira, "May I have my flute now?"

"Flute?" said Kira. "I thought you had it."

"Oh, no," Ahmed groaned. "What will I do now?"

Ask students to identify the people in the story. (Ahmed and Kira)

Ask them to identify the time and place where the story occurs. (long ago, in "Tune City")

Ask them to tell you what has happened so far. (The twins are going to play in a concert and Ahmed doesn't have his flute.)

Point out that students have identified *characters*—the main people or animals in a story; *setting*—the time and place of a story; and *plot*, the main things that happen in a story, which usually includes a problem that has to be solved.

Explain that characters, setting, and plot together are called *story structure*.

Model how to identify story structure in *Sing to the Stars*. Use the graphic organizer to chart the details.

Think Aloud

After reading the first two pages of the story, I can tell it takes place now, in a city. The author (or narrator) describes Ephram walking down the street; Mr. Washington says that he can hear Ephram's shoes tap the cement and hear Ephram on the roof from his open apartment window. The illustrations also show modern clothing.

Write the title *Sing to the Stars* on the story map. Ask students to name the characters in the story and record them on the story map. (*Ephram, Mr. Washington, Grandma*)

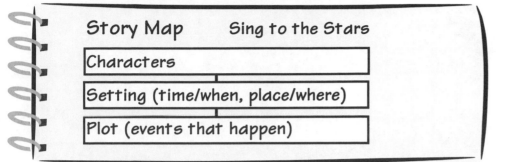

Story Map   Sing to the Stars

| Characters |
| Setting (time/when, place/where) |
| Plot (events that happen) |

Practice

Have students copy the story map. Guide students to list a few main events of the story, such as Ephram and Mr. Washington talk, Ephram discovers Mr. Washington played the piano, there is a power outage during the concert, Mr. Washington plays in the concert.

Apply

Have students keep track of story structure, with an eye to identifying characters, setting, and plot, in the Reader's Library selection *Ruthie's Perfect Poem* by Andrew Clements. Then have them complete the questions and activity on the Responding page.

LITERATURE FOCUS: 10–15 MINUTES

Revisit *Sing to the Stars* and *Ruthie's Perfect Poem*

Identify with students the various elements of story structure for *Sing to the Stars* and *Ruthie's Perfect Poem*. Also, help them to look for words with the VCCV pattern, such as *stammers, murmur*, (*Sing to the Stars*, pages 494 and 498) *bookcase*, and *wonderful* (*Ruthie's Perfect Poem*, pages 59 and 62).

Theme 5

Heroes

Selections

1 Happy Birthday, Dr. King!

2 Gloria Estefan

3 Lou Gehrig:
The Luckiest Man

Day 1

Objectives

- read words with prefixes and suffixes
- use the Phonics/Decoding strategy to decode longer words

Materials

- Teaching Master ES5-1
- Practice Master ES5-1
- Anthology: *Happy Birthday, Dr. King*

Technology

Get Set for Reading CD-ROM

Happy Birthday, Dr. King

Education Place

www.eduplace.com
Happy Birthday, Dr. King

Audiotape

Happy Birthday, Dr. King
Audiotape for **Heroes**

Lexia Phonics CD-ROM

Intermediate Intervention

PRETEACH

SKILL FOCUS: STRUCTURAL ANALYSIS 25–30 MINUTES

Prefixes and Suffixes

Warm-Up/Academic Language

Remind students that **prefixes** are word parts **added to the beginning of base words** or **word roots** and that **suffixes** are word parts that are **added to the end of them**. Point out that **adding a prefix or a suffix** can **change the meaning or part of speech**.

Teach

Write *review* on the board, and read it with students. Write this equation on the board: *re-* + *view* = *review*. Circle *view* and explain that it is a base word that means "to look at." Underline *re-* and tell students that it is a prefix that means "again." To *review* something means to "to look at it again." Point out that adding the prefix *re-* to the base word *view* adds the meaning "again."

Explain that adding a suffix, such as *-er*, also changes the meaning of a base word. Write this equation on the board: *view* + *-er* = *viewer*. Remind students that *-er* usually means "someone who." Elicit that *view* means "to look at" and *viewer* means "someone who looks at."

Demonstrate how the following prefixes and suffixes change the meaning of each base word shown on the chart. Have students help you to complete it.

Base Word	+ Suffix or Prefix	= New Word
penny: one cent	*-less*: without	penniless: without any money
govern: to rule	*-ment*: make a word a noun	government: a group of people who rule
trust: to depend on and believe in	*dis-*: not or opposite of	distrust: to doubt

Display the following sentence, and model how to decode *uncomplicated*: *Gavin rarely gets into a mess because his life is easy and <u>uncomplicated</u>.*

Think Aloud

I see the prefix un- *at the beginning of this word. I also see the* -ed *ending. I think that a final* e *was dropped before the ending was added. I cover the prefix and ending and add a final* e. *That leaves a familiar word:* complicate. *I know that* un *means "not," so that means* uncomplicated *is the opposite of* complicated. *That makes sense in the sentence. An easy life is an* uncomplicated, *or simple one.*

Guided Practice

Display or **distribute** Teaching Master ES5-1 and discuss the illustration.

Read the first dialogue with students and help them to underline the shared base word and the prefixes or suffixes.

Guide students to see that the meaning of the base word is changed by the addition of each prefix or suffix.

Repeat the procedure with the remaining dialogues.

Practice/Apply

Distribute Practice Master ES5-1 to students and review directions.

Ask students to complete the Practice Master independently.

Check students' responses to make sure they understand how prefixes and suffixes change word meaning.

LITERATURE FOCUS: 10–15 MINUTES

Preview *Happy Birthday, Dr. King!* Segment 1

Refer to the bottom of page 535 in the Teacher's Edition and preview with students Segment 1 of *Happy Birthday, Dr. King!* (pages 534–541).

Note the suggestions in the Extra Support boxes on Teacher's Edition pages 536, 539, and 540.

Day 2

Objectives

- identify causes and effects
- understand how one cause can lead to multiple effects
- learn which clue words can signal causes and effects

Materials

- Teaching Master ES5-2
- Practice Master ES5-2
- Anthology: *Happy Birthday, Dr. King!*

SKILL FOCUS: COMPREHENSION   25–30 MINUTES

Cause and Effect

Warm-Up/Academic Language

Explain that one thing can be the reason another thing happens. Tell students that this is called **cause and effect**. Point out that **effect** describes **what happened** and the **cause** explains **why it happened**. Point out that words such as *because, when, since, if, so*, and *as a result* **can signal cause and effect statements**.

Teach

Tell students that watching for signal words as they read can help them to identify cause-and-effect relationships. Write these clue words on the board, and read them with students: *because, when, since, if, so*, and *as a result*.

Write this sentence on the board, and point out the importance of the word *because*: *Jeremy missed school because he was sick.*

Read aloud the story below. Have students raise their hand when they hear a signal word.

Read Aloud

Mike searched all over because he had lost a library book. He looked under the bed so he could check in the pile that was always under there. He looked in his closet since it, too, was messy enough that the book could be buried in there. No library book appeared. Mike sadly counted the money he had saved because he knew he would have to pay for the lost book. He had just enough to replace it, but if he spent it all on the book, he wouldn't be able to buy the new game he had been saving for. He prepared to ride his bicycle to the library. He reached for his helmet. As a result, he noticed something strange on the shelf. "Yes!" said Mike, overjoyed since had found the missing book.

Display the following chart on the board. Guide students to help you complete the chart.

Cause	Effect
Mike had lost a library book.	He searched all over.
Mike needed to check the pile under his bed.	He looked under the bed.
Mike's closet was so messy that the book could be in it.	He looked in the closet.
Mike thought he'd have to pay for the book.	He counted the money.
Mike would have to pay for the book.	He wouldn't be able to afford the game he wanted.
Mike reaches for his bike helmet.	He noticed something strange on the shelf.
Mike found the missing book.	He was overjoyed.

Guided Practice

Display or **distribute** Teaching Master ES5-2, and discuss the illustration with students.

Read the selection with students and have them listen for signal words.

Help students to complete the cause-and-effect chart.

Practice/Apply

Distribute Practice Master ES5-2 to students and go over the directions.

Instruct students to complete the cause-and-effect chart independently.

Check to be sure all students understand the cause and effect skill by discussing the completed charts.

LITERATURE FOCUS: 10–15 MINUTES

Preview *Happy Birthday, Dr. King!* Segment 2

Refer to the bottom of page 542 in the Teacher's Edition and preview with students Segment 2 of *Happy Birthday, Dr. King!* (pages 542–549).

Note the suggestions in the Extra Support box on Teacher's Edition page 548.

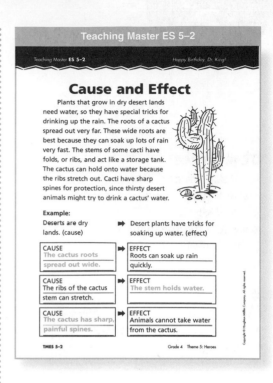

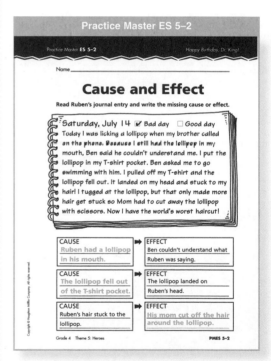

Day 3

SKILL FOCUS: STRUCTURAL ANALYSIS   25–30 MINUTES

Prefixes and Suffixes

Teach

Review that prefixes are word parts added to the beginnings of words and suffixes are word parts added to the ends of words. Remind students that adding a prefix or a suffix changes the meaning of a word and makes a new word.

Write the prefixes *re-*, *dis-*, and *un-* and the words *like*, *write*, and *happy* on the board and model how to combine the words and prefixes to make new words.

> **Think Aloud**
>
> *I can add these prefixes to words to make new words. If I add* re- *to* write, *I get* rewrite. *When I add* dis- *to* like, *I get* dislike. *When I add* un- *to* happy, *I get* unhappy. *In each case, the prefix changes the meaning of the word.*

Explain that the prefix *re-* means "again." The prefix *dis-* means "opposite." The prefix *un-* means "opposite" or "not."

Write *-ness*, *-ment*, *-ful*, and *-less* and the words *spot*, *improve*, *wonder*, and *sad* on the board and model how to combine the words and suffixes.

> **Think Aloud**
>
> *I know that suffixes are added to the ends of words. I can combine* sad *and* -ness *to make* sadness, *a word I know. I can also combine* improve *and* -ment *to make* improvement, wonder *and* -ful *to make* wonderful, *and* spot *and* -less *to make* spotless. *These are words I know. I can also see that the suffix changes the meaning of the word or how I can use it.*

Explain that the suffixes *-ment* and *-ness* both mean "state or quality of." The suffix *-ful* means "full of." The suffix *-less* means "without."

Objectives

- decode words with a prefix or a suffix *re-*, *dis-*, *un-*; *-ness*, *-ment*, *-ful*, *-less*
- identify the meaning of words with a prefix or a suffix *re-*, *dis-*, *un-*; *-ness*, *-ment*, *-ful*, *-less*

Materials

- Anthology: *Happy Birthday, Dr. King!*

Practice

Have students skim the selection to find one or more words with the following prefixes and suffixes: *re-, dis-, un-, -ment, -ful*. Ask them to write a definition for each word.

Apply

Give students the following words and have them use the prefixes *re-, dis-*, and *un-* and the suffixes *-ful, -less, -ment*, and *-ness* to make new words. They may use some words twice. Ask them to explain the meanings of the words they make.

LITERATURE FOCUS: 10–15 MINUTES

Review *Happy Birthday, Dr. King!*

Guide students through the Comprehension Skill Lesson for **Cause and Effect** on page 537 in the Teachers Edition.

SKILL FOCUS: GRAMMAR   25–30 MINUTES

Subject Pronouns

Teach

Encourage students to discuss what they learned from the story *Happy Birthday, Dr. King!* Then display the following sentences:

> The students learned a lot about Dr. King.
>
> We learned a lot about Dr. King.

Ask students how the sentences differ. Then underline *We* in the second sentence. Explain that *We* is a pronoun that can take the place of the subject *The students*. Review that a subject is who or what a sentence is about.

Have students write the following subject pronouns on index cards: *I, we, you, he, she, it, they*. Read aloud the following sentences and identify the subjects. Ask students to hold up a card to show the pronoun that can take the place of each subject.

> Jamal and Arthur were in trouble. (They)
>
> Mrs. Gordon gave them both a note from the principal. (She)
>
> Jamal took the note home. (He)
>
> The note said Jamal had been fighting. (It)

Practice

Ask students to look at the first sentence in the fourth paragraph on page 536. Then model how to replace subjects with subject pronouns.

Think Aloud

The first thing I do when I look at this sentence is try to figure out the subject. Jamal *is who the sentence is about, so* Jamal *must be the subject. Then I ask myself, Which subject pronoun can take the place of* Jamal? *The pronoun* He *might work. I'll try the pronoun in the sentence: He decided to go in the front door... That makes sense.* He *must be the correct subject pronoun.*

Objectives

- identify subject pronouns
- use subject pronouns in sentences

Materials

- Reader's Library: *Thanks to Sandra Cisneros*
- index cards

Encourage students to use this thinking process as they identify the subjects in these story sentences and replace them with pronouns:

p. 536 Maybe <u>Mom</u> won't ask me about school. (she)

p. 541 <u>Grandpa</u> Joe took a deep breath and began… (He)

p. 544 <u>That man</u> was Dr. King. (He)

p. 547 <u>Our class</u> could do something to show that fighting is not the way to get things done. (We)

Review, when finished, by asking: *What words are subject pronouns?* (I, we, you, he, she, it, they) *What does a subject pronoun do?* (It replaces the subject of a sentence.)

Apply

Ask students to write five sentences about the story. At least three sentences should contain subject pronouns. Have students exchange papers, underline the subject pronouns in each other's sentences, and name the subject for which each pronoun stands.

LITERATURE FOCUS: 10–15 MINUTES

Preview *Thanks to Sandra Cisneros*

Walk students through *Thanks to Sandra Cisneros* and discuss illustrations using words such as *recognized* and *experiences*.

Ask students to find cause-and-effect relationships within the sequence of illustrations. Guide them to think about how the presentation of the Sandra Cisneros book (pages 13–17) appears to be the cause of the main character's inspiration.

Day 5

Cause and Effect

Teach

Remind students that cause and effect exists when one event makes another event happen. We can find an effect by asking the question, *What happened?* We can find the cause by asking the question, *Why did this happen?*

Write these sentences on the board:

> The school was closed last Thursday.
>
> Last Thursday was Thanksgiving, a holiday.

Have students identify which sentence is a cause and which sentence is an effect. If they are having trouble, guide them through the process. First ask, *What happened?* (School was closed on Thursday.) Then ask, *Why did this happen?* (Thursday was a holiday.)

Point out that identifying causes and effects can help us better understand what we read. Knowing why things happen helps us understand how events are related to each other. Use this example to illustrate the point. Have students silently read the first paragraph of the introductory material on page 532. Ask, *What happened to Mrs. Parks?* (The police arrested her.) *Why did this happen?* (Mrs. Parks refused to move to the back of the bus.) Have students identify the cause and the effect and explain their reasoning.

Objectives

- recognize cause/effect relationships
- distinguish between cause and effect

Materials

- Anthology: *Happy Birthday, Dr. King!*
- Reader's Library: *Thanks to Sandra Cisneros*

Practice

Have students create a two-column chart with the heads Cause and
Effect. Tell them to complete this organizer as they read *Happy
Birthday, Dr. King!* They can record events in the Effect column. They
should summarize why each event happened in the Cause column.
Model this example. Direct students back to page 539 of the story. Ask,
What happened to Jamal in school? (His teacher gave him a pink
slip.) Ask, *Why did this happen?* (He fought with another boy over a
seat in the back of the bus.)

Work through the story with students if they are having trouble. Point
out important events. Ask students to explain why these events happened.

Apply

Have students keep track of cause and effect, with an eye to identifying
what happens and why it happens, in the Reader's Library selection
Thanks to Sandra Cisneros by Daniel Santacruz. Then have them complete the questions and activity on the Responding page.

LITERATURE FOCUS: 10-15 MINUTES

Revisit *Happy Birthday, Dr. King!* and *Thanks to Sandra Cisneros*

Review with students the cause-and-effect relationships presented in
Happy Birthday, Dr. King! and *Thanks to Sandra Cisneros.* Also, help
them to look for words with prefixes or suffixes such as *assignment,
disappeared, unhappy,* (*Happy Birthday, Dr. King!*, pages 536, 539,
542) *slowly, reminded,* and *experiences* (*Thanks to Sandra Cisneros,*
pages 12, 12, and 15).

Day 1

Objectives

- read words in which final *y* has been changed to *i*
- use the Phonics/Decoding Strategy to decode longer words

Materials

- Teaching Master ES5-3
- Practice Master ES5-3
- Anthology: Gloria Estefan

Technology

Get Set for Reading CD-ROM
Gloria Estefan

Education Place
www.eduplace.com
Gloria Estefan

Audiotape
Gloria Estefan
Audiotape for **Heroes**

Lexia Phonics CD-ROM
Intermediate Intervention

Changing Final *y* to *i*

Warm-Up/Academic Language

Remind students that in many **words ending in *y***, the ***y* is changed to *i* when an ending is added.** Explain that recognizing that a *y* was changed to *i* may help them to recognize and read long, unfamiliar words.

Teach

Write *cloudy* on the board, and read it aloud. Circle the base word *cloud* and underline the final *y*. Tell students that they will learn about adding endings to base words that have a final *y*.

Write these equations on the board:

cloudy + -er = cloudier

cloudy + -est = cloudiest

Circle the endings *-er* and *-est*. Point out that, in each word, the *y* changes to *i* before the ending is added.

Write *scurry* on the board. Ask volunteers to come to the board and write what happens when the endings *-es* and *-ed* are added to *scurry*. (scurries, scurried)

Remind students that removing an ending can often help them to figure out the meaning of longer words. Use the following sentence to explain: *You can recycle old telephone directories.*

Think Aloud

I see a word with the ending -es. I suspect that a final y *in the longer word was changed to* i *when the ending -es was added. If I put back the final* y, *I get the word* directory. *Now I see a base word that I recognize:* direct. *I try to sound out the whole word:* dih REKT oh rees. Directories. Directories *must be the plural of* directory. *That makes sense in the sentence.*

Write these words on the board: *jellied, parties, spicier, laziest*, and *tastiest*.

Have volunteers write the base word of each word on the board. (jelly, party, spicy, lazy, tasty)

Guided Practice

Display or **distribute** Teaching Master ES5-3 and discuss the format. Explain that headlines are often not complete sentences and that they use capital letters to begin nearly every word.

Ask students to find the word in each headline that ends in *i* + a suffix.

Help students to underline these words and to write the base word.

Ask students to compare the underlined and base words. Guide them to observe that, in each instance, the final *y* in the base word changes to *i* when an ending is added.

Practice/Apply

Distribute Practice Master ES5-3, and go over the illustration and directions.

Instruct students to complete the Practice Master independently.

Have students share their answers with the group.

Check students' responses to be sure they know to change *y* to *i* when adding endings to base words with final *y*.

LITERATURE FOCUS: 10–15 MINUTES

Preview *Gloria Estefan* Segment 1

Refer to the bottom of page 561 in the Teacher's Edition and preview with students Segment 1 of *Gloria Estefan* (pages 561–565).

Note the suggestions in the Extra Support boxes on Teacher's Edition pages 563 and 564.

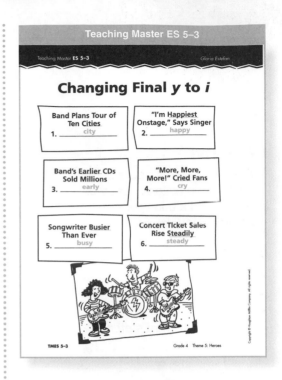

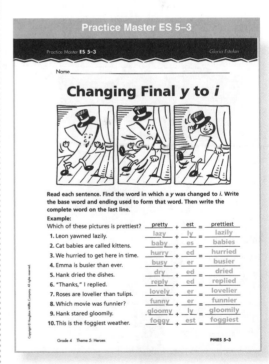

Day 2

Objective
- make judgments about a character's actions based on story details and your own opinions and values

Materials
- Teaching Master ES5-4
- Practice Master ES5-4
- Anthology: *Gloria Estefan*

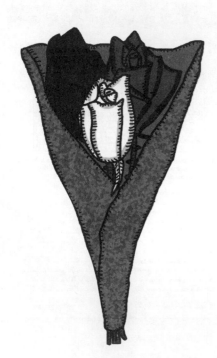

Making Judgments

Warm-Up/Academic Language

Tell students that they can **make judgments about characters in stories.** Explain that when readers make a judgment they ask themselves "Do I agree with this? Is this right or fair?" To make fair judgments, **readers use their own opinions and experiences** as well as **facts from the story.**

Teach

Discuss how students make judgments about people, ideas, and situations in real life. Elicit that they should use the person's actions and their own beliefs about what is right and wrong.

Read this story aloud:

Read Aloud

> Jordan was leaving the video store when he saw a car run into a cyclist. The woman on the bike fell to the ground. Luckily, her helmet remained on her head, but she was unable to stand back up. Jordan bolted back into the store. "I have to use the phone!" he yelled. Then Jordan calmly dialed 911. "A woman was hit by a car." Jordan said. He described where the parking lot was and an ambulance arrived right away.

Display the chart below on the board. Guide students to make a judgment about Jordan, using story details and their own values and experience. Sample responses are shown.

Question	Story Details	Own Opinions and Experiences	Judgment
What kind of person is Jordan?	Jordan got involved and acted quickly and calmly after he saw the bicyclist go down.	People should help each other whenever they can. It is good to know what to do in an emergency.	Jordan is a quick-thinker. I think he's a hero.

Guided Practice

Display or **distribute** Teaching Master ES5-4.

Read the story with students, asking them to think about Trisha's decision.

Help students fill out the chart and disuss the final entries.

Practice/Apply

Distribute Practice Master ES5-4 to students and go over the directions.

Instruct students to work independently to complete the Practice Master.

Ask students to discuss their judgments with a partner and then read their letters to each other.

Check students' ability to make judgments as they read by observing their responses.

LITERATURE FOCUS: 10–15 MINUTES

Preview *Gloria Estefan* Segment 2

Refer to the bottom of page 566 in the Teacher's Edition and preview with students Segment 2 of *Gloria Estefan* (pages 566–576).

Note the suggestions in the Extra Support boxes on Teacher's Edition pages 568, 573, and 576.

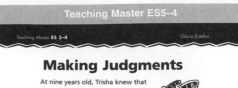

Teaching Master ES5–4

Teaching Master **ES 5–4**   *Gloria Estefan*

Making Judgments

At nine years old, Trisha knew that she wanted to be an Olympic figure skater. She had already won many impressive skating awards. She practiced at the rink four afternoons each week. Trisha loved to skate.

One day, Trisha was having a terrible practice. She couldn't get the hardest move of her new routine right. She fell a few times. Her coach told her to be patient and that she had time to get it right before her next competition. After she fell for the fifth time, Irisha yelled "I quit! I don't want to skate anymore!"

Question	Story Details	Own Opinions and Experiences	Judgment
Should Trisha quit skating because she fell a few times?	Trisha loves skating. She's won many awards. She's having trouble doing a very hard move so she quit.	Sometimes I say things I don't mean when I'm upset. Quitting something you love because of one problem is a mistake.	Trisha is making a bad decision. I hope she changes her mind.

TMES 5–4   Grade 4   Theme 5: Heroes

Copyright © Houghton Mifflin Company. All rights reserved.

Practice Master ES5–4

Practice Master **ES 5–4**   *Gloria Estefan*

Name _____

Making Judgments

Read the story. Then write a letter to Nelson to tell him what you think of his behavior. Give reasons for your opinion.

On his way to school, Dave saw a toy drum lying in the grass. He picked it up and beat it a few times. All of a sudden, a hand grabbed the drum. It was Nelson. He was always taking things away from people. "Give that back! I found it!" Dave yelled.

Nelson beat the drum. "Try and get it!" he called with a laugh as he ran away. Suddenly he tripped and fell on top of the drum. It broke. "OK, you can have it back," Nelson called.

Dave picked up the broken drum and tossed it into the trash.

Dear Nelson,

Sample response: I think it is wrong to take things from people without asking. How would you feel if someone grabbed something from you and broke it? I think you should be nicer from now on and think about other people's feelings.

Grade 4   Theme 5: Heroes   PMES 5–4

Copyright © Houghton Mifflin Company. All rights reserved.

Day 3

SKILL FOCUS: STRUCTURAL ANALYSIS   25–30 MINUTES

Changing Final *y* to *i*

Objective
• change final *y* to *i* when adding endings

Materials
• Anthology: *Gloria Estefan*

Teach

Review that when an ending or a suffix is added to a word that ends in a consonant plus *y*, the *y* changes to *i*. Explain to students that knowing how the spelling of the word changes will help them recognize words to which endings have been added.

Write the word *worry* and this sentence on the board and model changing the *y* to *i* before adding the ending: *Gloria was _____ that she would not have enough time to study.*

Think Aloud

I know that the word I want is worried. Worry *ends in a consonant plus* y. *So I know that when I write the word, I have to change the* y *to* i *before I add the ending* -ed. Worried *looks different from* worry, *but because I know that the* y *changes to* i, *I can recognize that the two words are forms of the same word. I have to remember to look closely at the words, though. If the word ended in a vowel plus* y, *I would just add the ending.*

Practice

Write the following words and endings on the board. Ask students to explain how they would add the endings to the words and how the new word would be spelled.

happy + -ness	happiness
steady + -ly	steadily
study + -ed	studied
day + -s	days

Apply

Write the following sentences. Have students copy the underlined words and write the base words and endings from which they were made.

That is the <u>silliest</u> hat I've ever seen.

Several <u>families</u> came to the party.

Do you know any <u>remedies</u> for poison ivy?

He finished the job <u>easily</u>.

The mayor <u>replied</u> to my letter.

Yesterday was a <u>glorious</u> day.

LITERATURE FOCUS: 10–15 MINUTES

Review *Gloria Estefan*

Guide students through the Comprehension Skill Lesson for **Making Judgments** on page 575 in the Teacher's Edition.

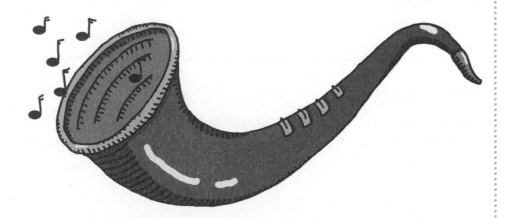

Day 4

Objectives
- identify object pronouns
- use object pronouns in sentences

Materials
- index cards
- Reader's Library: *Duke Ellington: A Life in Music*

Object Pronouns

Teach

Ask students to name three facts that they learned from the story about Gloria Estefan. Then write the following sentence on the chalkboard:

> The story gave <u>the students</u> facts about Gloria Estefan.

Ask students to change the sentence to make it tell about what happened to them. Have them replace the underlined words with a pronoun. (us) Then explain that the pronoun *us* is an object pronoun. Review that object pronouns come after action verbs.

Have students write the following object pronouns on index cards: *me, us, you, him, her, it, them*. Ask students to listen carefully as you read the following sentences. Identify the object in each sentence. Have students hold up a card to show the pronoun that can replace each object.

> A tour bus carried <u>Gloria, Emilio, and Nayib</u>. (them)
>
> A truck hit <u>the bus</u>. (it)
>
> The crash threw <u>Nayib</u> under a mountain of stuff. (him)
>
> The accident hurt <u>Gloria</u>. (her)

Practice

Have students look at the sentence on page 561 that begins, *By the time Gloria was two…* Then model how to replace objects with object pronouns.

Think Aloud

To figure out which object pronoun to use, I must first find the object of the sentence. The words the family *come after the verb* had settled. *The object of the sentence must be* the family. *Then I ask myself,* Which object pronoun can take the place of *the family? I'll try* them *in the sentence.* By the time Gloria was two years old, José Fajardo had settled them in Miami, Florida. *That makes sense. The object pronoun* them *must be correct.*

Have students use this thinking process as they identify the objects in these sentences from the story and replace them with pronouns:

p. 564 A few weeks after that, Emilio asked <u>Gloria</u> to join the band permanently. (her)

p. 566 Three months later, on September 1, 1978, she married <u>Emilio</u>. (him)

p. 567 The couple named <u>the boy</u> Nayib. (him)

p. 569 These two albums made <u>Gloria and the Miami Sound Machine</u> a success all over English-speaking America. (them)

Review, when finished, by having students name object pronouns. (me, us, you, him, her, it, them) **Ask** what an object pronoun does. (It replaces the object of a sentence.)

Apply

Have students use object pronouns in a brief written summary of the story. Students can exchange papers, underline each object pronoun, and name the object for which it stands.

LITERATURE FOCUS: 10–15 MINUTES

Preview *Duke Ellington: A Life in Music*

Walk students through *Duke Ellington: A Life in Music* and discuss illustrations using words such as *orchestra, improvise, honor, jazz,* and *elegant.*

Ask students to scan through the illustrations and make judgments about the feelings and actions of the people shown in the story.

Day 5

Objectives:
- weigh pros and cons to make judgments
- understand that there is no one correct judgment

Materials:
- Anthology: *Gloria Estefan*
- Reader's Library: *Duke Ellington: A Life in Music*

Making Judgments

Teach

Remind students that a judgment is an opinion based on personal values. Point out that readers make various judgments when they read. In some cases, we judge the actions of people who are the subjects of a written work. Some readers may decide that a person behaved wisely or was right in a certain situation. Other readers may think that the person behaved foolishly or was wrong. Because a judgment is based on personal values, there is no one correct judgment. However, readers should consider all the facts before making a judgment.

Tell students that one way to consider the facts is by listing the pros and cons of a person's behavior. *Pros* are facts that support the way a person behaved. *Cons* are facts that do not support the way a person behaved. Direct students back to pages 564–566 of *Gloria Estefan* to use the information on those pages to model using pros and cons to make a judgment.

Use a Think Aloud to model making a judgment about the fact that Gloria did not begin singing full time until she graduated from college.

Think Aloud

Pros: A full-time singing career would have interfered with Gloria's studies. Gloria had promised her mother that she would graduate from college. It is very hard to become a successful singer. Musicians are wise to get an education in case their music career does not go well.

Cons: Gloria had great talent. She loved to perform. She believed music was her true calling. Staying in college delayed her opportunity to pursue a music career. She loved Emilio, whose passion was music.

Ask students, *Do you think Gloria's decision to stay in college was wise?* Hold a class discussion. Encourage students to add other facts, pro or con, that they think should be considered. Afterwards, remind them that there is no one correct judgment.

Practice

Have students form opinions about other situations discussed in the selection. Remind them to consider all the facts. Tell them to list each fact as a pro or con before making a judgment. You might suggest that they think about the following situations: *Emilio quits his full-time job shortly after their first child is born. Record company officials decide to release the band's albums only in South America. Gloria decides to undergo a risky operation. Gloria turns down roles in movies.*

Hold class discussions. Encourage students to share their judgments with their classmates. Ask them to identify the facts they considered as pros and cons before forming an opinion.

Apply

Have students make judgments, with an eye to weighing pros and cons, in the Reader's Library selection *Duke Ellington: A Life in Music* by Erick Montgomery. Ask students to complete the questions and activity on the Responding page.

LITERATURE FOCUS: 10–15 MINUTES

Revisit *Gloria Estefan* and *Duke Ellington: A Life in Music*

Review with students the process of making judgments about characters' actions in *Gloria Estefan* and *Duke Ellington: A Life in Music*. Also, help students to look for words in which the final *y* has become an *i,* such as *worried, studies, parties,* (*Gloria Estefan,* all page 565), *families,* and *copied* (*Duke Ellington: A Life in Music,* pages 33 and 37).

Day 1

Objectives
- read words with the VCV pattern
- use the Phonics/Decoding strategy to decode longer words

Materials
- Teaching Master ES5-5
- Practice Master ES5-5
- Anthology: *Lou Gehrig: The Luckiest Man*

Technology

Get Set for Reading CD-ROM

Lou Gehrig: The Luckiest Man

Education Place

www.eduplace.com
Lou Gehrig: The Luckiest Man

Audiotape

Lou Gehrig: The Luckiest Man
Audiotape for **Heroes**

Lexia Phonics CD-ROM

Intermediate Intervention

PRETEACH

SKILL FOCUS: STRUCTURAL ANALYSIS — 25–30 MINUTES

VCV Pattern

Warm-Up/Academic Language

Remind students that a good way to read a **long, unfamiliar word** is to **divide it into syllables**. Readers can use the **pattern of vowels and consonants** to help them figure out how to **divide a word into syllables**. Point out that many words with the **vowel-consonant-vowel (VCV) pattern** can be **divided between the first vowel and the consonant**. When that happens, the **first vowel has a long sound**. Other words with this pattern can be **divided between the consonant and the second vowel**. When this happens, **the first vowel has a short sound**.

Teach

Write *tiger* on the board and read it with students. Underline the letters *i-g-e*. Label the VCV pattern. Explain that words with the VCV pattern are often divided into syllables between the first long vowel and the consonant: V/CV. Draw a slash between the *i* and *g* (ti/ger). Point out that the slash mark means a break in syllables. Have students say the word in syllables, *TIE gur.*

> 1. t i g e r
> 2. v c v
> 3. v/cv
> 4. ti/ger

Follow the same procedure with these words: *open, paper, okay.*

Explain that some words with the VCV pattern are divided after the consonant: VC/V. Tell students that the first vowel in words like this usually has a short vowel sound.

Display the following sentence and model how to decode *Lemon: Lemon sherbet is very refreshing on a hot day.*

Think Aloud

I have identified the VCV pattern. I first try dividing the word between the V and C. I blend the two word parts, using a long vowel sound for the e. LEE/mon. That doesn't sound right. I look at the word again. I think I'll try the short vowel sound, and divide the word after the consonant. LEM/on. Lemon. That makes sense in the sentence.

Write the following words on the board and have students come to the board to separate the syllables with a slash mark: *never, visit, parent.* (nev/er, vis/it, par/ent)

Guided Practice

Display or **distribute** Teaching Master ES5-5 to students and read the items on the shopping list with them.

Help students to locate and underline all the two-syllable words.

Ask students to identify whether the first vowel sound is long or short, and help them divide the syllables accordingly in the spaces given.

Practice/Apply

Distribute Practice Master ES5-5 to students and go over the directions.

Ask students to complete the Practice Master independently.

Check students' understanding of the VCV pattern by going over the responses as a group.

LITERATURE FOCUS: 10–15 MINUTES

Preview *Lou Gehrig: The Luckiest Man* Segment 1

Refer to the bottom of page 585 in the Teacher's Edition and preview with students Segment 1 of *Lou Gehrig: The Luckiest Man* (pages 584–591).

Note the suggestions in the Extra Support boxes on Teacher's Edition pages 586, 589, and 590.

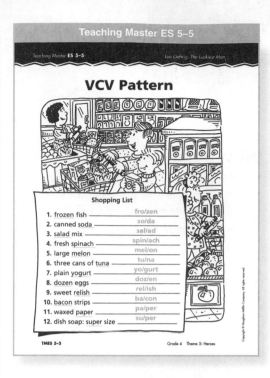

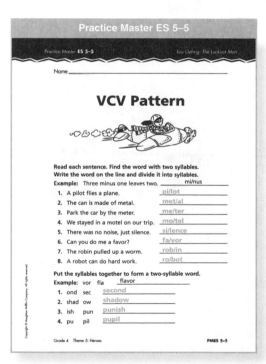

Day 2

Fact and Opinion

Objectives

- identify facts and opinions
- identify words that signal opinions
- understand that facts can be proven and opinions cannot

Materials

- Teaching Master ES5-6
- Practice Master ES5-6
- a real apple, or a picture of one
- Anthology: *Lou Gehrig: The Luckiest Man*

Warm-Up/Academic Language

Remind students that an **opinion is a feeling, idea,** or **belief** based on **what a person thinks about something.** An **opinion cannot be proved true or false.** Explain that **clue words** such as *great, amazing, unfair,* and *awful* may **signal opinions. A fact is a statement that can be checked and proven true or false.** Tell students that **being able to distinguish fact from opinion** will help them to **become smarter readers.**

Teach

Hold up an apple, and say:

- *This apple is a fruit.*

- *This apple tastes great!*

- *This apple was grown in Washington.*

- *Macintosh apples are the best.*

- *I bought the apple at the grocery store.*

Write each statement in the chart shown below, instructing students to identify it as a fact or opinion and to tell why they think so. Follow the procedure for all the statements.

Statement	Fact or Opinion?
This apple is a fruit.	fact; can be proven
This apple tastes great!	opinion; everyone has different tastes
This apple was grown in Washington.	fact; can be proven
Macintosh apples are the best.	opinion; everyone has different tastes
I bought the apple at the grocery store.	fact; can be proven

Point out signal words such as *great* and *best*, and lead students to see that each statement using one of these words is an opinion.

Guided Practice

Display or **distribute** Teaching Master ES5-6 and read the passage with students.

Help them complete the chart by identifying facts and opinions.

Ask students to suggest how they could prove statements they identify as facts and whether opinions use signal words such as *great* or *best*.

Practice/Apply

Distribute Practice Master ES5-6 to students and go over the directions with them.

Have students read the passage.

Tell students to complete the chart independently. Have them write the number of each sentence in the correct column.

Check students' understanding of Fact and Opinion by reviewing their responses.

LITERATURE FOCUS: 10–15 MINUTES

Preview *Lou Gehrig: The Luckiest Man* Segment 2

Refer to the bottom of page 566 in the Teacher's Edition and preview with students Segment 2 of *Lou Gehrig: The Luckiest Man* (pages 566–576).

Note the suggestions in the Extra Support boxes on Teacher's Edition pages 568, 573, and 576.

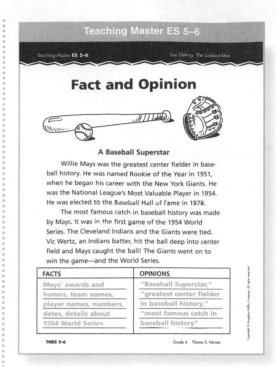

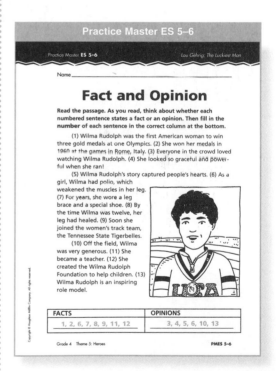

Day 3

SKILL FOCUS: STRUCTURAL ANALYSIS   25–30 MINUTES

VCV Pattern

Objective
- read words that have the VCV pattern

Materials
- Anthology: *Lou Gehrig: The Luckiest Man*

Teach

Review that many words have a VCV (Vowel/Consonant/Vowel) pattern. Remind students that when they come to a word with the VCV pattern, they can try to pronounce the word by giving the first vowel a long sound. If they do not recognize the word, they can then try the short sound.

Write this sentence on the board:
The scout offered Lou Gherig a good <u>salary</u>.

Think Aloud

When I look at the underlined word, I see that it has a VCV pattern. The first vowel might have a long sound, so I'll try that first. SALE-uh-re—no, that's not a word I recognize. Next I'll try the short sound of a, /ă/. I recognize the word salary, *and it makes sense in the sentence.*

Practice

Write the following sentences on the board and ask students to identify the words with a VCV pattern. Have volunteers pronounce them and explain how they decided whether the first vowel was long or short.

Lou Gehrig compiled an outstanding record. He was selected twice as the league's Most Valuable Player.

Help students identify *compiled, record, selected,* and *Player* as words with the VCV pattern. Call on volunteers to pronounce the words and tell whether the first vowel is long or short.

Apply

Write the following words on the board. Ask students to copy the words and underline the VCV pattern. Have them put a check next to the words in which the first vowel is long, and an *x* next to the words in which the first vowel is short.

remember	material
money	melody
decided	electrical
government	similarly

LITERATURE FOCUS: 10–15 MINUTES

Review *Lou Gehrig: The Luckiest Man*

Guide students through the Comprehension Skill Lesson for **Fact and Opinion** on page 589 in the Teacher's Edition.

Day 4

RETEACH
SKILL FOCUS: GRAMMAR · 25–30 MINUTES

Possessive Pronouns

Objectives
- identify possessive pronouns
- use possessive pronouns in sentences

Materials
- index cards
- Reader's Library: *Mark McGwire: Home Run Hero*

Teach

Discuss Lou Gehrig's early life with students. Ask them to recall how his mother felt about him joining the Yankees. Then display these sentences:

> Lou's mother wanted him to stay in college.
>
> His mother wanted him to stay in college.

Ask students what they notice about the proper noun *Lou's* in the first sentence. Help them recognize that the word ends with 's. The word is possessive. It tells whose mother. Then ask students to name the word in the second sentence that replaces *Lou's*. (His) Point out that *His* is a possessive pronoun.

Have students write these possessive pronouns on index cards: *my, our, your, his, hers, its, their*. Ask them to listen carefully as you read the following sentences. Identify the possessive in each sentence. Have students hold up a card to show the pronoun that can replace it.

The young boy's home was New York City. (His)
Christina Gehrig's dreams for Lou did not come true. (Her)
The players' manager sent Lou to bat for the shortstop. (Their)
Lou was one of baseball's most valuable players. (its)

Practice

Have students look at the second sentence on page 590. Then model how to use possessive pronouns.

Think Aloud

> *I know that words that end with 's are possessive. The name* Lou's *ends with 's. It tells whose. I know that I can replace a possessive noun with a possessive pronoun. The pronoun* His *might work. I'll try it in the sentence:* His constant play earned him the nickname Iron Horse. *That makes sense. The pronoun* His *must be the correct pronoun to use.*

Encourage students to use this process as they identify possessives in the story and replace them with possessive pronouns:

p. 590 He was selected again as the league's MVP in 1936. (its)

p. 592 On June 19, his thirty-sixth birthday, they told Lou's wife, Eleanor, what was wrong. (his)

Have students identify the possessive pronoun in each of these story sentences and name the noun for which it stands.

p. 586 Christina Gehrig had great hopes for her son Lou. (Christina Gehrig)

p. 594 Many of the players from the 1927 Yankees... came to honor their former teammate. (Yankees)

Review by asking students: *What words are possessive pronouns?* (my, our, your, his, hers, its, their.) *What does a possessive pronoun do?* (It replaces a possessive noun.)

Apply

Ask students to write a paragraph about Lou. Have them use at least three possessive pronouns in the paragraph. Students can exchange papers, underline each possessive pronoun, and name the possessive noun for which it stands.

LITERATURE FOCUS: 10 15 MINUTES

Preview *Mark McGwire: Homerun Hero*

Walk students through *Mark McGwire: Homerun Hero*, and discuss illustrations using words such as *outfield, record, rookie, injured, competition*, and *concentrate*.

Ask students to scan through the illustrations and locate an image that shows facts about Mark McGwire. (Page 47 shows his statistics.) Discuss how such facts differ from opinions.

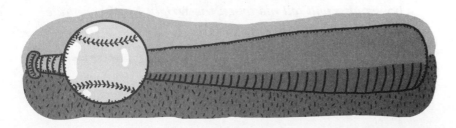

Day 5

Objectives:

- understand the meaning of facts and opinions
- distinguish between fact and opinion

Materials:

- Anthology: *Lou Gehrig: The Luckiest Man*
- Reader's Library: *Mark McGwire: Home Run Hero*

Fact and Opinion

Teach

Remind students that a fact is a statement that can be proved right or wrong. A fact usually can be checked in a reference source, such as an encyclopedia or an almanac. Often facts include statistical information, such as numbers and dates. An opinion states what someone thinks, feels, or believes. Mention that clue words sometimes appear before opinions. These clue words include *I think, everyone,* and *all the time.* You may agree or disagree with an opinion. However, you cannot prove it is true or false.

Write these sentences on the board:

> Lou Gehrig played baseball.
>
> Baseball is the best sport.

Point out that the first sentence is a fact. You can prove it is right by checking the information in a reference book, such as an encyclopedia or a book of baseball facts. The second sentence is an opinion. Some people may agree; others may disagree. However, the statement cannot be proved right or wrong.

Use the first paragraph in *Lou Gehrig: The Luckiest Man* to model identifying facts.

Think Aloud

I can check a reference work and find that Henry Ford sold his first automobile in 1903. This is a fact. Reference books also will tell me when the Wright Brothers made their first flight. This is a fact.

Practice

Have students identify other facts as they skim the selection. Discuss with them how they know that particular statements are facts. You might focus on the following information:

Lou never missed a day of school.

Lou played in 2,130 consecutive games.

He won Most Valuable Player Awards in 1927 and 1936.

Ask students whether they think the following statements are facts or opinions, and have them explain their answers.

Lou's mother thought games and sports were a waste of time.

She was convinced that [Lou] was ruining his life.

Fiorello La Guardia… said, "You are the greatest prototype of good sportsmanship and citizenship."

Apply

Have students keep track of fact and opinion, with an eye to identifying what can be proven right or wrong, in the Reader's Library selection *Mark McGwire: Home Run Hero* by Richard Merchant. Then have them complete the questions and activity on the Responding page.

LITERATURE FOCUS: 10–15 MINUTES

Revisit *Lou Gehrig: The Luckiest Man* and *Mark McGwire: Home Run Hero*

Review with students the process for distinguishing between facts and opinions for selected portions of *Lou Gehrig: The Luckiest Man* and *Mark McGwire: Home Run Hero.* Also, help students to look for multi-syllabic words with the VCV pattern, such as *beginnings, university, bonus, salary,* (*Lou Gehrig: The Luckiest Man*, pages 585, 588, 588, and 588) *uniform,* and *record* (*Mark McGwire: Home Run Hero*, pages 41, 43).

Theme 6

Nature: Friend and Foe

Selections

Day 1

Objectives

- read three-syllable words
- use the Phonics/Decoding strategy to decode longer words

Materials

- Teaching Master ES6-1
- Practice Master ES6-1
- Anthology: *Salmon Summer*

Get Set for Reading
CD-ROM

Salmon Summer

Education Place

www.eduplace.com
Salmon Summer

Audiotape

Salmon Summer
Audiotape for
Nature: Friend and Foe

Lexia Phonics
CD-ROM

Intermediate Intervention

PRETEACH

SKILL FOCUS: STRUCTURAL ANALYSIS   25–30 MINUTES

Three-Syllable Words

Warm-Up/Academic Language

Remind students that when they encounter a **three-syllable word**, they should look for familiar prefixes, suffixes, and base words or word roots. Explain that this will help them to **divide the longer word into smaller parts**. They can **sound out each individual part** and then **blend the roots together**.

Teach

Write the word *unhelpful* on the board. Point out that *unhelpful* is a three-syllable word that contains a prefix *un*, a base word *help*, and a suffix *ful*.

Circle the base word *help* and underline *un* and *ful*. Sound out and blend each of the three syllables. Then blend the three syllables together.

Repeat the procedure for *powerful, covering,* and *explorer*.

Tell students that recognizing base words in a compound word will help them read many three-syllable words. Write the word *grandmother* on the board and model. Remind students that *grandmother* is a compound word with two familiar base words.

Write the following words on the board: *discover, dependent, related, storytime, mistaken, protecting*.

Tell students that each word is a three-syllable word. Ask them to use what they know about prefixes, suffixes, base words and word roots to divide the words into syllables and then blend them together to say the words. *(dis/cov/er, de/pend/ent, re/lat/ed, stor/y/time, mis/tak/en, pro/tect/ing)*

Guided Practice

Display or **distribute** Teaching Master ES6-1 and read each book title and author with students. Discuss the humor in each author's name.

Help them to identify the three-syllable words in each title and write the words on the line below.

Have students identify any prefixes, suffixes, base words, or word roots in each word.

Guide students in placing slash marks between the syllables.

Practice/Apply

Distribute Practice Master ES6-1 to students and go over the directions.

Tell students to complete the Practice Master independently.

Check students' ability to decode three-syllable words by reviewing their responses.

LITERATURE FOCUS: 10–15 MINUTES

Preview *Salmon Summer* Segment 1

Refer to the bottom of page 635 in the Teacher's Edition and preview with students Segment 1 of *Salmon Summer* (pages 634–641).

Note the suggestions in the Extra Support boxes on Teacher's Edition pages 638 and 640.

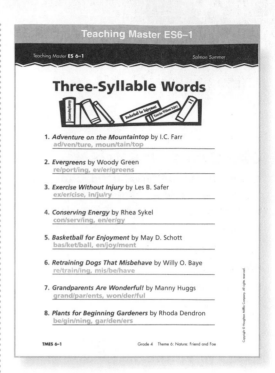

Teaching Master ES6–1

Teaching Master **ES 6-1**   *Salmon Summer*

Three-Syllable Words

1. *Adventure on the Mountaintop* by I.C. Farr
   ad/ven/ture, moun/tain/top

2. *Evergreens* by Woody Green
   re/port/ing, ev/er/greens

3. *Exercise Without Injury* by Les B. Safer
   ex/er/cise, in/ju/ry

4. *Conserving Energy* by Rhea Sykel
   con/serv/ing, en/er/gy

5. *Basketball for Enjoyment* by May D. Schott
   bas/ket/ball, en/joy/ment

6. *Retraining Dogs That Misbehave* by Willy O. Baye
   re/train/ing, mis/be/have

7. *Grandparents Are Wonderful!* by Manny Huggs
   grand/par/ents, won/der/ful

8. *Plants for Beginning Gardeners* by Rhoda Dendron
   be/gin/ning, gar/den/ers

TMES 6-1   Grade 4   Theme 6: Nature: Friend and Foe

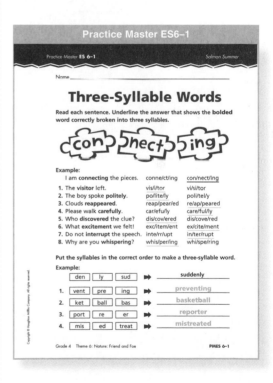

Practice Master ES6–1

Practice Master **ES 6-1**   *Salmon Summer*

Name _____

Three-Syllable Words

Read each sentence. Underline the answer that shows the **bolded** word correctly broken into three syllables.

con nect ing

Example:

I am **connecting** the pieces.	conne/ct/ing	con/nect/ing
1. The **visitor** left.	vis/i/tor	vi/si/tor
2. The boy spoke **politely**.	po/lite/ly	poli/tel/y
3. Clouds **reappeared**.	reap/pear/ed	re/ap/peared
4. Please walk **carefully**.	car/eful/ly	care/ful/ly
5. Who **discovered** the clue?	dis/cov/ered	dis/cove/red
6. What **excitement** we felt!	exc/item/ent	ex/cite/ment
7. Do not **interrupt** the speech.	inte/rr/upt	in/ter/rupt
8. Why are you **whispering**?	whis/per/ing	whi/spe/ring

Put the syllables in the correct order to make a three-syllable word.

Example:

den	ly	sud	➡	suddenly
1. vent	pre	ing	➡	preventing
2. ket	ball	bas	➡	basketball
3. port	re	er	➡	reporter
4. mis	ed	treat	➡	mistreated

Grade 4   Theme 6: Nature: Friend and Foe   PMES 6-1

SKILL FOCUS: COMPREHENSION   25–30 MINUTES

Following Directions

Objectives

- identify the materials needed to follow directions successfully
- identify steps in a set of directions

Materials

- Teaching Master ES6-2
- Practice Master ES6-2
- Anthology: *Salmon Summer*

Warm-Up/Academic Language

Point out that **following directions** is an important skill. Remind students that when they read directions they need to read them **all the way through**. Next, they should **gather the necessary materials**. Finally, **each step in the directions should be followed in order.**

Teach

Write the following instructions on the board:

> Write your name on your paper.
>
> Take out a pencil.
>
> Take out a piece of paper.

Read the directions with students and ask them if they would be able to follow the directions as presented. Lead students to recognize that the directions could not be followed because they are out of order.

Have students reread the set of directions, putting them in the correct order.

Call on three students to write the directions in order and to number the steps 1, 2, 3 as they go.

Explain that sometimes order words such as *first, next, then*, and *last* are used instead of numbers to explain the sequence of steps. Have other students edit the instructions on the board using order words.

Tell students to work with a partner to create a simple set of instructions, such as how to cut a piece of paper into four equal pieces, or how to draw a line that is exactly 6 inches long.

Ask partners to exchange directions with another pair. If time allows, have each pair follow the instructions they were given. Ask students to identify any ways in which the directions could be made clearer.

Guided Practice

Display or **distribute** Teaching Master ES6-2 and read the complete set of directions with students.

Have them gather the materials.

Reread the directions one step at a time, having students complete each step before continuing.

Have students share their creatures with the class and read their sentences aloud.

Practice/Apply

Distribute Practice Master ES6-2 to students and go over the directions and the decoding instructions with them.

Have students complete the Practice Master independently.

Check each student's understanding of how to follow directions as they share their work with the group.

LITERATURE FOCUS: | 10–15 MINUTES

Preview *Salmon Summer* Segment 2

Refer to the bottom of page 642 in the Teacher's Edition and preview with students Segment 2 of *Salmon Summer* (pages 642–647).

Note the suggestions in the Extra Support boxes on Teacher's Edition pages 643, 644, and 646.

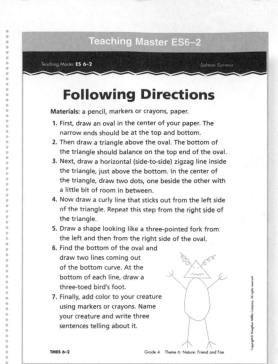

Teaching Master ES6–2

Teaching Master **ES 6–2**   *Salmon Summer*

Following Directions

Materials: a pencil, markers or crayons, paper.

1. First, draw an oval in the center of your paper. The narrow ends should be at the top and bottom.
2. Then draw a triangle above the oval. The bottom of the triangle should balance on the top end of the oval.
3. Next, draw a horizontal (side-to-side) zigzag line inside the triangle, just above the bottom. In the center of the triangle, draw two dots, one beside the other with a little bit of room in between.
4. Now draw a curly line that sticks out from the left side of the triangle. Repeat this step from the right side of the triangle.
5. Draw a shape looking like a three-pointed fork from the left and then from the right side of the oval.
6. Find the bottom of the oval and draw two lines coming out of the bottom curve. At the bottom of each line, draw a three-toed bird's foot.
7. Finally, add color to your creature using markers or crayons. Name your creature and write three sentences telling about it.

TMES 6–2   Grade 4   Theme 6: Nature: Friend and Foe

Copyright © Houghton Mifflin Company. All rights reserved.

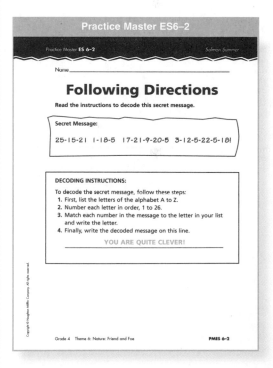

Practice Master ES6–2

Practice Master **ES 6–2**   *Salmon Summer*

Name _____

Following Directions

Read the instructions to decode this secret message.

Secret Message:

25-15-21 1-18-5 17-21-9-20-5 3-12-5-22-5-18!

DECODING INSTRUCTIONS:

To decode the secret message, follow these steps:
1. First, list the letters of the alphabet A to Z.
2. Number each letter in order, 1 to 26.
3. Match each number in the message to the letter in your list and write the letter.
4. Finally, write the decoded message on this line.

_____ YOU ARE QUITE CLEVER! _____

Copyright © Houghton Mifflin Company. All rights reserved.

Grade 4   Theme 6: Nature: Friend and Foe   **PMES 6–2**

Day 3

Three-Syllable Words

Teach

Review with students that words can be divided into syllables—parts of words that are pronounced as a unit. Remind them that when they decode longer words, they can get help by looking for base words, prefixes, suffixes, and endings. Point out that knowing different syllabication patterns helps them decode longer words.

Write the following sentence on the board and model how to decode words with three syllables: *Seagulls and other scavengers came to get the scraps of fish.* You may use the following Think Aloud:

Think Aloud

I don't recognize this word. But I see the VCV pattern and the -er ending, so that helps. I'll try pronouncing it. SKAY vuhng ers — *that doesn't sound right. I'll try another way:* SKA vuhng ers. *Still not quite right. I'll try once more.* SKAV uhn jers. *Now that sounds right.*

Practice

Write the following sentences on the board and have students practice decoding the underlined words: *Alex fishes the same way his <u>ancestors</u> did. There is an <u>abundance</u> of salmon for all.*

Help students to decode the words as necessary. Confirm the correct syllabication: an/ces/tors; a/bun/dance.

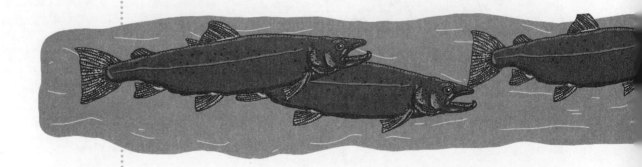

Objective

- read words with three syllables.

Materials

- Anthology: *Salmon Summer*

Apply

Write the phrases below on the board. Have students work with partners to decode the three-syllable words and divide them into syllables. Ask them to explain how knowing how to divide the words into syllables helped them.

1. made an illegal move
2. too judgmental
3. submitted her poem
4. rearrange the living room
5. watch the proceedings
6. demanded payment

LITERATURE FOCUS: 10–15 MINUTES

Review *Salmon Summer*

Guide students through the Comprehension Skill Lesson for **Following Directions** on page 643 in the Teacher's Edition.

Day 4

Objectives
- identify adverbs
- classify adverbs by type
- write sentences using adverbs correctly

Materials
- Reader's Library: *Peter's Harvest*
- index cards

Adverbs

Teach

Review with students that an adjective is a word that describes a noun or a pronoun. Tell them that another kind of describing word is called an adverb. An *adverb* can describe a verb.

Ask students for sentences that use an action verb to name three things they did after school yesterday, such as *I read. I played. I ran.* Have students tell how they did each action, when they did it, or where they did it. For example: *I read carefully. I played later. I ran far.*

Point out that students used an adverb to tell more about each verb. Extend this concept by telling them that adverbs are words that give us more information about an action verb or a form of the verb *be*. Adverbs tell *how, when,* or *where*.

HOW	WHEN	WHERE
angrily	always	downtown
carefully	finally	inside
fast	often	off
loudly	once	out
quickly	sometimes	there
sadly	then	upstairs

Have students write the words *how, when,* and *where* on index cards. After reading each sentence below, help students identify the adverb. Then have students hold up a card to designate the kind of adverb.

The salmon are running <u>now</u>. (when)
They swim <u>around</u>. (where)
Alex and his father <u>quickly</u> set their net. (how)

Emphasize these points with students.

- Adverbs can come before or after the verbs they describe.
- Most adverbs telling *how* end with *-ly*.

Practice

Encourage students to identify and classify adverbs in these sentences.

<u>Now</u> they must finish landing today's catch. (when)

The fish are heading <u>upstream</u> to mate. (where)

He feels another nibble and tugs <u>hard</u>. (how)

With help from his father, Alex pulls the halibut <u>aboard</u>. (where)

Apply

Ask students to write a paragraph telling about something they like to do with another family member, such as fishing, cooking, or playing a sport. Tell them to include at least five adverbs in their writing. Have students exchange papers and underline the adverbs in each other's writing. Ask them to classify each adverb.

LITERATURE FOCUS:　　　　　　　　　　　　10–15 MINUTES

Preview *Peter's Harvest*

Walk students through *Peter's Harvest* and discuss illustrations using words such as *grains, harvest,* and *experiences*.

Ask students to find illustrations that show activities for which it would be important to follow directions. (pages 18–19)

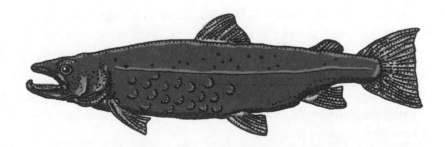

Day 5

SKILL FOCUS: COMPREHENSION   25–30 MINUTES

Following Directions

Objectives
• follow directions in order
• recognize order words

Materials
• Anthology: *Salmon Summer*
• Reader's Library: *Peter's Harvest*

Teach

Post these steps for following directions on the board or chart paper:

> 1. Read all directions carefully.
> 2. Be sure you understand each step. If you don't, ask questions.
> 3. Gather any necessary materials.
> 4. Follow each step in order.
> 5. Finish each step before going on to the next.

Review each step in turn. Point out that the third step may not always apply. Illustrate by noting that you need materials to make objects or follow recipes, but you do not need materials to follow written directions to a friend's house. Ask students if they have any questions. Use this example to stress the importance of following directions in order:

<u>How To Ride a Bike</u>

1. Use your foot to lift the kickstand away from the ground.

2. Use your feet to push the pedals and move the bike forward.

3. Steer the bike by moving the handlebars from side to side with your hands.

4. Apply the brakes to slow down or stop the bike.

Discuss with students what will happen if the first step is skipped or if the steps are not followed in order. (The bike will not move unless the kickstand is lifted.) Ask what might happen if a person fails to read all the directions. (The rider could have an accident.) Tell students that writers sometimes use order words to help readers recognize the correct sequence, or order, in which steps take place. These order words include *first, next,* and *finally.*

Practice

Have students reread the details on page 638. Ask, *What is the first step Alex must follow?* (Put on gloves.) *What might happen if he skips this step?* (He could cut his hands.) Direct students to the second paragraph on page 642. Write these terms on the board: *clean, smoke, hang out to dry.* Work through with students how order words could be used to show the steps Alex follows in preparing the fish. (First, he cleans them. Next, he smokes them. Finally, he hangs them out to dry.) Ask, *What might happen if the first step was skipped?* (Possible answers: The fish might not cure properly, or people might get sick after eating it.)

Apply

Direct students to the second paragraph on page 645. Have them list the steps Alex follows when he goes fishing. (He baits the hook. He attaches a sinker. He hangs the line overboard.) Ask, *What would happen if the steps were not followed in order?* (The hook would float on the surface. The fish would not come for the bait.) Tell students to add order words that give clues to the sequence. Repeat the process for reeling in a fish. (He feels for a nibble. He tugs hard. He pulls the line in.)

Have students identify and use order words when describing directions, in the Reader's Library selection *Peter's Harvest* by Anne Sibley O'Brien. Ask students to complete the questions and activity on the Responding page.

LITERATURE FOCUS: 10–15 MINUTES

Revisit *Salmon Summer* and *Peter's Harvest*

Review with students examples of following directions described in *Salmon Summer* and *Peter's Harvest*. Also, help them to look for three-syllable words, such as *ancestors, scavengers, abundance,* (*Salmon Summer*, pages 637, 640, and 642) *wonderful, September*, and *family* (*Peter's Harvest*, pages 6, 9, and 11).

Day 1

Objectives

- read words with the suffixes *-less*, *-ness*, and *-ion*
- use the Phonics/Decoding strategy to decode longer words

Materials

- Teaching Master ES6-3
- Practice Master ES6-3
- Anthology: *Wildfires*

Technology

**Get Set for Reading
CD-ROM**

Wildfires

Education Place

www.eduplace.com
Wildfires

Audiotape

Wildfires
Audiotape for
Nature: Friend and Foe

Lexia Phonics

CD-ROM

Intermediate Intervention

Suffixes *-less*, *-ness*, and *-ion*

Warm-Up/Academic Language

Remind students that **suffixes** are word parts that are **added to the end of base words** and **root words**. Point out that suffixes can **change a word's meaning** or its **part of speech.** Explain that the suffix *-less* adds the meaning **"without"** to a base word's meaning. Point out that the **suffixes *-ness*, and *-ion* make a base or root word a noun.**

Teach

Write the suffix *-less* on the board. Then write the word *painless*. Underline the suffix and lead students to see the base word *pain*.

Elicit that *painless* means "without pain." Then write the following equation on the board: *pain + -less* = without pain

Repeat the procedure with the words *hopeless, sleepless*, and *soundless*.

Write the suffixes *-ness* and *-ion* on the board. Then write the words *darkness* and *suggestion*. Read each word for students and point out that the suffix *-ion* is pronounced /shun/. Tell students that the suffixes *-ness* and *-ion* make a word a noun.

Underline each suffix and lead students to see that the base word *suggest* is a verb and *dark* an adjective and that these parts of speech change with the addition of *-ness* or *-ion*.

Ask students to help you create new words using the suffixes *-less*, *-ness*, and *-ion*. Write the following words on the board:

• speech + less	=	speechless
• worth + less	=	worthless
• express + ion	=	expression
• impress + ion	=	impression
• kind + ness	=	kindness
• good + ness	=	goodness

Guided Practice

Display or **distribute** Teaching Master ES6-3 and read the passage with students.

Guide students to underline each word with a *-less, -ness,* or *-ion* suffix and identify the base word in each underlined word. Point out the spelling changes in *creation, happiness,* and *combination.*

Discuss how the addition of each suffix changed the meaning or part of speech of the base word.

Practice/Apply

Distribute Practice Master ES6-3 to students, and go over the directions.

Remind students to look out for words requiring spelling changes. (dizziness)

Have students complete the Practice Master independently.

Check all students' responses to make sure they can decode words with *-less, -ness,* and *-ion* suffixes.

LITERATURE FOCUS: 10–15 MINUTES

Preview *Wildfires* Segment 1

Refer to the bottom of page 661 in the Teacher's Edition and preview with students Segment 1 of *Wildfires* (pages 660-671).

Note the suggestions in the Extra Support boxes on Teacher's Edition pages 666, 667, and 670.

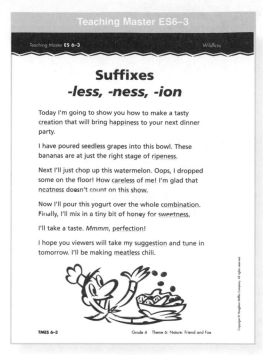

Teaching Master ES6–3

Teaching Master ES 6–3   Wildfires

Suffixes
-less, -ness, -ion

Today I'm going to show you how to make a tasty creation that will bring happiness to your next dinner party.

I have poured seedless grapes into this bowl. These bananas are at just the right stage of ripeness.

Next I'll just chop up this watermelon. Oops, I dropped some on the floor! How careless of me! I'm glad that neatness doesn't count on this show.

Now I'll pour this yogurt over the whole combination. Finally, I'll mix in a tiny bit of honey for sweetness.

I'll take a taste. *Mmmm,* perfection!

I hope you viewers will take my suggestion and tune in tomorrow. I'll be making meatless chili.

TMES 6–3   Grade 4   Theme 6: Nature: Friend and Foe

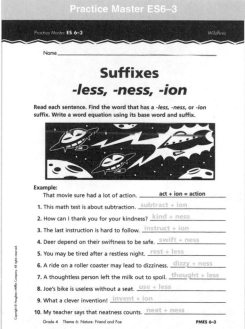

Practice Master ES6–3

Practice Master **ES 6–3**   Wildfires

Name

Suffixes
-less, -ness, -ion

Read each sentence. Find the word that has a *-less, -ness,* or *-ion* suffix. Write a word equation using its base word and suffix.

Example:
That movie sure had a lot of action.   **act + ion = action**

1. This math test is about subtraction. subtract + ion
2. How can I thank you for your kindness? kind + ness
3. The last instruction is hard to follow. instruct + ion
4. Deer depend on their swiftness to be safe. swift + ness
5. You may be tired after a restless night. rest + less
6. A ride on a roller coaster may lead to dizziness. dizzy + ness
7. A thoughtless person left the milk out to spoil. thought + less
8. Joe's bike is useless without a seat. use + less
9. What a clever invention! invent + ion
10. My teacher says that neatness counts. neat + ness

Grade 4   Theme 6: Nature: Friend and Foe   PMES 6–3

Day 2

Objectives
- identify the relationship between topic and main idea
- identify how supporting details explain the main idea

Materials
- Teaching Master ES6-4
- Practice Master ES6-4
- Anthology: *Wildfires*

SKILL FOCUS: COMPREHENSION   25–30 MINUTES

Topic, Main Idea, Supporting Details

Warm-Up/Academic Language

Explain to students that the **topic is what a selection is about.** Remind them that the **main idea** of a paragraph **is the key point the writer wants to make.** Point out that the **main idea** is often **stated in the first sentence** of a paragraph, but it may appear in **any part** of the paragraph. In some cases, readers may have to draw conclusions to identify the main idea. Tell students that **supporting details** give more **specific information about the main idea.**

Teach

Tell students that you will read a paragraph about why fire drills are important. Ask them what your finished paragraph will be about. (Why fire drills are important) Explain that they have identified the topic of your paragraph. Write the topic on the board, then read the following paragraph aloud:

Read Aloud

> Fire drills are important because they show us what to do in case of an emergency. Fire drills can happen at any time, so we need to learn which exits to use no matter where we are in a building. Practicing fire drills helps us not to panic when there is an emergency. Fire drills also help us to know where to go once we get outside a building.

Reread the paragraph and ask students to tell you the main idea and write it on the board. (Fire drills are important because they show what to do in case of an emergency.)

Guide students to see that each of the sentences that follow the main idea are supporting details. Point out that the supporting details give more detailed information about the main idea.

Write each of the supporting details on the board. (learn which exits to use; practice helps us not to panic; help us to know where to go once we get outside)

Guided Practice

Display or **distribute** Teaching Master ES6-4, and read the passage with students.

Reread the first paragraph and ask students to identify its topic, main idea, and supporting details.

Help students to fill in the graphic organizer.

Follow a similar procedure with the second paragraph of the passage.

Practice/Apply

Distribute Practice Master ES6-4 to students and go over the directions with them.

Have students complete the Practice Master independently.

Check students' responses to make sure they can identify topic, main idea, and supporting details.

LITERATURE FOCUS: 10–15 MINUTES

Preview *Wildfires* Segment 2

Refer to the bottom of page 672 in the Teacher's Edition and preview with students Segment 2 of *Wildfires* (pages 672–681).

Note the suggestions in the Extra Support boxes on Teacher's Edition pages 676 and 680.

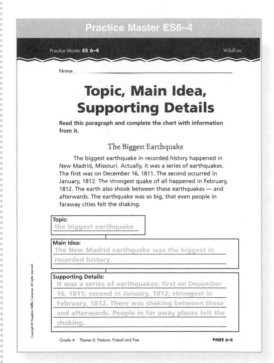

Day 3

Objective
- read words with suffixes *-less*, *-ion*, *-ness*.

Materials
- Anthology: *Wildfires*

SKILL FOCUS: STRUCTURAL ANALYSIS   25–30 MINUTES

Suffixes *-less*, *-ion*, *-ness*

Teach

Review that suffixes are word parts added to the ends of base words that add to or change the meaning of the words. The suffix *-less* means "without." The suffix *-ion* means "action or process of." The suffix *-ness* means "condition or quality of." Remind students that they can use their knowledge of suffixes to help them decode longer words. By removing the suffix and looking at the base word, they can often figure out what the longer word means.

Write the following sentences on the board and model how to decode words with suffixes: *Firefighters felt helpless as the fire approached the building. The firefighters felt a sense of helplessness as the fire came closer.* You may use the following Think Aloud to model for students:

Think Aloud

When I see the word helpless, *I recognize the suffix* -less. *I know that it means "without," so* helpless *means "without help." I know both* help *and* -less, *and it makes sense in the sentence. Now let me look at this longer word,* helplessness. *It has two suffixes,* -less *and* -ness. *But I can break it down in the same way. The firefighters felt the condition of being* without help, *or* helpless. *By knowing the suffixes, I could figure out the meaning of the word.*

Practice

Write the following sentence on the board and have students decode the underlined word: *Many forest fires are caused by carelessness.*

Apply

Give students the words below and have them use the suffixes *-less, -ion,* and *-ness* to make new words. They may use some words twice. Ask them to explain the meanings of the words they make.

vacate	fond	motion	taste
digest	donate	lonely	faith
ill	eager	construct	close
polite	rest	thoughtful	express

LITERATURE FOCUS: 10–15 MINUTES

Preview *Wildfires*

Guide students through the Comprehension Skill Lesson for **Topic, Main Idea, Supporting Details** on page 663 in the Teacher's Edition.

Day 4

Objectives

- identify adverbs that compare
- form adverbs that compare, using *-er, -est, more,* and *most*
- write sentences using adverbs that compare correctly

Materials

- Reader's Library: *Landslides*

Comparing with Adverbs

Teach

Remind students that adjectives are used to compare people, places, and things. Tell them that adverbs are also used to make comparisons. Explain that the ending *-er* is often added to short adverbs to compare two actions. Tell them to use *-est* to compare three or more actions.

Write the sentences below on the board, using the names of three volunteers. Have them demonstrate the actions.

> (Name A) walked fast. (one action)
>
> (Name B) walked faster than (Name A). (two actions)
>
> (Name C) walked fastest of all. (three or more actions)

Ask students to identify the adverbs in the sentences. (fast, faster, fastest) Point out that these adverbs compare how the volunteers walked. Explain that for most adverbs that end with *-ly,* you use *more* to compare two actions. Use *most* to compare three or more actions. Then change the adverbs in the sentences to *slowly, more slowly, most slowly.*

Read aloud the groups of sentences below. Have students form the adverb that best completes each sentence.

After the fire, parts of the forest _____ returned to life. (quickly)

Some parts returned _____ than others. (more quickly)

Which part returned _____ of all? (most quickly)

Practice

Ask students to identify the adverbs in sentences from the story. Have them name the comparative and superlative forms of each adverb.

Page 664 "Animals are <u>rarely</u> killed in forest fires." (more rarely, most rarely)

Page 672 "After a fire, burned areas <u>quickly</u> burst into life." (more quickly, most quickly)

Page 675 "The pink flowers of fireweed <u>soon</u> appeared." (sooner, soonest)

Apply

Tell students to write a comparison of three things. Have them include adverbs that compare in their writing. Ask them to read aloud their comparison. Encourage listeners to raise their hand whenever they hear an adverb that compares.

LITERATURE FOCUS: 10–15 MINUTES

Preview *Landslides*

Walk students through *Landslides*, and discuss illustrations using words such as *boulders, landslides, erosion,* and *geologists*.

Ask students to find the illustrations and photographs that best show the main idea of a selected paragraph.

Day 5

RETEACH

SKILL FOCUS: COMPREHENSION · 25_30 MINUTES

Topic, Main Idea, Supporting Details

Teach

Remind students that the *topic* is the subject about which the author is writing. The *main idea* is the most important idea that the writer wants readers to understand about the topic. *Supporting details* are pieces of information that explain or that tell more about the main idea. Supporting details may include facts and examples. Use a weather forecast to illustrate these concepts, for example:

Think Aloud

Think about a TV weather report on a nice day. The topic is the weather. The main idea is the weather is pleasant. Supporting details may include these facts: The sun is shining. The temperature is warm. There is a cool breeze.

Point out that in a longer piece of writing such as one paragraph (or a group of paragraphs) may have a topic, a main idea, and supporting details that explain this main idea. Have students reread the first paragraph of *Wildfires* on page 662. Then, model the concept using the Think Aloud.

Think Aloud

The topic is wildfires. *The main idea in the first paragraph is that* wildfires are frightening. *Sentences 2-4 provide details supporting the main idea.*

Have students reread paragraphs 3-5 on pages 662-664. Model the concept with the following Think Aloud:

Objective

• identify topics, main ideas, and supporting details.

Materials

• Anthology: *Wildfires*
• Reader's Library: *Landslides*

Think Aloud

The topic in these paragraphs is fire. *The main idea is stated in the first sentence:* Fire needs fuel, oxygen, and heat. *The other sentences in these paragraphs provide supporting details that explain this main idea.*

Practice

Point out that the topic of the entire selection is *wildfires*. Then explain that students are going to focus on passages that are one to three paragraphs long. Have them identify the topic, main idea, and supporting details within these shorter passages. You might include these excerpts: **paragraph 2, page 664** (Topic: forest fires; Main Idea: Some forest fires benefit plants and animals; Details: other information); **paragraph 3, page 664** (Topic: Fighting forest fires; Main Idea: This sometimes harms growth and increases risk; Details: other information); **paragraphs 1–3, page 672** (Topic: The Yellowstone Park Fire of 1988; Main Idea: Burned areas quickly recovered; Details: Facts about plant and animal life).

Apply

Have students repeat the process using other passages that are one to three paragraphs in length. You might consider pairing students who are having trouble with others who seem to have mastered the concept and its application.

Have students keep track of topic, main idea, and details, with an eye to identifying each of them, in the Reader's Library selection *Landslides* by Linda Hartley. Ask students to complete the questions and activity on the Responding page.

LITERATURE FOCUS: 10–15 MINUTES

Revisit *Wildfires* and *Landslides*

Review with students the process of identifying topic, main idea, and supporting details in *Wildfires* and *Landslides*. Also, help them to look for words with the suffixes *-ion, -ness,* and *-less,* such as *reaction, wilderness, carelessness, hopeless,* (*Wildfires*, pages 662, 664, 666, and 670) *erosion, action,* and *predictions* (*Landslides*, pages 26, 27, and 30).

Day 1

Skylark

Objectives

• read words with the root *graph* or *tract*
• use the Phonics/Decoding strategy to decode longer words

Materials

• Teaching Master ES6-5
• Practice Master ES6-5
• Anthology: *Skylark*

Get Set for Reading CD-ROM

Skylark

Education Place

www.eduplace.com
Skylark

Audiotape

Skylark
Audiotape for
Nature: Friend and Foe

Lexia Phonics CD-ROM

Intermediate Intervention

Word Roots *graph, tract*

Warm-Up/Academic Language

Tell students that **word roots** are **word parts** that **have meaning**, but can not always stand on their own. Explain that **knowing the meaning** of a word root can **help students read longer, unfamiliar words.** Point out that the **word root** *graph* **means "to write, draw, or record,"** and the **word root** *tract* **means "to pull."**

Teach

Write the word *photograph* on the board. Frame the word root *graph* and remind students that the root means "to write, draw, or record" by writing the meaning on the board.

Lead students to define *photograph* as an image recorded on film.

Follow a similar procedure for the word *tractor*. Remind students that the root *tract* means "to pull." Guide students to define *tractor* as a machine designed for pulling farm machinery.

Display a chart like the one shown. Work with students to fill out the chart. Identify and discuss the meaning of the new word formed in the third column by giving students context clues as well as helping them to use the meaning of each root and word part.

Root	+ Word Part = Longer Word	
graph	*para*	The sentences in the first paragraph are all written about the same main idea.
graph	*auto*	The author signed her autograph by writing her name on my book.
tract	*ex-*	The miners worked to extract the copper from deep in the ground.
tract	*re-*	I will retract my statement by apologizing and telling her I didn't mean what I said.

Provide additional words for the chart as time allows. Additional words might include, *graphics, geography, attract,* and *contract (v.)*.

Guided Practice

Display or **distribute** Teaching Master ES6-5, and read the passage with students.

Go over the illustrations to review the word roots and their meanings.

Help students to fill out the chart.

Discuss the meaning of each *graph* and *tract* word.

Practice/Apply

Distribute Practice Master ES6-5 to students and review the word roots and their meanings.

Explain the directions and tell students to complete the Practice Master independently.

Check all students' responses to be sure they can decode words with *graph* and *tract*.

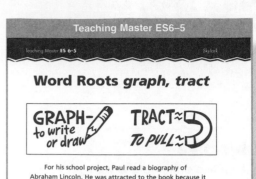

Teaching Master ES6–5

Teaching Master **ES 6-5**   *Skylark*

Word Roots *graph, tract*

GRAPH– to write or draw   TRACT≈ TO PULL≈

For his school project, Paul read a biography of Abraham Lincoln. He was attracted to the book because it was thin and had lots of pictures. But once Paul began to read it, nothing could distract him.

Then Paul made a poster to show what he had learned. He wrote several information-filled paragraphs. He extracted parts of Lincoln's speeches and letters. He traced Lincoln's autograph and made copies of photographs. Paul used computer graphics for the title and headings. It was the best project Paul had ever done.

graph	tract
biography	attracted
paragraphs	distract
autograph	extracted
photographs	
graphics	

TMES 6-5   Grade 4 Theme 6: Nature: Friend and Foe

Preview *Skylark* Segment 1

Refer to the bottom of page 689 in the Teacher's Edition and preview with students Segment 1 of *Skylark* (pages 688–695).

Note the suggestions in the Extra Support boxes on Teacher's Edition pages 690, 691, and 694.

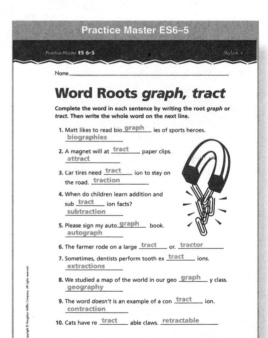

Practice Master ES6–5

Practice Master **ES 6-5**   *Skylark*

Name_____

Word Roots *graph, tract*

Complete the word in each sentence by writing the root *graph* or *tract*. Then write the whole word on the next line.

1. Matt likes to read bio <u>graph</u> ies of sports heroes.
   <u>biographies</u>

2. A magnet will at <u>tract</u> paper clips.
   <u>attract</u>

3. Car tires need <u>tract</u> ion to stay on the road. <u>traction</u>

4. When do children learn addition and sub <u>tract</u> ion facts?
   <u>subtraction</u>

5. Please sign my auto <u>graph</u> book.
   <u>autograph</u>

6. The farmer rode on a large <u>tract</u> or. <u>tractor</u>

7. Sometimes, dentists perform tooth ex <u>tract</u> ions.
   <u>extractions</u>

8. We studied a map of the world in our geo <u>graph</u> y class.
   <u>geography</u>

9. The word *doesn't* is an example of a con <u>tract</u> ion.
   <u>contraction</u>

10. Cats have re <u>tract</u> able claws. <u>retractable</u>

Grade 4 Theme 6: Nature: Friend and Foe   PMES 6-5

Day 2

Making Inferences

Objective

- combine story details with personal knowledge and experience to understand what characters are like

Materials

- Teaching Master ES6-6
- Practice Master ES6-6
- Anthology: *Skylark*

Warm-Up/Academic Language

Remind students that **writers do not always specifically state all the information** they expect readers to understand. Sometimes it is **up to readers to figure out story events** for themselves. Explain that readers **make inferences** by thinking about the **information the writer provides** and by using what they know from **their own experience.**

Teach

Read aloud the following passage to students:

Read Aloud

> Melinda checked the starting times. Then she called Grace. "Good news," Melinda said. "My mom said she'd drive us." The two girls got to the theater 10 minutes early. After buying their tickets, Melinda and Grace stopped at the snack bar. Melinda carried the popcorn while Grace carried the drinks. They found some good seats and settled in to watch the previews.

Guide students to complete a chart like the one shown on the next page. Tell students that they should use a combination of thinking about story details and their own personal experience to figure out a piece of information that the writer of the passage did not include. When students have completed the chart, point out that nowhere in the passage does it directly state that the girls are going to see a movie.

WHERE DID MELINDA AND GRACE GO?	HOW DO YOU KNOW?
to see a movie	**Details:** starting times in a newspaper, theater, tickets, snack bar, popcorn, watch previews
	Experience: This is what I do when I go to a movie.

Guided Practice

Display or **distribute** Teaching Master ES6-6 and read the passage with students.

Help students to suggest inferences that could be made from the passage and to identify the clues that helped them to make their inferences.

Practice/Apply

Distribute Practice Master ES6-6 to students and go over the directions with them.

Ask them to read the story and complete the Practice Master independently.

Check students' responses to make sure they can make inferences.

LITERATURE FOCUS: 10–15 MINUTES

Preview *Skylark* Segment 2

Refer to the bottom of page 696 in the Teacher's Edition and preview with students Segment 2 of *Skylark* (pages 696–703).

Note the suggestions in the Extra Support boxes on Teacher's Edition pages 699, and 702.

Teaching Master ES6–6

Teaching Master ES 6–6   *Skylark*

Making Inferences

Lauren and Rose were picnicking in a field, but soon a thunderstorm made them run for shelter. Rose suggested the girls stand under a nearby tree.

"No, no!" said Lauren. "Never get under a tree during a thunderstorm! Let's run for the car."

Suddenly, lightning flashed and a great BOOM shook them. Lauren pointed to the tree. Flames were shooting out of the branches. Rose's eyes opened wide. "You saved my life!" said Rose.

What can I infer?	How can I tell that?
Lauren knows more than Rose about storm safety.	Lauren knows that a car is safer than a tree.
Lightning struck the tree	Light and a boom; tree catches fire.
Rose feels amazed. She knows she could have been hurt.	Her eyes open wide when she sees the burning tree.
Rose feels grateful to Lauren	Rose says: "You saved my life." I would feel the same.

TMES 6–6   Grade 4   Theme 6: Nature: Friend and Foe

Practice Master ES6–6

Teaching Master ES 6–6   *Skylark*

Making Inferences

Lauren and Rose were picnicking in a field, but soon a thunderstorm made them run for shelter. Rose suggested the girls stand under a nearby tree.

"No, no!" said Lauren. "Never get under a tree during a thunderstorm! Let's run for the car."

Suddenly, lightning flashed and a great BOOM shook them. Lauren pointed to the tree. Flames were shooting out of the branches. Rose's eyes opened wide. "You saved my life!" said Rose.

What can I infer?	How can I tell that?
Lauren knows more than Rose about storm safety.	Lauren knows that a car is safer than a tree.
Lightning struck the tree	Light and a boom; tree catches fire.
Rose feels amazed. She knows she could have been hurt.	Her eyes open wide when she sees the burning tree.
Rose feels grateful to Lauren	Rose says: "You saved my life." I would feel the same.

TMES 6–6   Grade 4   Theme 6: Nature: Friend and Foe

Day 3

Objectives

- identify the root words *graph* and *tract*
- define the root words *graph* and *tract*

Materials

- Anthology: *Skylark*

Roots *graph, tract*

Teach

Challenge students to unscramble this mystery word on a piece of paper: *graph bio er.* Remind students that *-er* is a suffix, a word part added at the end of a word, and that *graph* is a root meaning "write." Offer a clue: This word means "someone who writes about other people's lives." Ask a volunteer to write the word on the board, and have students read it aloud.

Model decoding *extract* with the following Think Aloud: *The dentist will extract Paul's baby tooth.*

Think Aloud

I can see two word parts I know in this word. I know the prefix ex-, *and I recognize the root* tract. *If I put them together, I get* eks TRAKT. *Knowing what these word parts mean helps me decide that* extract *means "to pull out."*

Practice

Have students underline the root they recognize for each of the following words. Then, ask them to pronounce the word: *photograph, autograph, tractor, distract, paragraph.*

Apply

Write the word parts listed on the next page on the board and ask students to fill in either *graph* or *tract* to complete each word. Then have students give the meaning of each word they create.

bio_____y

auto_____

sub_____ion

geo_____y

dis_____ion

phono_____

photo_____

Review *Skylark*

Guide students through the Comprehension Skill Lesson for **Making Inferences** on page 691 in the Teacher's Edition.

Day 4

RETEACH

SKILL FOCUS: GRAMMAR   25–30 MINUTES

Objectives

- identify prepositions and prepositional phrases
- use prepositions and prepositional phrases in sentences

Materials

- Reader's Library: *Whiteout*
- index cards

Prepositions and Prepositional Phrases

Teach

Explain that prepositions show relationships between other words. Discuss the different relationships between *walked* and *mountain* in these sentences:

Amy walked <u>up</u> a mountain.

Amy walked <u>by</u> a mountain.

Review some of these common prepositions with students.

COMMON PREPOSITIONS

about	before	except	of	through
above	behind	for	off	to
across	below	from	on	under
after	beside	in	out	until
along	by	inside	outside	up
around	down	into	over	with
at	during	near	past	without

Point out that adverbs should not be confused with prepositions. Adverbs tell more about a verb. Prepositions are followed by an object that answers the question *Who?* or *What?*

Amy walked up. (adverb) *Amy walked up a mountain.* (preposition)

Explain that a preposition relates some other words in the sentence to the noun or the pronoun that follows the preposition. The noun or the pronoun that follows a preposition is the *object of the preposition*.

Miguel went to <u>the zoo</u>. (object of the preposition *to*)

Tell students that the preposition and its object form a *prepositional phrase: Tia's plane <u>flew above the city</u>*. Then, read aloud the sentences below. Have students write the preposition in each sentence on an index card and hold it up. Ask them to name the entire prepositional phrase.

Life on a prairie farm was hard. (on; on a prairie farm)

Coyotes roamed near the livestock. (near; near the livestock)

Strong storms swept over the land. (over; over the land)

Practice

Using a Think Aloud, model how to identify prepositions and prepositional phrases in the story. Have students look at the first sentence of the story on page 690.

Think Aloud

As I read this sentence, I see the word in. *I think* in *is a preposition, but I'll check to make sure. I look at the words that follow* in *and ask,* Do these words tell in whom or in what? *The words* the kitchen *tell what Sarah and the writer are in. So* in *must be a preposition. The words* in the kitchen *are the prepositional phrase.*

Have students continue with the rest of the paragraph.

Apply

Ask students to write a brief summary of *Skylark*. Have them use prepositional phrases in the sentences they write.

LITERATURE FOCUS: 10–15 MINUTES

Preview *Whiteout*

Walk students through *Whiteout* and discuss illustrations using words such as *blizzard, whiteout,* and *swelling*.

Ask students to identify illustrations from which they can make inferences about the character's feelings or story events.

Day 5

Objectives

- make inferences
- use personal experience and story clues to write a character study

Materials

- Anthology: *Skylark*
- Reader's Library: *Whiteout*

Making Inferences

Teach

Review inferences with students. Remind them that writers may intentionally leave information out of stories. They do this to make reading more fun and to get readers more involved in a story. Readers make a guess about an event or a character. They base their guess on personal knowledge and clues in the story. A guess based on this kind of information is called an *inference*. Use this example to illustrate how we use personal knowledge to make inferences in real life: *The teacher gives a written report back to my friend. My friend smiles. Without being told, I make the inference that my friend has received a good grade on the report.* Ask students to think of and share other examples.

Have students reread page 690 of *Skylark*. Then model how readers use story clues and personal knowledge to make inferences about characters and events in stories. Use the following Think Aloud.

Think Aloud

The story is set on the prairie. The weather is hot. I can infer from story clues that it is summer. Anna asks if Sarah remembers the wildflowers and the roses. Personal knowledge tells me flowers still should be blooming. Something, maybe lack of rainfall, must have killed them. Anna asks if Sarah remembers singing. I know that people sing when they are happy. I can infer from what Anna says and what I know that she and Sarah are sad.

Practice

Work through events in the story to have students make other inferences: A coyote comes into the yard in search of water (page 690). (Inference: Natural water sources must have dried up, or a wild animal would not do this.) Sarah says that the coyote wanted water, "just like us" (page 692). (Inference: It has not rained for a long time, and the family is worried about survival.) Anna does not call Sarah "mother" when speaking, but she refers to her as "mother" in the book (page 696). (Inference: Anna loves Sarah and thinks of her as her mother, but she is shy about saying so.)

Help students, as necessary, to use personal knowledge and story clues to make other inferences about plot events.

Apply

Have students write a character study of Sarah based on inferences. Tell them to use a word web to organize their ideas. They can write Sarah in the center of the web. On spokes radiating from the center circle, they should write traits and evidence that support their inferences. Some examples might include *touching Anna's hair—affectionate* (page 690); *concern for the coyote—gentle* (page 692); *dancing at the party—fun-loving* (page 695); *saving the cows from the fire—brave* (page 700).

Have students share how they used personal knowledge and story clues to make inferences about Sarah's character.

Have students keep track of inferences, with an eye to understanding character and events, in the Reader's Library selection *Whiteout* by Kay Livorse. Ask students to complete the questions and activity on the Responding page.

LITERATURE FOCUS: 10–15 MINUTES

Revisit *Skylark* and *Whiteout*

Review with students the process for making inferences about characters' feelings in *Skylark* and *Whiteout*. Also, help them to look for words with the roots *graph* and *tract*, such as *phonograph*, and *photograph* (*Skylark*, page 695).

Base Words and Endings
-er and *-est*

The Greatest Dog in Town

Our dog Rex is the greatest dog in town. He's braver than any other dog. He's also noisier than any dog! He gets hungrier and thirstier than any of our friends' dogs. He's got the wettest nose and the sharpest ears in the neighborhood. High fives for Rex! No, wait a minute — highest fives for Rex!

Copyright © Houghton Mifflin Company. All rights reserved.

Name_____

Base Words and Endings
-er and *-est*

Write a sentence using each of the numbered words.

1. loud
2. louder
3. loudest

_____
_____
_____
_____
_____
_____

1. strong
2. stronger
3. strongest

_____
_____
_____
_____
_____
_____

1. silly
2. sillier
3. silliest

_____
_____
_____
_____

Copyright © Houghton Mifflin Company. All rights reserved.

Story Structure

Characters   ### Setting

Harry   Dog   Florida yard

Harry lived in Florida. One hot day, an old dog with a limp showed up in his yard. The dog panted and whined. It fell over onto the grass.

"I can't take you home or to a vet," said Harry, "but I can give you a bowl of water."

That was all the dog needed. When it finished drinking, it got up and walked away.

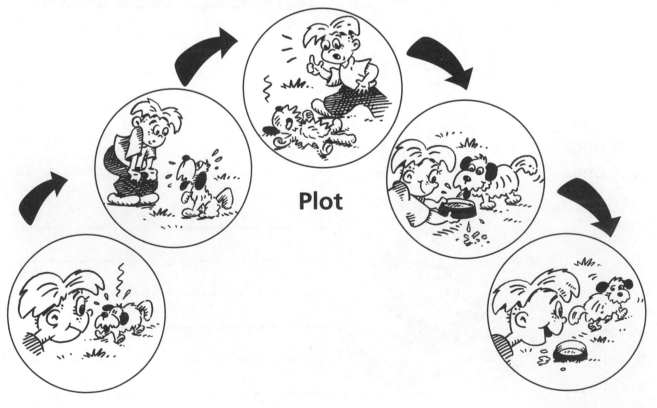

Plot

Copyright © Houghton Mifflin Company. All rights reserved.

Name_____

Story Structure

Read the following story and then fill in the missing information.

Kim lives in New York City with her dog, Herb. One day, she was bouncing a ball when suddenly it disappeared. She looked everywhere for it. All of a sudden, Herb appeared with the ball in his mouth, wagging his tail. "I guess you want to play," said Kim. Herb barked. So Kim and Herb had a game of fetch until they both got too tired to play anymore.

Characters: _____   **Setting:** _____

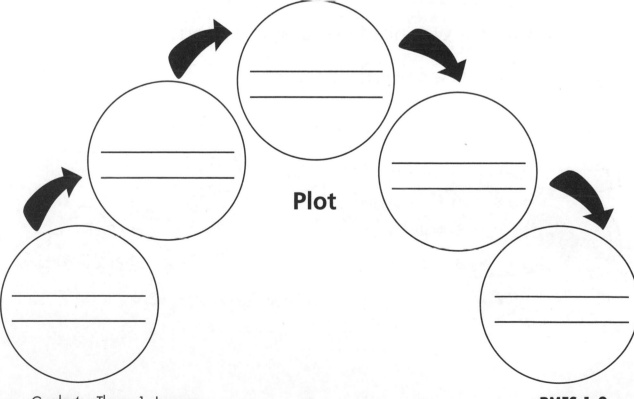

Plot

Copyright © Houghton Mifflin Company. All rights reserved.

Suffixes *-ly* and *-y*

My First Airplane Ride

Last week I had my first airplane ride. As my sister and I waited to take off, my heart beat **nervous**. The plane raced down the runway. I held on **tight** to my sister. I couldn't believe how **quick** we were moving! After take off, I **real** was glad that it wasn't too **cloud** to see the tiny cars below. By the time lunch was served, I was **bare** nervous anymore. I stared out the window so **eager** that I **hard** ate. Just when I thought I beat my fear of flying, the ride got **awful bump**. The pilot said **cheerful** that it was nothing to worry about. I'm **certain** glad that it was a smooth landing!

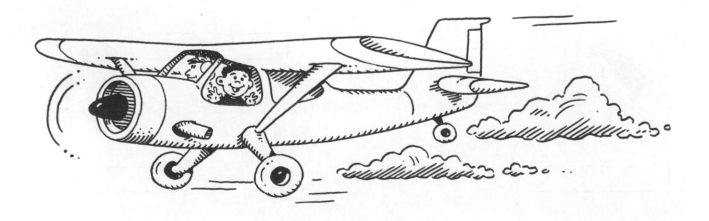

Copyright © Houghton Mifflin Company. All rights reserved.

Name_____

Suffixes *-ly* and *-y*

Read the base words in the box. For each of the sentences shown, choose a base word and *-ly* or *-y* to form a word that best fits in the blank space.

itch	happy	slow	nervous	rain
sleep	friend	loud	bright	

1. When my Uncle Lenny asked me if I wanted to go camping, I _____ said yes.

2. The ride went so _____ that I got bored.

3. Soon I was so _____ that I fell asleep and had a dream.

4. In my dream, Uncle Lenny and I went on a hike, but had to turn back because it was so _____.

5. I brushed against some poison ivy and got all _____ around my ankles.

6. Still dreaming, I heard a cranky bear roar _____.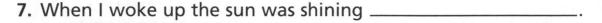

7. When I woke up the sun was shining _____.

8. My uncle looked at me and said in a _____ way, "Are you ready to put up the tent?"

9. "Uncle Lenny," I said _____. "Tell me something. There aren't any *bears* around here, are there?"

Copyright © Houghton Mifflin Company. All rights reserved.

Author's Viewpoint

The Visit, Part 1

Yuck! My cousin Heidi is spending the whole month with us. I just know Mom will make me take her everywhere. She'll embarrass me in front of my friends. Last year when she visited she touched all my stuff and lost one of my CDs. And all those dumb questions she asked! She's only two years younger than I am — but two years make a big difference! To make matters worse, last night Mom asked me if I'd share my room with Heidi. What could I say? Of course I had to say yes.

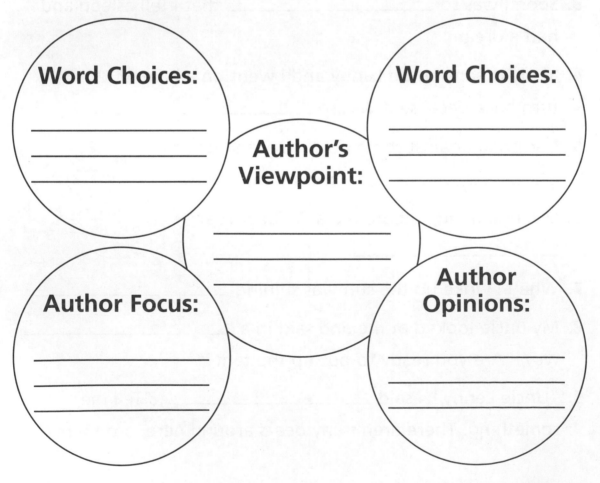

Copyright © Houghton Mifflin Company. All rights reserved.

Name_____

Author's Viewpoint

The Visit, Part 2

Read the story and complete the web with details that support the author's viewpoint.

It's Heidi's first night here, and she's sad. "I miss my friends and my cat," she said. I didn't know what to say. I began to feel sorry for her. Suddenly, I got an idea. I left and returned with Zoe, my cat. I held some string and Zoe jumped up to grab it. Heidi giggled. She said we should teach Zoe to fetch like her cat back home. Soon, Zoe was learning a new trick! Maybe Heidi's visit wouldn't be so bad after all. I guess people can change.

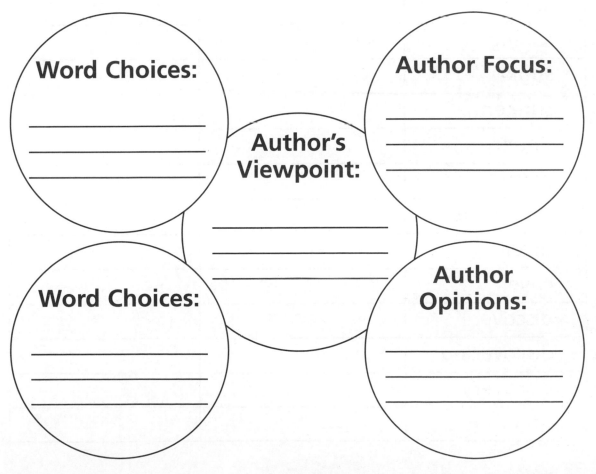

Copyright © Houghton Mifflin Company. All rights reserved.

Syllabication

Word	Syllables	Number of Syllables
sail	sail	
sailing	sail/ing	
sunk		
sunken		
under		
water		
underwater		
diver		
cover		
discover		
discovering		
discovery		
ocean		

Copyright © Houghton Mifflin Company. All rights reserved.

Name _____

Syllabication

Divide the words below into syllables, and write them on the lines.

Example: boating = ___boat / ing___

1. wreckage = _____

2. passage = _____

3. passenger = _____

4. floated = _____

5. steering = _____

6. sinkable = _____

7. unsinkable = _____

8. iceberg = _____

For each word below, write the number of vowel sounds in the word, then write the number of syllables.

Example: thunder: vowel sounds __2__ / syllables __2__

1. **swimming:** vowel sounds ____ / syllables ____

2. **diving:** vowel sounds ____ / syllables ____

3. **beneath:** vowel sounds ____ / syllables ____

4. **seashore:** vowel sounds ____ / syllables ____

5. **disaster:** vowel sounds ____ / syllables ____

6. **overboard:** vowel sounds ____ / syllables ____

7. **voyager:** vowel sounds ____ / syllables ____

8. **depart:** vowel sounds ____ / syllables ____

Copyright © Houghton Mifflin Company. All rights reserved.

Text Organization

Special Features	Description
	Tell what the text is about
	A set of main ideas and supporting details
	Tell you what each section is about by breaking the text up into smaller parts
	Present information from the text in a visual way
	Describe an illustration with one or two words
	A longer description of a photo or illustration; may be one or more sentences
	Present extra, interesting information about the text; are often on the side of the main text

Copyright © Houghton Mifflin Company. All rights reserved.

Name_____

Text Organization

Read the text below and then write a short journal entry for the next day of the boat trip. Use a heading, text, an illustration, and a caption.

My Sailing Journal

the steering wheel

the anchor

Friday: And we're off!

My friend Sasha's dad has his own sailboat. Today we're all leaving for a three-day sailing trip. I've never slept on a boat before. There's not much room but it's cozy on the boat. The radio says that we can expect great weather. I can't wait to do some star-gazing later tonight.

Saturday: Rough seas!

The weather report was wrong! Today we sailed through a scary storm. Sasha's dad told us to put our life jackets on and stay in the cabin. I was worried that I'd get sick! Luckily, the storm passed quickly. By the time we returned upstairs, the sun was out and there was a big rainbow.

_____

_____

_____

_____

_____

Copyright © Houghton Mifflin Company. All rights reserved.

Word Roots *tele* and *rupt*

tele = "over a distance" rupt = "break"

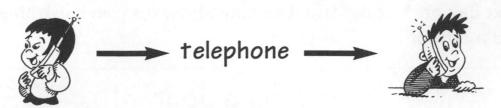

1. telephone = a machine that carries sound from far away

2. television = _____

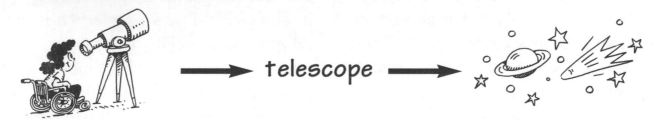

3. telescope = _____

4. interrupt = _____

_____

5. erupt = _____

_____

Copyright © Houghton Mifflin Company. All rights reserved.

Name _____

Word Roots *tele* and *rupt*

Below is a list of *tele* and *rupt* words. Choose the word which makes the most sense and write it in the blank spaces provided.

television	telephone	interrupt
telescope	disrupt	erupt

1. Even though my friend Alex moved far away, we still talk on the _____.

2. An astronomer uses a _____ to view stars that are millions of miles away.

3. Watching the volcano _____ was like seeing its top explode.

4. My sister complains that I always _____ her when she speaks.

5. I won't throw the paper airplane because it will

   _____

   the class.

6. The thing I like best about watching the news on _____ is that I can see what is happening in far away places.

Copyright © Houghton Mifflin Company. All rights reserved.

Noting Details

- A detail can give important information which explains an idea, or tells about a character's feelings.

- A detail can give less important information for background or just to set the scene.

Detail 1: I am so upset with my sister Rosa today!

Detail 2: Her snoring kept me awake last night, and today I am tired.

Detail 3: I overslept and will be late for school!

Detail 4: We are having cereal and juice for breakfast.

Detail 5: I am not speaking to Rosa this morning.

Detail 6: I am wearing a blue sweater today.

Detail	Is the detail important?	Why or why not?
1		
2		
3		
4		
5		
6		

Copyright © Houghton Mifflin Company. All rights reserved.

Name_____

Noting Details

Read the story and fill in the charts below.

      Later that day, when Mrs. Keating called on me, I was so tired from not sleeping last night that I didn't even answer! At recess, the kids played kickball. I sat down to rest with my friend Mark under the big oak tree. It was a cool, sunny day. The leaves were turning orange. Mark told me the story of a movie he saw but I fell asleep. "Sara!" shouted Mark. "Wake up! You slept through the best part of the story!" I said I was sorry. Then we all went inside.

Important Detail # 1	
Important Detail # 2	
Important Detail # 3	

Background Detail # 1	
Background Detail # 2	
Background Detail # 3	

Copyright © Houghton Mifflin Company. All rights reserved.

Contractions

In a contraction, the apostrophe is a mark that stands for a missing letter or letters.

1. I <u>could not</u> believe it!   I <u>couldn't</u> believe it!
2. <u>It is</u> fun to learn the piano.   <u>It's</u> fun to learn the piano.
3. I <u>did not</u> understand.   I <u>didn't</u> understand.
4. <u>That is</u> so cool!   <u>That's</u> so cool!
5. <u>What is</u> wrong?   <u>What's</u> wrong?

6. We <u>should not</u> do that. _____

7. I <u>was not</u> talking. _____

8. I <u>have not</u> asked. _____

9. <u>I am</u> almost ready _____

10. <u>We are</u> going to school _____

Copyright © Houghton Mifflin Company. All rights reserved.

Name_____

Contractions

Read the sentences below. Write the contraction form of the underlined words.

Example: We <u>were not</u> in a hurry.   weren't _____

1. We <u>would not</u> make it in time. _____

2. <u>It is</u> too cold to go swimming. _____

3. <u>We are</u> going to the mall. _____

4. That <u>is not</u> the correct answer. _____

5. <u>He will</u> be five minutes late. _____

6. Please <u>do not</u> do that. _____

Read the sentences below. Each contraction is underlined. Write out the full words for each contraction.

Example: <u>It's</u> no problem.   It is _____

7. <u>He's</u> my best friend. _____

8. She <u>doesn't</u> know the way. _____

9. Bonnie <u>couldn't</u> find her keys. _____

10. <u>I'm</u> so hungry! _____

11. We <u>aren't</u> interested. _____

12. <u>I've</u> got five dollars. _____

Copyright © Houghton Mifflin Company. All rights reserved.

Sequence of Events

Signal words are clues that can tell you when events
occur in the story.

finally	while	first	once	meanwhile	later	next
when	after	earlier	as	afterward	during	before

"Before" words	"During" words	"After" words
_____	_____	_____
_____	_____	_____
_____	_____	_____
_____	_____	_____
_____	_____	_____
_____	_____	_____
	_____	

Copyright © Houghton Mifflin Company. All rights reserved.

Name_____

Sequence of Events

Below are a group of signal words. Insert the correct ones in the sentences below.

later	before	during	next	as
afterwards	after	first	finally	earlier

1. _____ in the summer, Carlos and his best friend Brian had decided to start a club.

2. _____ they could start the club, they had to do some planning.

3. "_____, we need to decide what our club will be about," said Carlos.

4. "_____ we'll need to choose a place to meet," said Brian.

5. "And _____ that, we'll need to think of a cool name for our club," replied Carlos.

6. _____ the boys began to work, word about the club spread around the neighborhood.

7. _____ their time planning and building the club, the boys had fun.

8. _____ that month, Carlos and Brian held their first meeting.

9. _____ the two boys said they couldn't believe how many people came to join.

10. "Now we're _____ a real club!" said Brian.

Copyright © Houghton Mifflin Company. All rights reserved.

Word Roots
sign and *spect*

> ***sign*** = a sign or mark   ***spect*** = to look at

On our way to Aunt Beatrice's house for a visit, I saw a big sign for a circus.

"Can we please stop, Dad?" I asked, respectfully.

"Sure," answered Dad. We entered a big tent. There were big, bright designs on the sides of the tent. The seats were full of spectators. Mom put on her spectacles to get a better look. My sister said she suspected the show would have acrobats. "Why do you think so?" I asked her. "Because I inspected the sign very carefully," she said. Just then the lights began to blink on and off, signaling that the show was about to begin. I knew it would be spectacular.

Spect	*Sign*
_____	_____
_____	_____
_____	_____

Copyright © Houghton Mifflin Company. All rights reserved.

Name_____

Word Roots
sign and *spect*

Choose the correct words from the box below and fill in the
blanks for each picture and definition.

spectrum	inspect	design	spectator
spectacle	resign	signal	signature

1. _____ =  = a drawing or pattern

2. _____ = = an amazing show

3. _____ =  = to give up or quit
a job

4. _____ =  = a person's hand-
written name

5. _____ = = to examine closely

6. _____ = = something that gives
information such as a
command or warning

7. _____ = = to watch something

8. _____ = = the full range of colors

Copyright © Houghton Mifflin Company. All rights reserved.

Making Inferences

Story Detail:	Own Experience:	I Can Infer That:
Before leaving for camp, Sean gave his dog Boomer a hug. "Make sure when you walk him, you hold on to the leash tightly," Sean told his mom.	_____ _____ _____ _____ _____ _____ _____ _____	_____ _____ _____ _____ _____ _____ _____
Later, Sean got a letter from home. "Boomer is doing well, but he misses you. I hold on tightly when I walk him, just like you said."	_____ _____ _____ _____ _____ _____	_____ _____ _____ _____ _____

Copyright © Houghton Mifflin Company. All rights reserved.

Name_____

Making Inferences

Read the passage in the first column, and fill out the second and third columns. Give reasons for your answers.

Story Detail:	I would feel:	Sean feels:
On his first day at camp, Sean didn't know anyone. He had no one to talk to or sit with at lunch.	_____ Reason: _____ _____ _____ _____ _____	_____ Reason: _____ _____ _____ _____ _____
After lunch the children went for a hike. Sean's hiking partner was Anthony. He was friendly. They were in the same cabin, too.	_____ Reason: _____ _____ _____ _____ _____	_____ Reason: _____ _____ _____ _____ _____
The boys heard a sound and froze. A moose stepped in front of them. Sean stared and said, "Wow."	_____ Reason: _____ _____ _____ _____	_____ Reason: _____ _____ _____ _____

Copyright © Houghton Mifflin Company. All rights reserved.

Suffixes *-er, -or,* and *-ist*

-er
-or } someone who
-ist

1. Anya <u>survived</u> the shipwreck.   Anya is a <u>survivor</u>.

2. Zack <u>plays</u> the guitar.   Zack is a <u>guitarist</u>.

3. Eric <u>acts</u> in plays.   Eric is an <u>actor</u>.

4. Dennis <u>writes</u> the plays.   Dennis is a <u>writer</u>.

5. Marika <u>inspects</u> buildings.   Marika is a
                                                           building <u>inspector</u>.

6. Mohammed is someone who practices <u>science</u>.
   Mohammed is a _____.

7. James is someone who <u>designs</u> magazines.
   James is a magazine _____.

8. Anne is someone who <u>reports</u> for a newspaper.
   Anne is a newspaper _____.

9. Trisha is someone who <u>operates</u> a telephone.
   Trisha is a telephone _____.

Copyright © Houghton Mifflin Company. All rights reserved.

Copyright © Houghton Mifflin Company. All rights reserved.

Name_____

Suffixes *-er, -or,* and *-ist*

Complete the chart below using the *-er, -or,* and *-ist* endings.

Someone who...		...is called a(n)
1. runs		_____
2. teaches		_____
3. makes art		_____
4. sails		_____
5. drives		_____
6. plays piano		_____
7. swims		_____
8. directs a movie		_____

Making Generalizations

A generalization is a statement that is true most of the time. It often uses words such as *all, few, often, some, rarely, never, always, many,* or *most.*

     A tropical rain forest is a forest of tall trees that gets a lot of rain. Some rain forests get over 250 inches of rain in one year! Rain forests are always warm. The temperature rarely goes over 93 degrees or drops below 68 degrees. Rain forests remain green all year long. The tallest trees block out much of the light below. Most rain forests are near the equator. Tropical rain forests have more species, or types, of plants and animals in them than any other places in the world.

Question: *What are most rain forests like?*

Details	Generalization
_____	_____
_____	_____
_____	_____
_____	_____

Copyright © Houghton Mifflin Company. All rights reserved.

Making Generalizations

Read the paragraph and fill out the generalization chart below.

Many tropical rain forests are in danger. They may be cut down by people who want to use the land for farming, mining, or building. In some countries, there are now so many people, that they need more land for cities. In other places, people cut down the forests for the wood from the trees.

Question: *Why are rain forests in danger?*

Details	Generalization
_____	_____
_____	_____
_____	_____
_____	_____
_____	_____
_____	_____
_____	_____

Copyright © Houghton Mifflin Company. All rights reserved.

Possessives

Have you seen a blue hat? It's my sister's hat. Its brim is very wide. She needs it back because she's going to Norway next week and Norway's weather is very cold.

Do you have my son's glasses? I think he left them here last week. Or was it at the doctor's office? Oh, dear. Now I can't remember. He might have left them in his father's car, too.

Where is my hamster, Denny? He used to be my friend Marc's but he gave Denny to Lisa. Lisa's cat almost ate him, so her Dad said to give Denny to her cousins. Denny had a rough time at the cousins' house. They fought over him, so they gave him to me.

Lost and Found

Copyright © Houghton Mifflin Company. All rights reserved.

Name_____

Possessives

Rewrite each of the following sentences using a possessive.

1. That scooter belongs to John.

   _____

2. Hey, there goes the dog that belongs to Terry.

   _____

3. That store is owned by the Goldmans.

   _____

4. The food that Mae-lin cooks is the best.

   _____

Rewrite these sentences without using a possessive.

5. The dog's collar is too tight.

   _____

6. Have you seen Melody's pictures?

   _____

7. Martha's horse is beautiful.

   _____

8. My family's home has many plants.

   _____

Copyright © Houghton Mifflin Company. All rights reserved.

Categorize and Classify

My name is Elaine. I have so many cousins! Will you help me keep track of them? My cousins Robbie and Ricky live in Florida. My cousins Katie, Richard, and Joshua live in California. My cousin Beth lives in Canada. My cousins Leo, Hannah, and Dan live in Vermont. Finally, my cousins Connie and Rona live in New York.

Who Lives Where?

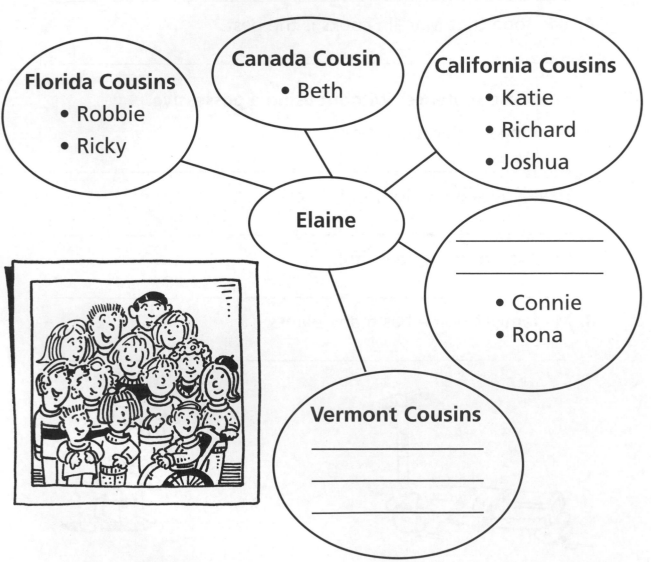

Florida Cousins
- Robbie
- Ricky

Canada Cousin
- Beth

California Cousins
- Katie
- Richard
- Joshua

Elaine

_____
_____
- Connie
- Rona

Vermont Cousins
_____
_____
_____

Copyright © Houghton Mifflin Company. All rights reserved.

Name_____

Categorize and Classify

Read about Cheryl's activities. Answer the questions below.

Monday: school drama club, do homework, family dinner
Tuesday: school soccer practice, family dinner
Wednesday: homework, family dinner, play on computer
Thursday: school soccer practice, homework, family dinner
Friday: homework, family dinner
Saturday: see movie with friends, family dinner, do some drawings, watch TV with sister
Sunday: visit grandmother with family, roller-skate in park with friends, family dinner

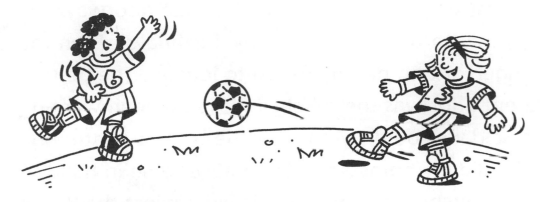

1. What are things Cheryl does for school?

_____

_____

2. What are things Cheryl does for fun during her free time?

_____

_____

3. What are things Cheryl does with her family?

_____

_____

Copyright © Houghton Mifflin Company. All rights reserved.

Compound Words

Last Saturday was my birthday! My family took me
to a cool restaurant downtown. After the meal, my dad
whispered something in the waiter's ear. Soon, a giant
cake was wheeled out from the kitchen doorway.
Everyone started to sing "Happy Birthday." Even the
strangers sitting nearby began to join in. The best
present I got was the baseball glove I'd been wanting.
Dad said we could try it out in the backyard later on —
after I did my homework. That glove came in handy for
the double-header my team played against the Ravens
later that week!

1. _____   6. _____

2. _____   7. _____

3. _____   8. _____

4. _____   9. _____

5. _____   10. _____

Copyright © Houghton Mifflin Company. All rights reserved.

Name_____

Compound Words

Pick a word from the box and write it on the line to complete the compound words in the sentences.

down	step	yard	pack	drive
thing	side	shoe	way	good

1. Simon walked down the hall_____.

2. He paused by the window to tie his _____lace.

3. He could hear his father singing out _____.

4. His father was busy doing some _____work.

5. He made a funny face at Simon from the _____way.

6. Simon laughed and went _____stairs.

7. Simon smiled and greeted his _____mother.

8. Simon ate his cereal and kissed her _____-bye.

9. Just as he shut the door, he felt like he had forgotten some_____.

10. "My back_____!" he remembered and raced back to his room.

Copyright © Houghton Mifflin Company. All rights reserved.

Noting Details

Yesterday Jean was walking home from school, humming quietly. It was a bright, chilly day. Suddenly, a little dog came up to her. "Follow me," he said, in a strange, low voice. Jean couldn't believe it! Was this dog really talking to her? Just then a cloud passed by the sun, making it colder and darker. Jean didn't know what to do.

"Well, what are you waiting for?" said the dog. "We've got things to see!"

The dog started walking away. "Am I going to let a little dog boss me around?" Jean asked herself. But, before she knew it, she was racing to catch up to him!

Most Important Details	Why Important?
_____	_____
_____	_____
_____	_____

Copyright © Houghton Mifflin Company. All rights reserved.

Name_____

Noting Details

Read the story below and fill in the web with the most important details about the story setting.

Soon Jean caught up to the little dog in front of a big white house. Behind the house was a leafy yard blooming with bright, colorful flowers. "Follow me," said the dog. He led Jean into what looked like a tiny doghouse.

She couldn't believe her eyes. The doghouse was as big as a palace inside! A small train rolled by on some tracks. The dog climbed onto the train and said, "Hop in! So, do you like the place?"

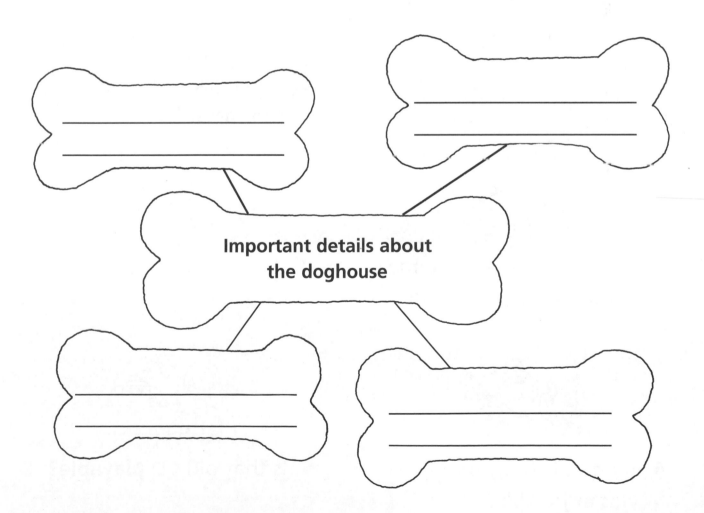

Important details about the doghouse

Copyright © Houghton Mifflin Company. All rights reserved.

Words with the Suffix *-able*

1. Glass vases are **breakable**.

5. Leslie's new puppy is **lovable**.

2. Kay's dress is **washable**.

6. Dominick tried to get **comfortable**.

3. My father gave me some **valuable** baseball cards.

7. Tyrone's riddle is not **solvable**.

4. Juan's birthday party was **enjoyable**.

8. Is that old CD **playable**?

Copyright © Houghton Mifflin Company. All rights reserved.

Copyright © Houghton Mifflin Company. All rights reserved.

Name _____

Words with the Suffix *-able*

Fill in each blank with the word that completes the definition for the bolded word above it.

1. The fireworks were **viewable** from our front porch.

   The fireworks were able to be _____

   from the porch.

2. The animal doctor said that my cat Nico is **curable**.

   Nico is able to be _____.

3. Sonia is **reachable** by email.

   Sonia is able to be _____.

4. Maura's home-cooked meal was very **enjoyable**.

   Maura's meal was able to be _____.

5. At first mom didn't think my story was **believable**.

   Mom didn't think the story was able to be _____.

6. Mia's handwriting is hardly **readable**.

   Mia's handwriting is not able to be _____.

7. The CD had so many scratches that it was not **playable**.

   The CD was not able to be _____.

8. Judy talked so quietly during her speech that it was not **understandable**.

   Judy's speech was not able to be _____.

Compare and Contrast

1. Both Tyler and Jess have pets, but Tyler has a cat and
Jess has a dog.

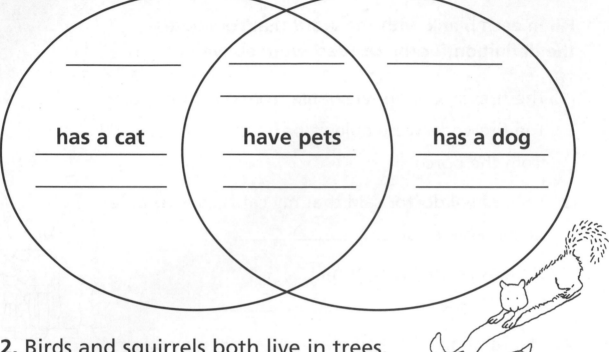

has a cat   have pets   has a dog

2. Birds and squirrels both live in trees,
but birds can fly and squirrels can't.

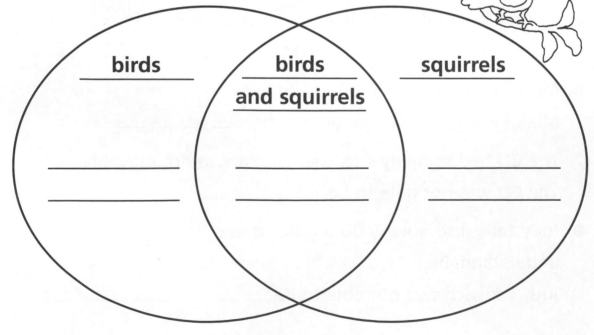

birds   birds
and squirrels   squirrels

Copyright © Houghton Mifflin Company. All rights reserved.

Name_____

Compare and Contrast

The story below compares and contrasts two students. Complete the diagram so that it tells how the two children are alike and how they are different.

Derek and Erin both like sports, but Derek likes soccer and Erin likes basketball. They go to the same school, but Erin is in Ms. Talbot's class, and Derek is in Mr. Alvarez's class. They both like school, but Erin enjoys reading the most and Derek likes math the most.

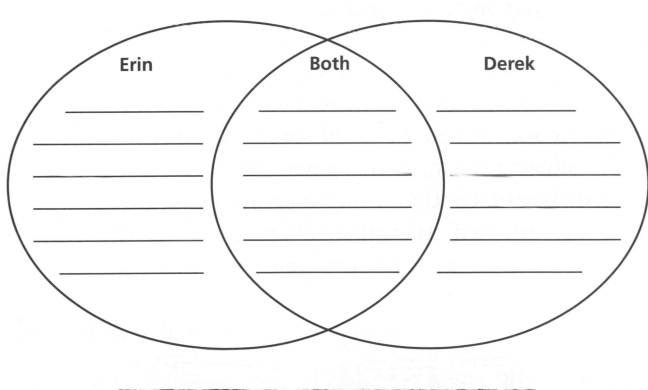

Erin   Both   Derek

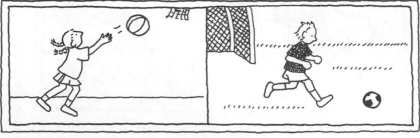

Copyright © Houghton Mifflin Company. All rights reserved.

Words with *-ed* and *-ing*

1. My mom and dad are grocery (shopped, shopping) right now.

   My mom and dad (shopped, shopping) for a new radio last weekend.

2. Last Thanksgiving, my grandmother (baked, baking) bread.

   My grandmother is (baked, baking) a cake for my sister's birthday.

3. Are you (wrapped, wrapping) the gifts?

   Who (wrapped, wrapping) the gifts?

4. Sophie (cleaned, cleaning) her room earlier.

   Sophie is (clean, cleaning) her room now.

5. I (danced, dancing) with Bianca at the party.

   I am (danced, dancing) with Bianca.

6. This winter, we are (vacationed, vacationing) in Bermuda.

   Last summer, we (vacationed, vacationing) in Paris.

Last summer in Paris

This winter in Bermuda

Copyright © Houghton Mifflin Company. All rights reserved.

Name_____

Words with -ed or -ing

Write the base word for each of the following words.
Then use the word with *-ed* or *-ing* in a short sentence.

1. hopped

Base word: _____

_____

2. racing

Base word: _____

_____

3. laughing

Base word: _____

_____

4. pulled

Base word: _____

_____

5. saving

Base word: _____

_____

6. dragging

Base word: _____

_____

7. scored

Base word: _____

_____

8. mixed

Base word: _____

_____

Copyright © Houghton Mifflin Company. All rights reserved.

Fantasy and Realism

1. The corn grew until it was taller than I was. **Realism**
   The corn grew taller than a skyscraper. **Fantasy**

2. It was so cold that the cows were giving ice cream instead of milk. _____
   It was cold, but we went to the barn and milked the cows anyway. _____

3. The farmer down the road wasn't very friendly.
   _____

   The farmer down the road was so mean, he once stopped a tornado just by yelling at it. _____

4. The tomatoes we put on our sandwiches were so juicy that they made the bread soggy. _____
   We had to wear raincoats to eat our tomatoes because they squirted so much juice. _____

5. The dog growled and said, "Don't even think about petting me right now!" _____
   The look on the dog's face told me not to pet her.

   _____

Copyright © Houghton Mifflin Company. All rights reserved.

Name_____

Fantasy and Realism

Tell whether each of the short passages below uses fantasy or realism. Give a reason for your answer.

1. When I got up this morning, I went into the bathroom. I looked into the mirror and said, "Boy, am I tired!"

   "Better wake up!" my reflection replied. "You've got a long day ahead."

   Fantasy or realism? _____

   Why? _____

2. I was trying to watch a video, but my brother wouldn't stop talking. So I pointed the remote control at him and pressed "pause." He froze. Finally, I watched the movie in peace.

   Fantasy or realism? _____

   Why? _____

Copyright © Houghton Mifflin Company. All rights reserved.

Suffix *-ible*

Question: Are you able to make sense of the plan?

Answer: Yes, the plan seems *sensible*.

Q: Are you able to bend this wire?

A: Yes, the wire is flexible.

Q: Are we permitted to whisper?

A: Yes, whispering is permissible.

Q: Can we divide this number by two?

A: Yes, it is divisible by two.

Q: Are you able to see to the bottom?

A: Yes, the bottom is visible.

Q: Can you believe what you are hearing?

A: No, it's too incredible*!*

Copyright © Houghton Mifflin Company. All rights reserved.

Name_____

Suffix *-ible*

Write the meaning of each bolded word in the blank.

Example:

What are the **permissible** moves in this game? _____able to be done_____

1. That old banana is not **edible**. _____

2. The plan seems **possible**. _____

3. If it wasn't so cloudy, the stars would be **visible**.

   _____

4. Her story was too odd to be **credible**. _____

Add *-ible* to the base word in bold. Write the new word on the line.

Example:

Most umbrellas are _____collapsible_____. **collapse**

1. That movie was really _____. **terror**

2. The sports car has a _____ roof. **convert**

3. A _____ jacket can be worn inside out. **reverse**

4. We chose a useful and _____ gift. **sense**

Copyright © Houghton Mifflin Company. All rights reserved.

Predicting Outcomes

Tonya's Clumsy Day

Tonya was telling Grandma about all the things that had gone wrong that day.

Tonya said, "I was talking to my friends and I didn't see the big mud puddle. I slipped and fell right into it. At lunch, I didn't realize that my usual table had been moved. I placed my lunch where the table should have been and it dropped on the floor."

"You just need to be more careful and pay attention," suggested Grandma.

"I guess so!" said Tonya. She bent down to pull out a carton of juice from the refrigerator. With her other hand, she felt around the countertop for a glass.

Prediction:

_____

_____

_____

Copyright © Houghton Mifflin Company. All rights reserved.

Name_____

Predicting Outcomes

Read the story about the two brothers.
Then answer the questions below.

Brian and his younger brother Roy were playing outside. "Look out!" Brian shouted suddenly. "There's a spider on your shoulder!"

Roy screamed. "Where? Where? Oooh, get it off!"

Brian began laughing. "Just kidding," he said.

Then Brian shouted again. "Look out! A spider is on your leg!"

Roy cried, "Where is it?"

Brian laughed. "Just kidding," he said.

Later, the boys were going inside. "Look out!" Brian shouted. "A spider is hanging in the doorway!"

1. What do you think will happen next? Write what Roy will say and do. _____

_____

_____

2. What helped you make that prediction?

_____

_____

_____

Copyright © Houghton Mifflin Company. All rights reserved.

Prefixes *re-, mis-, ex-*

Bess: Your story was exciting! I liked the part where the robot made the ship explode. I didn't expect that to happen.

Phil: Are there any parts I should rewrite?

Bess: You repeated the word *very* in these sentences. Maybe you should replace one or two.

Phil: OK. I'll revise this part. Did you misunderstand any parts? Are there any misspelled words?

Bess: I didn't see any other mistakes. It's a great story. I'd like to reread it.

Copyright © Houghton Mifflin Company. All rights reserved.

Name_____

Prefixes *re-, mis-, ex-*

Read each sentence. Find the word in the box that has the same meaning as the **bolded** word or words. Write the word on the line.

review	misprint	extreme
retold	except	misbehave

Let me **explain** my **mistake**, and **redo** the job.

1. The book has a **printing mistake** on page 2. _____

2. Everyone is here **but** Kerry. _____

3. Please **look again** at your notes. _____

4. Even a trained dog may **behave badly**. _____

5. The tale was **told again** by a new storyteller. _____

6. Polar bears stay warm in the **very great** cold. _____

Underline the word that fits in the sentence. Write it on the line.

1. What is the _____ amount? (exact, react)

2. Mom _____ her glasses and can't find them. (misplaced, replaced)

3. Think back to _____ the events. (miscall, recall)

4. Try not to _____ the radio. (excuse, misuse)

Grade 4   Theme 4: Problem Solvers   **PMES 4-3**

Copyright © Houghton Mifflin Company. All rights reserved.

Problem Solving

Lee looked out the window at the snowy landscape. He saw Jim and Kara pulling their sleds.

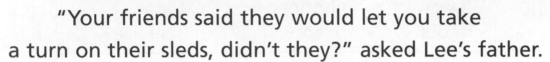

"I wish I had a sled," said Lee.

"Your friends said they would let you take a turn on their sleds, didn't they?" asked Lee's father.

"Yes," said Lee. "I'll catch up with them." Lee opened the closet to find his jacket. He saw a big cardboard box and got an idea. Lee pulled out the sides of the box and made a flat shape. He asked his father for two plastic trash bags and some packing tape.

Lee covered the flat cardboard with the trash bags. He smoothed out the bags and used the tape to hold them in place. The sled was finished!

Lee's sled was so fast and so smooth that Jim and Kara asked to ride on it over and over again.

Problem: _____	
Solution: _____	
Step 1: _____	
Step 2: _____	
Step 3: _____	
Step 4: _____	

Copyright © Houghton Mifflin Company. All rights reserved.

Name_____

Problem Solving

Read the story. Then complete the chart.

"Don't bounce that ball in the house!" said Chris's mother. "Our downstairs neighbors will get headaches!"

Chris put down the ball. A snowstorm had kept her inside since Friday. Now it was Sunday, and the snow was still falling. Chris wanted to do something active.

Then Chris got an idea. She stuffed three pairs of socks into one sock. She measured her room. Every three feet, she put a line of tape on the floor. Then she cut off the top of an empty plastic milk jug. She hung the jug from the closet door.

"Now I can practice shooting baskets," Chris said.

Problem: _____
_____
_____
Solution: _____
Step 1: _____
Step 2: _____
Step 3: _____

Copyright © Houghton Mifflin Company. All rights reserved.

Prefixes *pre-, con-, com-*

100%
preshrunk
cotton

It's so easy to
prepare this
precooked
rice.

Just combine
the mix, eggs,
and milk.

End computer
confusion!
Connect and
communicate
with just one
click.

CAR LOT

A complete
breakfast in
one box.

These
pre-owned
cars are
beyond
compare!

Copyright © Houghton Mifflin Company. All rights reserved.

Name_____

Prefixes *pre-, con-, com-*

Complete each sentence with a word from the box.

prefix	preschool	prejudge
predict	preview	

1. I know what the movie will be about because I saw the

   _____.

2. It is not fair to _____ someone before you know

   the facts.

3. When you place a _____ before a base word, it

   changes the meaning.

4. Children may attend _____ before they enter

   elementary school.

5. I could _____ the ending before it happened

   because I learned how to do that in school last week.

Complete each sentence with a word from the box.

compete	concert
contain	complain

1. Those jars _____ jam.

2. Who will _____ in the bike race?

3. Mr. Perez enjoyed the band's _____

4. The neighbors may _____ about the noise.

Copyright © Houghton Mifflin Company. All rights reserved.

Drawing Conclusions

Who is Oro?

Something awakened Manny. He sat up in bed suddenly, and his eyes flew open. Then he heard the gentle groan of floorboards—*creak, creak, creak*. Manny opened his eyes wider. The room was completely dark. For just a moment, Manny saw two yellow circles glowing near the floor. Then he saw a leaping shadow. He felt something flop at the foot of the bed. Soon he heard a soft, purring sound. He sighed, "Oh, it's just Oro." Manny went back to sleep.

Detail: _____

+ **Detail:** _____

+ **Detail:** _____

+ **Detail:** _____

=

Conclusion: _____

Copyright © Houghton Mifflin Company. All rights reserved.

Name_____

Drawing Conclusions

Read the story, then fill out the graphic organizer below. What is Simon's favorite food? Write your conclusion in the bottom box. Write the details that added up to that conclusion.

Simon entered the kitchen. He sniffed the air. "Mmmmm," he said. He peeked into the oven. He saw red sauce gleaming on top of flat dough. He saw yellow cheese sizzling.

"Are there onions and green peppers on it?" Simon asked.

"Yes. And pepperoni, too," answered Simon's grandmother.

Simon smacked his lips. "I can't wait to crunch that crust!" he said.

Detail: _____
+ Detail: _____
+ Detail: _____
+ Detail: _____
=
Conclusion: _____

Copyright © Houghton Mifflin Company. All rights reserved.

VCCV Pattern

Birds welcome the day.
Twitter, chatter, chirp, and squawk.
Come to the concert!

A faint drum patters.
A horn murmurs, flutes whisper.
Then the cymbals crash!

When the jazz trumpet
sings—picture silver glitter.
See bright notes shimmer.

_____

_____

_____

Copyright © Houghton Mifflin Company. All rights reserved.

Name_____

VCCV Pattern

**Read each sentence. Find the word with two syllables.
Write the syllables with a slash dividing them.**

Example:

Do you like to combine ham and eggs? _____com/bine_____

1. Leaves scatter in the wind.   _____

2. It's a perfect day for a jog.   _____

3. I heard a sudden noise.   _____

4. Please practice the song.   _____

5. The friends collect coins.   _____

6. My sister sings well.   _____

Say each syllable. Combine them to make two 2-syllable words.

Example:

	pose	com	pur		compose	purpose
1.	con	tain	nect	➤	_____	_____
2.	der	lad	won	➤	_____	_____
3.	son	les	per	➤	_____	_____
4.	rect	cor	ner	➤	_____	_____
5.	net	mag	bon	➤	_____	_____
6.	pet	trum	car	➤	_____	_____

Copyright © Houghton Mifflin Company. All rights reserved.

Story Structure
The Farmer's Lesson

Long ago, in a land far away, a farmer worried that his five sons argued too much. One day, the farmer showed his sons a thick bundle of sticks. He told each son to try to break the sticks in half. Each failed. Then the farmer untied the bundle and gave one stick at a time to his sons. Each stick was easily broken.

"My sons," said the farmer, "you are like these sticks. Together, you are strong. Apart, you are weak."

The sons learned the lesson and never fought again.

Characters: _____	Setting: _____

Plot

Problem: _____

Events: _____

_____

_____

_____

_____

_____

Solution or Ending: _____

Copyright © Houghton Mifflin Company. All rights reserved.

Name_____

Story Structure

Read the story and fill out the chart below.

Long ago, a cruel general was about to attack a small village by the sea. "Only your cleverness can save you," he told the villagers. "Make a drum that can beat without being hit with a stick or a hand. If you can do that, my army will leave you in peace."

"The general knows we can't make it," cried the villagers. "It's just an excuse to attack us!"

Then the oldest woman of the village stepped forward. "I can solve the riddle," she said. "Make the drum with two sides of paper. Before fixing the sides in place, put a bee inside the drum. The bee will beat its wings against the sides."

The drum was made and the village was left in peace.

Characters: _____ _____	Setting: _____ _____
Plot **Problem:** _____ _____ _____ **Events:** _____ _____ **Solution:** _____	

Copyright © Houghton Mifflin Company. All rights reserved.

Prefixes and Suffixes

Copyright © Houghton Mifflin Company. All rights reserved.

Name_____

Prefixes and Suffixes

Underline the word that fits in the sentence. Write it on the line.

Example:

Did you see the ___replay___ of the home run?
(replay, playful)

1. Ed was sorry he had been _____.
   (thoughtful, thoughtless)

2. People may frown when they are _____.
   (happiness, unhappy).

3. Gentle rocking can feel _____.
   (restful, unrest)

4. The coach treated everyone with _____.
   (fairness, unfair)

5. We hope for peace and _____.
   (discontent, contentment)

6. A broken hammer is _____.
   (useless, useful)

7. The cat pounced with a sudden _____.
   (remove, movement)

8. Jana _____ the story three times.
   (retold, untold)

Copyright © Houghton Mifflin Company. All rights reserved.

Cause and Effect

Plants that grow in dry desert lands need water, so they have special tricks for drinking up the rain. The roots of a cactus spread out very far. These wide roots are best because they can soak up lots of rain very fast. The stems of some cacti have folds, or ribs, and act like a storage tank. The cactus can hold onto water because the ribs stretch out. Cacti have sharp spines for protection, since thirsty desert animals might try to drink a cactus' water.

Example:

Deserts are dry lands. (cause) ➡ Desert plants have tricks for soaking up water. (effect)

CAUSE		EFFECT Roots can soak up rain quickly.

➡

CAUSE The ribs of the cactus stem can stretch.		EFFECT

➡

CAUSE		EFFECT Animals cannot take water from the cactus.

Copyright © Houghton Mifflin Company. All rights reserved.

Name_____

Cause and Effect

Read Ruben's journal entry and write the missing cause or effect.

Saturday, July 14 ☑ Bad day   ☐ Good day
Today I was licking a lollipop when my brother called
on the phone. Because I still had the lollipop in my
mouth, Ben said he couldn't understand me. I put the
lollipop in my T-shirt pocket. Ben asked me to go
swimming with him. I pulled off my T-shirt and the
lollipop fell out. It landed on my head and stuck to my
hair! I tugged at the lollipop, but that only made more
hair get stuck so Mom had to cut away the lollipop
with scissors. Now I have the world's worst haircut!

CAUSE	EFFECT
_____	Ben couldn't understand what Ruben was saying.

CAUSE	EFFECT
_____	The lollipop landed on Ruben's head.

CAUSE	EFFECT
Ruben's hair stuck to the lollipop.	_____

Copyright © Houghton Mifflin Company. All rights reserved.

Changing Final *y* to *i*

**Band Plans Tour of
Ten Cities**

1. _____

**"I'm Happiest
Onstage," Says Singer**

2. _____

**Band's Earlier CDs
Sold Millions**

3. _____

**"More, More,
More!" Cried Fans**

4. _____

**Songwriter Busier
Than Ever**

5. _____

**Concert Ticket Sales
Rise Steadily**

6. _____

Copyright © Houghton Mifflin Company. All rights reserved.

Name_____

Changing Final *y* to *i*

Read each sentence. Find the word in which a *y* was changed to *i*. Write the base word and ending used to form that word. Then write the complete word on the last line.

Example:

Which of these pictures is prettiest? ___pretty___ + ___est___ = ___prettiest___

1. Leon yawned lazily. _____ + ____ = _____

2. Cat babies are called kittens. _____ + ____ = _____

3. We hurried to get here in time. _____ + ____ = _____

4. Emma is busier than ever. _____ + ____ = _____

5. Hank dried the dishes. _____ + ____ = _____

6. "Thanks," I replied. _____ + ____ = _____

7. Roses are lovelier than tulips. _____ + ____ = _____

8. Which movie was funnier? _____ + ____ = _____

9. Hank stared gloomily. _____ + ____ = _____

10. This is the foggiest weather. _____ + ____ = _____

Copyright © Houghton Mifflin Company. All rights reserved.

Making Judgments

At nine years old, Trisha knew that she wanted to be an Olympic figure skater. She had already won many impressive skating awards. She practiced at the rink four afternoons each week. Trisha loved to skate.

One day, Trisha was having a terrible practice. She couldn't get the hardest move of her new routine right. She fell a few times. Her coach told her to be patient and that she had time to get it right before her next competition. After she fell for the fifth time, Trisha yelled "I quit! I don't want to skate anymore!"

Question	Story Details	Own Opinions and Experiences	Judgment
Should Trisha quit skating because she fell a few times?			

Copyright © Houghton Mifflin Company. All rights reserved.

Name_____

Making Judgments

Read the story. Then write a letter to Nelson to tell him what you think of his behavior. Give reasons for your opinion.

On his way to school, Dave saw a toy drum lying in the grass. He picked it up and beat it a few times. All of a sudden, a hand grabbed the drum. It was Nelson. He was always taking things away from people. "Give that back! I found it!" Dave yelled.

Nelson beat the drum. "Try and get it!" he called with a laugh as he ran away. Suddenly he tripped and fell on top of the drum. It broke. "OK, you can have it back," Nelson called.

Dave picked up the broken drum and tossed it into the trash.

Dear Nelson,

_____

_____

_____

_____

_____

_____

Copyright © Houghton Mifflin Company. All rights reserved.

VCV Pattern

Shopping List

1. frozen fish —————————————

2. canned soda —————————————

3. salad mix —————————————

4. fresh spinach —————————————

5. large melon —————————————

6. three cans of tuna —————————————

7. plain yogurt —————————————

8. dozen eggs —————————————

9. sweet relish —————————————

10. bacon strips —————————————

11. waxed paper —————————————

12. dish soap: super size —————————————

Copyright © Houghton Mifflin Company. All rights reserved.

Name_____

VCV Pattern

Read each sentence. Find the word with two syllables.
Write the word on the line and divide it into syllables.

Example: Three minus one leaves two. _____ mi/nus _____

1. A pilot flies a plane. _____

2. The can is made of metal. _____

3. Park the car by the meter. _____

4. We stayed in a motel on our trip. _____

5. There was no noise, just silence. _____

6. Can you do me a favor? _____

7. The robin pulled up a worm. _____

8. A robot can do hard work. _____

Put the syllables together to form a two-syllable word.

Example: vor   fla   _____ flavor _____

1. ond   sec   _____

2. shad   ow   _____

3. ish   pun   _____

4. pu   pil   _____

Copyright © Houghton Mifflin Company. All rights reserved.

Fact and Opinion

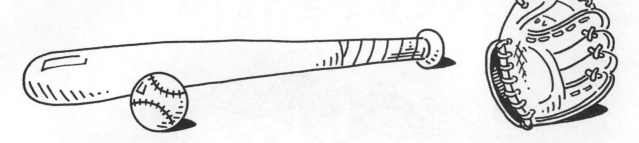

A Baseball Superstar

Willie Mays was the greatest center fielder in baseball history. He was named Rookie of the Year in 1951, when he began his career with the New York Giants. He was the National League's Most Valuable Player in 1954. He was elected to the Baseball Hall of Fame in 1979.

The most famous catch in baseball history was made by Mays. It was in the first game of the 1954 World Series. The Cleveland Indians and the Giants were tied. Vic Wertz, an Indians batter, hit the ball deep into center field and Mays caught the ball! The Giants went on to win the game—and the World Series.

FACTS	OPINIONS
_____	_____
_____	_____
_____	_____
_____	_____
_____	_____

Copyright © Houghton Mifflin Company. All rights reserved.

Name_____

Fact and Opinion

Read the passage. As you read, think about whether each numbered sentence states a fact or an opinion. Then fill in the number of each sentence in the correct column at the bottom.

(1) Wilma Rudolph was the first American woman to win three gold medals at one Olympics. (2) She won her medals in 1960 at the games in Rome, Italy. (3) Everyone in the crowd loved watching Wilma Rudolph. (4) She looked so graceful and powerful when she ran!

(5) Wilma Rudolph's story captured people's hearts. (6) As a girl, Wilma had polio, which weakened the muscles in her leg. (7) For years, she wore a leg brace and a special shoe. (8) By the time Wilma was twelve, her leg had healed. (9) Soon she joined the women's track team, the Tennessee State Tigerbelles.

(10) Off the field, Wilma was very generous. (11) She became a teacher. (12) She created the Wilma Rudolph Foundation to help children. (13) Wilma Rudolph is an inspiring role model.

FACTS	OPINIONS
_____	_____

Copyright © Houghton Mifflin Company. All rights reserved.

Three-Syllable Words

1. *Adventure on the Mountaintop* by I.C. Farr

_____

2. *Evergreens* by Woody Green

_____

3. *Exercise Without Injury* by Les B. Safer

_____

4. *Conserving Energy* by Rhea Sykel

_____

5. *Basketball for Enjoyment* by May D. Schott

_____

6. *Retraining Dogs That Misbehave* by Willy O. Baye

_____

7. *Grandparents Are Wonderful!* by Manny Huggs

_____

8. *Plants for Beginning Gardeners* by Rhoda Dendron

_____

Copyright © Houghton Mifflin Company. All rights reserved.

Name_____

Three-Syllable Words

Read each sentence. Underline the answer that shows the **bolded** word correctly broken into three syllables.

Example:

    I am **connecting** the pieces.   conne/ct/ing   <u>con/nect/ing</u>

1. The **visitor** left.   vis/i/tor   vi/si/tor
2. The boy spoke **politely**.   po/lite/ly   poli/tel/y
3. Clouds **reappeared**.   reap/pear/ed   re/ap/peared
4. Please walk **carefully**.   car/efu/ly   care/ful/ly
5. Who **discovered** the clue?   dis/cov/ered   dis/cove/red
6. What **excitement** we felt!   exc/item/ent   ex/cite/ment
7. Do not **interrupt** the speech.   inte/rr/upt   in/ter/rupt
8. Why are you **whispering**?   whis/per/ing   whi/spe/ring

Put the syllables in the correct order to make a three-syllable word.

Example:

     | den | ly | sud | ➤   **suddenly** _____

1. | vent | pre | ing | ➤ _____

2. | ket | ball | bas | ➤ _____

3. | port | re | er | ➤ _____

4. | mis | ed | treat | ➤ _____

Copyright © Houghton Mifflin Company. All rights reserved.

Following Directions

Materials: a pencil, markers or crayons, paper.

1. First, draw an oval in the center of your paper. The narrow ends should be at the top and bottom.
2. Then draw a triangle above the oval. The bottom of the triangle should balance on the top end of the oval.
3. Next, draw a horizontal (side-to-side) zigzag line inside the triangle, just above the bottom. In the center of the triangle, draw two dots, one beside the other with a little bit of room in between.
4. Now draw a curly line that sticks out from the left side of the triangle. Repeat this step from the right side of the triangle.
5. Draw a shape looking like a three-pointed fork from the left and then from the right side of the oval.
6. Find the bottom of the oval and draw two lines coming out of the bottom curve. At the bottom of each line, draw a three-toed bird's foot.
7. Finally, add color to your creature using markers or crayons. Name your creature and write three sentences telling about it.

Copyright © Houghton Mifflin Company. All rights reserved.

Name_____

Following Directions

Read the instructions to decode this secret message.

Secret Message:

25-15-21   1-18-5   17-21-9-20-5   3-12-5-22-5-18!

DECODING INSTRUCTIONS:

To decode the secret message, follow these steps:
1. First, list the letters of the alphabet A to Z.
2. Number each letter in order, 1 to 26.
3. Match each number in the message to the letter in your list and write the letter.
4. Finally, write the decoded message on this line.

_____

Copyright © Houghton Mifflin Company. All rights reserved.

Suffixes
-less, -ness, -ion

Today I'm going to show you how to make a tasty creation that will bring happiness to your next dinner party.

I have poured seedless grapes into this bowl. These bananas are at just the right stage of ripeness.

Next I'll just chop up this watermelon. Oops, I dropped some on the floor! How careless of me! I'm glad that neatness doesn't count on this show.

Now I'll pour this yogurt over the whole combination. Finally, I'll mix in a tiny bit of honey for sweetness.

I'll take a taste. *Mmmm*, perfection!

I hope you viewers will take my suggestion and tune in tomorrow. I'll be making meatless chili.

Copyright © Houghton Mifflin Company. All rights reserved.

Name_____

Suffixes
-less, -ness, -ion

Read each sentence. Find the word that has a *-less*, *-ness*, or *-ion* suffix. Write a word equation using its base word and suffix.

Example:

That movie sure had a lot of action. _____ act + ion = action _____

1. This math test is about subtraction. _____

2. How can I thank you for your kindness? _____

3. The last instruction is hard to follow. _____

4. Deer depend on their swiftness to be safe. _____

5. You may be tired after a restless night. _____

6. A ride on a roller coaster may lead to dizziness. _____

7. A thoughtless person left the milk out to spoil. _____

8. Joe's bike is useless without a seat. _____

9. What a clever invention! _____

10. My teacher says that neatness counts. _____

Copyright © Houghton Mifflin Company. All rights reserved.

Topic, Main Idea, Supporting Details

Fire Safety at Home

Always stay safe while using portable heaters. Place heaters more than three feet away from people, pets, and furniture. Check the wire on your heater to make sure it is not torn.

Watch out for other fire hazards. Never run an extension cord under a rug or behind curtains. Keep trash in covered bins. Store flammable items like paint thinner far from any heating sources.

Topic: _____

Main Idea, Paragraph 1:	Main Idea, Paragraph 2:
_____ _____	_____ _____
Supporting Details:	Supporting Details:
_____ _____ _____ _____	_____ _____ _____ _____

Copyright © Houghton Mifflin Company. All rights reserved.

Name_____

Topic, Main Idea, Supporting Details

Read this paragraph and complete the chart with information from it.

The Biggest Earthquake

The biggest earthquake in recorded history happened in New Madrid, Missouri. Actually, it was a series of earthquakes. The first was on December 16, 1811. The second occurred in January, 1812. The strongest quake of all happened in February, 1812. The earth also shook between these earthquakes — and afterwards. The earthquake was so big, that even people in faraway cities felt the shaking.

Topic:

_____

Main Idea:

_____

_____

Supporting Details:

_____

_____

_____

_____

_____

Copyright © Houghton Mifflin Company. All rights reserved.

Word Roots *graph, tract*

For his school project, Paul read a biography of Abraham Lincoln. He was attracted to the book because it was thin and had lots of pictures. But once Paul began to read it, nothing could distract him.

Then Paul made a poster to show what he had learned. He wrote several information-filled paragraphs. He extracted parts of Lincoln's speeches and letters. He traced Lincoln's autograph and made copies of photographs. Paul used computer graphics for the title and headings. It was the best project Paul had ever done.

graph	tract

Copyright © Houghton Mifflin Company. All rights reserved.

Name_____

Word Roots *graph, tract*

Complete the word in each sentence by writing the root *graph* or *tract*. Then write the whole word on the next line.

1. Matt likes to read bio_____ ies of sports heroes.

_____

2. A magnet will at _____ paper clips.

_____

3. Car tires need _____ ion to stay on

the road. _____

4. When do children learn addition and

sub _____ ion facts?

_____

5. Please sign my auto_____ book.

_____

6. The farmer rode on a large _____ or. _____

7. Sometimes, dentists perform tooth ex _____ ions.

_____

8. We studied a map of the world in our geo _____ y class.

_____

9. The word *doesn't* is an example of a con _____ ion.

_____

10. Cats have re _____ able claws. _____

Copyright © Houghton Mifflin Company. All rights reserved.

Making Inferences

Lauren and Rose were picnicking in a field, but soon a thunderstorm made them run for shelter. Rose suggested the girls stand under a nearby tree.

"No, no!" said Lauren. "Never get under a tree during a thunderstorm! Let's run for the car."

Suddenly, lightning flashed and a great BOOM shook them. Lauren pointed to the tree. Flames were shooting out of the branches. Rose's eyes opened wide. "You saved my life!" said Rose.

What can I infer?	How can I tell that?

Copyright © Houghton Mifflin Company. All rights reserved.

Name_____

Making Inferences

Read the story and fill out the chart

"We're lost! We'll never get back to camp!" yelled Garth.

"Try to stay calm," said Andy quietly. "We have to cross this river. I know that camp is on the other side."

"I want to give up!" complained Garth. "I can't take another step!"

"We crossed this river before," Andy said. "There was a bridge at a narrow spot. We just have to follow the river until we find it. We'll be fine."

Words to describe Garth:	Why I think that:
_____	_____
_____	_____
_____	_____
Words to describe Andy:	**Why I think that:**
_____	_____
_____	_____
_____	_____

Copyright © Houghton Mifflin Company. All rights reserved.

A	E	I	M	R	V
A	E	I	N	R	W
A	E	J	N	S	W
B	F	J	O	S	X
B	F	K	O	T	X
C	G	K	P	T	Y
C	G	L	P	U	Y
D	H	L	Q	U	Z
D	H	M	Q	V	Z

Copyright © Houghton Mifflin Company. All rights reserved.

Letter Cards

a	e	i	m	r	v
a	e	i	n	r	w
a	e	j	n	s	w
b	f	j	o	s	x
b	f	k	o	t	x
c	g	k	p	t	y
c	g	l	p	u	y
d	h	l	q	u	z
d	h	m	q	v	z

Letter Cards

Copyright © Houghton Mifflin Company. All rights reserved.